ies, Lies and the War on Terror

About the Authors

Paul Todd read philosophy at the University of East Anglia and has a doctorate from the University of Middlesex. A historian of the Cold War specializing in the Middle East, he has done research at the US National Security Archives and was editor of *The Gulf Report* monthly at the Gulf Centre for Strategic Studies in London. He is the author of *World Power and Global Reach: US Security Policy in Southwest Asia* and co-author of *Global Intelligence: The World's Secret Services Today*.

Jonathan Bloch was born in Cape Town, South Africa. He studied law at the University of Cape Town and the London School of Economics. He was politically active in South Africa and remains involved in Southern African causes. He is now a London-based businessman and a Liberal Democrat councillor in the London Borough of Haringey. He is the co-author of *British Intelligence and Covert Action*, *KGB/CIA*, and *Global Intelligence: The World's Secret Services Today* and a contributor to *Dirty Work 2: The CIA in Africa*.

The late **Patrick Fitzgerald**, journalist and researcher, wrote extensively on intelligence and national security for the *New Statesman*, *Economist*, *New Scientist*, *Tribune* and other publications. He co-authored *British Intelligence and Covert Action* and *Stranger on the Line*. This book owes much to his humour and trenchant insights, which he is sadly no longer here to pursue.

Spies, Lies and the War on Terror

Paul Todd, Jonathan Bloch & Patrick Fitzgerald

ZED BOOKS
London & New York

Spies, Lies and the War on Terror was first published in 2009 by
Zed Books Ltd, 7 Cynthia Street, London N1 9JF, UK
and Room 400, 175 Fifth Avenue, New York, NY 10010, USA

www.zedbooks.co.uk

Designed and typeset in Monotype Jansen
by illuminati, Grosmont, www.illuminatibooks.co.uk

Cover designed by Andrew Corbett

Printed and bound in the UK by MPG Biddles, King's Lynn

Distributed in the USA exclusively by Palgrave Macmillan, a division
of St Martin's Press, LLC, 175 Fifth Avenue, New York, NY 10010, USA

ISBN 978 1 84277 830 2 Hb
ISBN 978 1 84277 831 9 Pb

Contents

To all the victims of the War on Terror

Acronyms and abbreviations

ABW	Agencja Bezpieczenstwa Wewnetrznego (Poland, domestic intelligence)
ADVISE	Analysis, Dissemination, Visualization, Insight and Semantic Enhancement (USA)
AEI	American Enterprise Institute
AFRICOM	Africa Command (US military formations covering Africa)
AIPAC	American Israel Public Affairs Committee
AISE	Agenzia Informazioni e Sicurezza Esterna (Italy, foreign intelligence)
AISI	Agenzia Informazioni e Sicurezza Interna (Italy, domestic intelligence)
AM	Al Muhajiroun
AW	Agencja Wywiadu (Poland, foreign intelligence)
AWAC	Airborne Warning and Control System
BCCI	Bank of Credit and Commerce International
BfV	Bundesamt für Verfassungsschutz (Germany, domestic intelligence)
BMD	Ballistic Missile Defence
BND	Bundesnachrichtendienst (Germany, foreign intelligence)

CBW	Chemical and Biological Warfare
CENTCOM	Central Command (US military formations covering the Middle East region)
CFSP	Common Foreign and Security Policy (EU)
CIA	Central Intelligence Agency
CIC	Coalition Information Centre
CIFA	Counterintelligence Field Activity (USA, Department of Defense)
CLI	Committee for the Liberation of Iraq
CNI	Centro Nacional de Inteligencia (Spain, intelligence)
COG	Continuity in Government (USA)
COSI	Standing Committee on Internal Security (EU)
DCRI	Direction Centrale du Renseignement Intérieur (France, domestic intelligence)
DGSE	Direction Générale de la Securité Extérieure (France, foreign intelligence)
DIS	Dipartimento delle Informazioni per la Sicurezza
DSPB	Defense Science Policy Board
DST	Direction de la Surveillance du Territoire (France, domestic intelligence)
ECHR	European Convention on Human Rights
EIJ	Egyptian Islamic Jihad
EUCOM	European Command (US military formations covering Europe)
EUISS	European Union Institute for Security Studies
EURODAC	EU Automated Fingerprint Identification System
EUROPOL	European Police Office
FCO	Foreign & Commonwealth Office
FEMA	Federal Emergency Management Agency
FIS	Front Islamique du Salut (Algeria)
FISA	Foreign Intelligence Surveillance Act
GAO	General Accounting Office
GCHQ	Government Communications Headquarters (UK, signals intelligence)

GIA	Groupe Islamique Armé (Algeria)
GWOT	Global War On Terror
HUA	Harkat ul-Ansar
HVA	Hauptverwaltung Aufklärung (former East Germany, foreign intelligence)
IAEA	International Atomic Energy Commission
ICCPR	International Convention on Civil and Political Rights
ICG	Iraq Communications Group (UK)
IIS	Iraqi Intelligence Service
INA	Iraqi National Accord
INC	Iraqi National Congress
INR	Bureau of Intelligence and Research, US State Department
INTDIV	Intelligence Division (EU Military Staff)
IO	Information Operations
IOTF	Information Operations Task Force
ISI	Inter-Services Intelligence (Pakistan)
JHA	Justice and Home Affairs (EU)
JIC	Joint Intelligence Committee (UK)
JINSA	Jewish Institute for National Security Affairs
JITF	Joint Iraq Task Force (CIA)
JTAC	Joint Terrorism Analysis Centre (UK)
KLA	Kosovo Liberation Army
LfV	Landesbehörden für Verfassungsschutz (Germany, domestic provincial intelligence)
MAIF	Military Architecture Information Framework
MCA	Military Commissions Act (USA)
MEK	Mujahideen-e Khalq (Iran)
MOD	Ministry of Defence (UK)
MoU	Memorandum of Understanding
MPA	Metropolitan Police Authority (UK)
MPRI	Military Professional Resources Inc. (USA)
NCTC	National Counterterrorism Center (USA)

NIE	National Intelligence Estimate (USA)
NIF	National Islamic Front (Sudan)
NORTHCOM	Northern Command (US military formations covering North America)
NSA	National Security Agency (US, signals intelligence)
NSC	National Security Council (USA)
NSDD	National Security Decision Directive
OGC	Office of Global Communications (USA)
OIC	Organization of the Islamic Conference
OSI	Office of Strategic Influence (US Department of Defense)
OSINT	Open Source Intelligence
OSP	Office of Special Plans (Pentagon)
PACOM	Pacific Command (US military formations covering Asia and the Pacific)
PAIC	Popular Arab and Islamic Conference
PCTE	Policy Counterterrorism Evaluation (US Department of Defense)
PDD	Presidential Decision Directive
PDPA	People's Democratic Party of Afghanistan
PFLP	Popular Front for the Liberation of Palestine
PJAK	Partîya Jîyana Azadîya Kurdistanê (Party for a Free Life in Kurdistan)
PKK	Partîya Kerkerên Kurdistan (Kurdistan Workers' Party)
PLO	Palestine Liberation Organization
PNAC	Project for a New American Century
PNR	Passenger Name Record
PSYOPS	Psychological Operations
PTA	Prevention of Terrorism Act (UK)
RG	Renseignements Généreaux (France, domestic intelligence units)
SAIC	Science Applications International Corp. (USA)
SALT	Strategic Arms Limitations Talks

SCIRI	Supreme Council for the Islamic Revolution in Iraq
SDA	Stranka Democratske Akcije (Democratic Action Party, Bosnia)
SERE	Survival, Evasion, Resistance, Escape
SIAC	Special Immigration Appeals Commission
SIGINT	Signals Intelligence
SIS	Schengen Information System
SISMI	Servizio per le Informazioni e la Sicurezza Militare (Italy, military intelligence)
SITCEN	Situation Centre (EU CSFP)
SOCOM	Special Operations Command (US military special forces)
SOUTHCOM	Southern Command (US military formations covering Central and South America)
STRATCOM	Strategic Command (US strategic military formations, including nuclear and space-based systems)
SWIFT	Society for Worldwide Interbank Financial Telecommunication
TALON	Threat and Local Observation Notice (US Department of Defense)
TIA	Total Information Awareness
TSP	Terrorist Surveillance Program (US National Security Agency)
TWRA	Third World Relief Agency
UNPROFOR	UN Protection Force (Bosnia)
USD/I	Undersecretary for Defense/Intelligence (US Department of Defense)
USIA	US Information Agency
WHIG	White House Iraq Information Group
WINPAC	Weapons Intelligence and Arms Control Center (CIA)
WMD	Weapons of Mass Destruction
WTC	World Trade Center

The sleep of reason

At the start of World War II, Winston Churchill, the newly appointed British prime minister, warned of the coming of a new dark age in the event of Nazi victory, one made 'ever blacker by the lights of a perverted science'. Now, in the light of what has been proclaimed as the start of 'World War Four'[1] (the Cold War making up the numbers), many would find the concept disturbingly apt for the current era. As US Vice President Dick Cheney blandly defended 'having to work on the dark side' in sanctioning scientifically based US torture of its growing band of 'enemy combatants',[2] the prospect of a fresh combination of high technology driven by irrationalism has again taken centre stage.

In what follows, we show how what has widely been termed 'faith-based'[3] decision-making has taken hold since the launch of the War on Terror. Aside from individual convictions, this has rested on faith in the capacity of media mastery to influence events. But a key enabling factor has been the use of intelligence to legitimize expedient and often illegal policies of military adventure and civil repression. In the post-Iraq–9/11 world, the role of intelligence agencies – and of intelligence itself – has undergone dramatic transformation as a tool of statecraft. In this short study, we explore the fast-moving expansion of intelligence in the shifting front lines of the War on Terror, and the parallel moves away from a publicly proclaimed intelligence role in law enforcement towards its becoming a means for circumventing laws and conventions which, as George W. Bush famously observed, were 'designed for another era'.

Perpetual war

A major focus of this work is the extent to which the now-tainted concept of 'War on Terror' has seamlessly emerged from the shell of the Cold War, which was supposedly consigned to history with the fall of the Berlin Wall, a theme surprisingly underexplored to date. As the nineteenth-century philosopher Georg Hegel well knew, the 'cunning of history' has a record of reasserting itself, not least in the law of unintended consequences. And here the Bush administration's wars in Afghanistan and Iraq provide textbook confirmation for future historians. In the one instance, crisis was brought on by policy consciously sidelining available intelligence – regarding the Taliban, al-Qaeda and the aims of Pakistan and Saudi Arabia; in the other, intelligence was simply massaged and fabricated to fit predetermined policy – notably, regarding the desire to conduct pre-emptive war as an approach both to perceived threat and to US standing in general. In every case, the result was near-total reversal for the stated main aim – of demonstrating unchallengeable US power.

In reconfiguring the intelligence process to service the emerging strategic doctrine of pre-emptive war, the main losers were, as we will show, the authors of the project itself. At first, this was simply dismissed as one more transaction cost in the grand scheme of things. As one 'senior White House aide' was to remark to *New York Times* columnist Ron Suskind, people (like him) still in 'the reality-based community' were outpaced by events. 'That's not the way the world works anymore. We are an empire now. And when we act, we create our own reality.'[4] But as the awful face of that reality unfolded, with media saturation of the Abu Ghraib horror movie conjoined with the hitherto unimaginable prospect of looming military defeat, even those most committed to an open-ended War on Terror were to admit things had gone badly wrong.

Yet for the Bush administration – and no less for its principal foreign ally in Downing Street and Whitehall – the problem was viewed first and foremost as one of presentation. And, as we shall see, this was to push strategic communications and media management to the fore in a fashion unseen even at the height of the Cold War itself.

The new absolutism

Intelligence and its role in public policy are the major themes of this work. But, in a wider sense, we chart the progress of a distinctive secular trend. For as governments worldwide move out of public service provision and state macro-management, there is a parallel move towards micro-management in hitherto private and civic realms. Here, with the burgeoning of surveillance and state intrusion in general under the guise of counterterrorism, fighting crime or indeed public health, we consider how the increasing merger of state and corporate intelligence functions and method-ology seeks to address the ruptures of globalization with ever more draconian social control.

In charting the spread of what Amnesty International has termed a 'shadow system of justice' – found in torture, 'rendition', secret prisons and detention without trial – we consider how the inherent reversal of the principle of legal burden of proof is mir-rored in a corruption of the intelligence process. Secret evidence is by its very nature unaccountable and, in the embattled legal realm, unsafe. Moreover, information obtained under duress is liable to reflect precisely the whims of the interrogator. Indeed, this fairly uncontroversial principle has been widely used by actual – as opposed to innocently seized – terrorist detainees to field false information. Notable among these, as we shall see, was the 'high-value' al-Qaeda captive Ibn Sheikh al-Libbi, whose wholly untrue account of Osama bin Laden's links with Saddam Hussein was to trigger the Iraq invasion.

Sheikh al-Libbi, of course, was pushing an open door. But the 9/11 aftermath has seen a new stance of victimhood take increasing hold across the USA and elsewhere. And with public tolerance for curbs on long-held civil liberties have come political efforts to outflank institutional opposition to overturning established practice in intelligence-informed decision-making. The establishment of covert units within government in the USA, the UK and Israel, as we outline below, took place within a novel methodological mandate: to affect a reversal in the requirement to establish a scientific burden of proof, in a step-change from analysis to marketing. We review how notions of preventive self-defence, results-driven intelligence and 'custodial interview' have come together in ways that have indeed challenged the 'reality-based community', and, by overturning both legal norms and considered military doctrine, have opened paths to a new ideology where anything goes.

The opening chapter undertakes an in-depth examination of a highly significant, if generally understated, force in the securing of Cold War primacy for the West – radical Islamism. Here, we map out how the conjuncture of the final Cold War phase in the 1970s and 1980s took issue – all too well – with the parallel, exponential growth of transnational Islamism in the same period. We detail the rise of Islamist charities and financial institutions in bankrolling the Afghan jihad and their renewed alliance with

Western intelligence in the Balkans conflict. In this little-known episode, we outline how jihadi networks, which later included al-Qaeda, became deeply embedded across Europe, the USA and globally. And we focus on what has arguably been the critical ground in today's 'War on Terror': the nexus between Pakistan's Inter-Services Intelligence (ISI), Saudi funding and the ambiguous relations of both with intelligence and government policy in the USA and the UK.

In Chapter 2, we look to the expanding role of 'strategic communications' in implementing – and determining – the course of policy. The drive by the Pentagon to transform spin, propaganda and perception management into a 'core military competency' is examined in depth and related to efforts to establish the 'information battle-space' as a fresh field for domination. We trace how the burgeoning UK/US media campaign behind the promotion of the Iraq War and the War on Terror in general was geared to the needs of marketing strategy and the political/electoral timetable. In this, the non-stop pace of changes and the backstairs battles in the government machinery are linked to the trail of manufactured intelligence and, in parallel, the mushrooming network of lobbies and think-tanks brought on board by the Bush administration. In particular, we spotlight the joint efforts of the Bush team and Britain's Tony Blair in delivering the international credibility essential to the domestic selling of policy.

Chapter 3 takes up a broader analysis of the Cold War roots of the War on Terror and considers how the strategic discourse of nuclear annihilation has led to the promotion of starkly construed 'zero sum' views on security policy – domestic and international – in the United States. We consider how the apparently total US victory in the Cold War had inspired a drive for 'full-spectrum dominance' in any conceivable field of conflict and the establishment of a position of permanent ascendancy. We track how strategies of pre-emptive war have emerged from nuclear planning doctrine and how these have complemented the radical new doctrine of absolute presidential power in the United States – and the seemingly irresistible rise of the Pentagon in dictating not only foreign but also domestic policy. We outline the new institutional framework of the US military's domestic presence, assess the growing implications for civil liberties, and look at the technological drivers of the spread of mass surveillance – and the closely fought battle to rein them in.

In chapters 4 and 5 we look at the wider War on Terror arena of the UK and European Union. The UK – as a crucial legitimating factor for the War on Terror in its diplomatic and general 'brand' linkages – is the subject of Chapter 4, where we consider the domestic use of the terrorist threat as a promotional and political tool. We assess the increasing politicization of the police, security forces and civil servants in pushing government policy and examine the role of spin and manipulation in government itself. A main focus here is how the Blair government systematically used the terror threat after 9/11 to roll back civil liberties across the board and institute a raft of authoritarian policies on deportation, the use of secret evidence and detention without trial. We examine some of the more unsavoury overseas alliances forged in the process of pursuing the War on Terror and the creeping absorption of Britain within the global network of black sites, torture flights and rendition.

It is the opaque but hugely influential area of pan-EU security and intelligence decision-making that is addressed in our fifth chapter. In one of the first major studies of this little-understood transnational process, we outline how the leading European powers have systematically used both the threat and the reality of terror in mobilizing wider goals for military, intelligence and legislative integration. A particular focus is the unprecedented moves to set up cross-European databases and establish procedures for mass surveillance, in conjunction with parallel efforts in the

USA. We consider how closed-door decision-making and the drive towards ever-increasing social control are combining to produce a vast, Atlantic-wide 'surveillance society'. In considering the EU's counterterrorism policies, we also see how, despite public denial, EU nations have been fully complicit in the seizure and detention of those deemed terrorist suspects by the US authorities, and how the expanding NATO structure has been used to secure an oblique but highly significant new front in the War on Terror.

Finally, we take an overview of the now widely questioned War on Terror narrative, assessing its gains, losses and – critically – how far the whole enterprise has not only strengthened the hand of unaccountable politics and the reach of bureaucratic power, but has played to the agendas of the terrorists themselves.

I

Intelligence and Islamism

We won the Cold War for you. (Pervez Musharraf, 2006)

Islamism and the Cold War

The attacks in New York and Washington DC of 11 September 2001 brought a global movement, radical Islamism, from the desks of intelligence analysts and specialist political commentators to the very centre of world attention. To be sure, awareness of internationally focused Islamist networks and their proclaimed intentions for global jihad against 'Jews and Crusaders' – and a wide range of other targets, including the USA in general – had been repeatedly brought home in a series of spectacular actions. The attacks in Lebanon (1983), the earlier 1993 World Trade Center bomb plot, bombings in Saudi Arabia in 1995–96, car-bombings of the US embassies in East Africa in August 1998, and the crippling of the destroyer USS *Cole* in Aden in 2000, had placed the issue at the top of the intelligence agenda in London, Paris and Washington. The Clinton administration had in 1996 formed a specific 'Issue Station' at the CIA, devoted to Osama bin Laden and had also laid the basis for the international 'rendition' of suspected terrorists in Presidential Decision Directive (PDD) 39, of June 1995.[1]

In addition to the organized jihadi strain, there is the fast-spreading phenomenon of a more demotic 'street' Islamism, conjoining generational and identity politics with real and perceived grievances spanning discrimination against Muslim communities in the West and international concerns in Iraq, Palestine and across the Muslim world. Whilst this broad mix has often provided the milieu for transition to activism and militant groups, it is nevertheless important to distinguish between mainstream Islam – diverse, historically polyglot and culturally rooted – and the much more rigidly construed world of 'Islamism'. Although Islamism is itself subject to innumerable schisms and intense doctrinal faction – by no means all of which espouse violent jihad – there is common ground in literalist interpretations of sacred texts and rigorously enforced social micro-management. More ominously for the West, there is also loose but widespread agreement on replacing existing regimes in the Muslim countries with more Islamist ones, an agenda that finds significant support among influential networks within Muslim countries themselves.

What concerns us here is the conjunction between organized, transnational Islamism, given its current form under essentially Saudi influence – and, above all, funding – and the interests of Western powers. Historically, this has been a marriage of convenience, to be sure, but it is one whose outcomes have returned to haunt its erstwhile sponsors in wholly unpredictable ways.

If the rise of al-Qaeda – accurately portrayed at a recent conference as 'basically a new form of war-making entity'[2] – and of global networks of Islamist insurgency or 'terrorism' in general is almost entirely due to the revolution in IT-based communications,[3] the unifying thread of Islamism itself, while avowedly anti-modern, owes much to US/allied efforts in the Cold War and the spread of globalization. Although emerging from the same politico-economic ruptures of the early twentieth century that gave rise to communism, fascism and, indeed, Zionism, the Islamist revival led by such figures as Hassan al-Banna in Egypt and Maulana Maududi in (what later became) Pakistan was long viewed by colonial and then Cold War Western powers as a useful ally against communism and Third World nationalism in general. This was, almost reflexively, taken on board as an element in the management of world affairs, despite the total, almost visceral, opposition to Western values, political structures and social mores evident from the very beginning.

In many recent works, notably the wide-ranging 2005 study *Devil's Game* by US analyst Robert Dreyfuss,[4] much attention has been paid to the systematic cultivation of Islamist movements such as the Muslim Brotherhood (al-Ikhwan al-Muslimin) and the Shi'a clerical establishment of pre-revolutionary Iran. Here, both existing and emergent currents of Islamism were viewed by authorities in London and Washington as innately conservative forces against nationalism, socialism and the once-vibrant Third World coalition of 'non-aligned' nations. Even after the 1978–79 Iranian Revolution, the attempted coup in Saudi Arabia at the Grand Mosque in Mecca in November 1979,[5] the intensive assaults on civil liberties in Pakistan following the military takeover in 1977 by General Zia, and the assassination of pro-Western Egyptian leader Anwar al-Sadat in 1981, the rising current of international Islamism was still viewed through the essentially unchanged Cold War prism.

The turn of the 1970s, indeed, saw the unfolding of a massive lobby campaign by US neoconservatives and their allies aimed at the supposedly new threat from the Soviet Union. With the 1980 election of Ronald Reagan, and much UK support from Margaret Thatcher, the geopolitical focus of what was becoming known as the 'New Cold War'[6] was the region from the Horn of Africa through the Gulf to Afghanistan. Clearly, enduring US interests

– oil, support for Israel, actual Soviet gains in the region – played their contributory role, but for a small yet increasingly influential section of the renascent US right, a greater prize was on offer: by using the predominantly conservative Islamic states in the Middle East as an ideological – and, soon, military – tool, the USA could move against the Soviet Union itself through its 'weak underbelly' – the rapidly growing Muslim populations of Central Asia.

If the February 1979 revolution in Iran – an event quite un-connected to any Soviet efforts, notwithstanding much neo-conservative spinning – had propelled the region into public consciousness, it had also, for some, demonstrated the mobilizing power of Islamist ideology. Zbigniew Brzezinski, the influential national security adviser to President Jimmy Carter, believed that Russian standing in the so-called 'Arc of Crises' could be decisively challenged by mobilizing the religious right,[7] notably through such groupings as the Organization of the Islamic Con-ference (OIC). One of many transnational pan-Islamic institu-tions to emerge on a tide of oil revenues in the 1960s and 1970s period, the OIC was set up in 1969 by Saudi King Faisal, in explicit opposition to Nasser-style Arab nationalism and to the spread of communism, 'originated by a vile Jew',[8] and its main secular exemplar, the Soviet Union. Following the December 1979 Soviet invasion of Afghanistan, the OIC convened an emergency session on 27–29 January 1980 in Islamabad. Strongly condemning the 'Soviet military aggression against the Afghan people' and calling for diplomatic non-recognition of the pro-Soviet PDPA (Peoples Democratic Party of Afghanistan) regime, the 36-nation grouping voted to suspend Afghanistan's membership and also endorsed President Carter's call for a boycott of the forthcoming Moscow Olympics. At the UN, the budding US/OIC coalition had secured a 104:18 majority, including 57 officially 'non-aligned' representatives, 'strongly deploring the recent armed intervention into Afghanistan'. In addition there were 17 abstentions, with the abstaining Islamic states and even the PLO offering no support for the Russian position.[9]

With the USA facing a virtually unprecedented diplomatic windfall in its Cold War struggle, the Carter administration moved swiftly to secure long-planned-for basing and military pre-positioning agreements in the Horn and Gulf regions. However, though Jimmy Carter had declared the Gulf a 'vital US national interest' in the January 1980 State of the Union Address and had established a 'Rapid Deployment Force' for intervention in the region, these were essentially long-term projects, with little immediate effect.[10] To have significant strategic impact on the ground, the US administration was obliged to turn to a long-standing, though until recently out of favour, ally – Pakistan.

Although the USA had endorsed a series of military regimes in Islamabad since the 1950s, the July 1977 coup of General Zia ul-Haq had been condemned by the new Carter administration. Pakistan's nuclear weapons programme had led to a suspension of military aid and relations worsened still further with the February 1979 execution of former prime minister Ali Bhutto and the burning down by mobs of the US embassy. In early February 1980, however, a high-level US delegation arrived in Islamabad, headed by Brzezinski and deputy secretary of state Warren Christopher, offering $400 million in military aid and declaring the Soviet Union 'a threat to the peace and security of Pakistan, the region and the world.'[11] Whilst General Zia was happy enough to accept US commendations of Pakistan's 'leadership' at the Islamic Conference and the UN, the scale of US military aid on offer, modest due to US concern not to offend India, was rejected as 'peanuts'. Zia was offered private assurances, however, that much more aid would be forthcoming from 'friendly countries' where congressional oversight did not apply. Principal among these were Egypt and Saudi Arabia, both of which also featured on Brzezinski's February itinerary. The Russian move had, indeed, given US hawks in the administration – notably Brzezinski himself and defense secretary Harold Brown – precisely what they wanted in terms of a new strategy for encirclement of the Soviet Union. Brown had arrived in Beijing on 5 January to formalize the growing level of US–China military cooperation. Beijing had been funnelling increasing levels of aid to the Afghan insurgency since 1978 and was a major backer of Pakistan.

If the moves towards renewed Cold War militancy in South Asia can be plainly seen in the later Carter administration – with Brzezinski calling for US aid for Afghan insurgents from July 1979 in the (all too successful) hope of provoking a Soviet 'Vietnam'[12] – the US alliance with Islamist radicalism would be greatly strengthened during the two terms of Ronald Reagan. The Afghan war was expanded into the CIA's greatest ever operation, with some $5 billion of direct US aid, matched 'dollar for dollar' by Saudi Arabia, and a level of arms and equipment shipments peaking at 60,000 tonnes per year by the late 1980s.[13] Of equal significance was the massive provision of military training. Although some Afghani fighters were taken directly to US Special Forces establishments such as Fort Bragg, most training took place in border areas of Pakistan, where a large programme was run under the direction of the (US-trained) Pakistan Inter-Services Intelligence (ISI) with help from China, Israel and Britain's MI6.[14]

At the CIA's Langley headquarters, a relatively junior logistics officer, Mike Vicars, had devised a plan to channel most of the CIA's direct aid to a 100,000 strong elite force of 'techno-guerrillas' (out of a total of some 400,000 fighters in the field). For these, the Agency set up a programme of over twenty different courses, each lasting up to a month, and covering a comprehensive range of irregular warfare techniques. In this way the Afghan fighters were introduced to the latest US thinking on every kind of operation from urban sabotage to large combined-arms ambushes. Also introduced were the latest developments in US communications technology – burst transmitters and frequency-changing radios which could evade detection – and, particularly after Reagan's 'by all means available' National Security Decision Directive (NSDD) 166 of November 1984 – advanced Stinger ground-to-air missiles.[15] More controversial – information about which was strongly suppressed at the time – was the instruction given in randomized urban terror methodology, aimed at the Soviet garrisons increasingly confined in Afghan cities. Here, matters were contracted to the British and the ISI. As CIA South Asia operations director Gust Avarakotos recalls, 'I told them to just teach the Mujahideen how to kill: pipe bombs, car bombs. But don't ever tell me how you're doing it in writing. Just do it.'[16] To circumvent further the even remote possibility of inquiry from a continuously supportive US Congress, Britain's cash-strapped MI6 began receiving a regular CIA subsidy. 'The Brits were eventually able to buy things that we couldn't because it infringed on murder, assassinations and indiscriminate bombings', Avarakotos observes; 'they basically took care of the "How to kill people" department.'[17]

Despite the chaos attending the end of the Afghan War, the CIA and their congressional backers maintained the flow of arms and money to the Afghan mujahideen for a further two years after the January 1989 Russian withdrawal. The final instalment – some $200 million in the Defense Appropriations bill for FY 1992 – was augmented by a large shipment of Soviet-era weaponry captured after the 'Desert Storm' Iraq campaign.[18] If many in Congress were beginning to question the wisdom of arming obvious warlords such as Hezb-i-Islami leader Gulbuddin Hekmatyar, doubts were sidelined until the end of the first Bush administration, to avoid offending Saudi Arabia. However, whilst the incoming Clinton administration lacked the decades-long intimacy with the House of Saud enjoyed by the oil-magnate Bush family, help would soon be sought again from Riyadh to bankroll a new Islamist insurgency – Bosnia.

Blowback from the Balkans: al-Qaeda in Europe

As recently declassified US intelligence reveals, the break-up of Yugoslavia along ethnic-sectarian lines was looking an increasing likelihood to US and European governments by the turn of the 1980s, and with it the prospect of 'serious inter-communal conflicts' and a level of violence long-lasting, 'intractable and bitter'. Also correctly predicted in the October 1990 joint CIA/National Intelligence Council Report was the extreme reluctance of the Western powers, and the USA in particular, to become actively involved.[19] Whilst this hands-off approach was to continue to the end of the George H. Bush administration, preoccupied by the 1991 Gulf War and the forthcoming 1992 US elections, a new alliance was emerging between the increasingly pressed Bosnian Muslim government of Alijas Izetbegovic and Washington's principal Gulf ally, Saudi Arabia.

To be sure, the ruling Democratic Action Party (Stranka Democratske Akcije – SDA) of Bosnia and, to an extent, Izetbegovic personally, were at least publicly supportive of pluralism in Bosnia and seeking support from the West and a range of secular parties in Bosnia itself. From the outset, however, the growing conflict in the Balkans was drawing attention from the fast-spreading Islamist movement – increasingly dispersed after the fall of the Afghan PDPA government in 1992 – and their major international sponsors in the Gulf. Following the 6 April 1992 recognition of Bosnia's independence by the USA and European Community (EC) and the outbreak of heavy internecine fighting in the Serb-dominated north and the capital Sarajevo, delegations from a range of Islamist activist organizations, including the established Egyptian Islamic Jihad (EIJ)/Tansim al-Jihad of Ayman al-Zawahiri and the nascent al-Qaeda, began arriving in Bosnia and neighbouring Croatia.[20] In addition to the growing influx of volunteers, the SDA was able to secure much-needed arms shipments and funding from ostensibly humanitarian-based Islamic NGOs. Chief among these were the Chicago-based Benevolence International Foundation, the Muwafaq Foundation and the Third World Relief Agency (TWRA), based in Vienna and the main regional coordinating body.[21]

In this widely cast network, the structural linkage between the Afghan War and conflict in Bosnia as the drivers of militant Islamism can clearly be seen. The Bosnian efforts were able to draw upon the existing network of Islamic charities and banking, which had undergone massive expansion during the Afghan War. But the latter's ambiguities, at least in relation to the West, were soon to reappear. As later US court cases would reveal, Benevolence International, established to funnel aid to the Afghan fighters in the 1980s in conjunction with the al-Kiffa centre in Brooklyn, New Jersey, was also the base of Omar Abdul Rahman, who subsequently was convicted in the USA for the 1993 World Trade Center bombing. Muwafaq (Blessed Relief), another legacy of the war, had been managed by a powerful Saudi banking family, which also had substantial interests in the collapsed bank BCCI, a major backer of Islamist causes.[22] At an interstate level, however, perhaps the most significant of these foundations was the TWRA,[23] whose major state sponsor, Sudan, was then run by an Islamist military coalition under General Omar al-Bashir and the National Islamic Front, led by radical cleric Hassan al-Turabi.

The 'National Salvation Revolution' of 1989, which brought al-Turabi to power in Khartoum, was very much in step with the general upsurge of militant Islam at the turn of the decade. In parallel with the successful Sudan coup, insurgency flared in Egypt over the period 1990–97 – stoked by Tansim and its larger rival Ga'amat al-Islamiyyi – and a further Islamist front opened in Algeria after the annulment of the 1991–92 elections. Key common features – which would recur influentially in Bosnia – were the returning influx of seasoned fighters from the Afghan War and the ready availability of funding from the burgeoning Islamic banking network and Islamist NGOs. The cash nexus here was again the Gulf and Saudi Arabia. As Alex de Waal observes in a 2004 study, there was 'vast and indiscriminate Saudi funding of any educational, charitable or developmental activities that could claim the Salafi [fundamentalist] label'.[24]

Sudan, under the charismatic al-Turabi, was to emerge as the key state actor in Islamist politics in the Levant and Horn of Africa region, hosting an eclectic range of activists including, after 1992, Osama bin Laden. Here, the de Waal study notes, 'Sudan is a key intermediary in the export of Salafism through Islamic philanthropy. Uniquely among Arab-speaking countries, in the 1970s Sudan possessed a substantial professional class familiar with the operation of international relief and development agencies.'[25] It was thus to Sudan and an old ally, diplomat and NIF leader Elfathi Hassanien-Omal-Fathi and his Vienna-based Third World Relief Agency, that President Izetbegovic was to turn as the Bosnian conflict exploded in 1992. Concurrently with the funding stream, TWRA became a central coordinating hub for arms shipments transiting from Sudan, along with the flow of Afghan veterans exiled there in Osama bin Laden's growing network of camps and business enterprises.[26]

In keeping with his ambitions to become the 'Islamic Lenin',[27] al-Turabi was on uniquely good terms with both Iran and the major Shi'a militant groups, such as Hizbollah, and virtually all the Sunni/Salafist organizations, as well as Iraq – supported by Sudan in the 1991 Gulf War – and a range of Arab militant groupings. In 1990, Sudan abolished visa requirements for all Arab nationals; in 1991, al-Turabi founded the 'Popular Arab and Islamic Conference' (PAIC) as a direct rival to the Saudi-dominated Organization of Islamic Conference. By the time of its December 1993 sitting, the PAIC had expanded to include Hamas, George Habash's Popular Front for the Liberation of Palestine (PFLP), the Abu Nidal group, Front Islamique du Salute (FIS) of Algeria, Egypt's Jemaah Islamiya and EIJ/Tansim and representatives from Iran. Also present were delegates from Kosovo – later to re-emerge as the Kosovo Liberation Army (KLA) – and from Bosnia. It was the Iran/EIJ combination that would figure strongly in the Bosnian War. Despite the many doctrinal differences, EIJ had maintained a cordial relationship with Iran's Pasdaran revolutionary guards corps in the early 1990s, with Ayman al-Zawahiri appearing as a frequent house guest of both Iranian intelligence chief Ali Fallahian and Ahmad Vahidi, head of the Qods Force, a special operations unit based in Lebanon's Bekaa valley.[28]

With the spread of hostilities in Bosnia in early 1992, an alliance of sympathetic states was formed to overcome the September 1991 UN arms embargo. Here, Iran, Pakistan and Turkey were to emerge as the main suppliers, with financial backing from Brunei, Malaysia and Saudi Arabia.[29] A main transit point was Sudan, which also provided volunteers from the pool of expatriate Afghan fighters. Some estimates say that up to 10,000 mujahideen passed through Bosnia, many to disappear into the wider European hinterland. Although Sudan was placed on the US State Department's list of 'State Sponsors of Terrorism' in August 1993, the growing arms traffic through Khartoum was subject to tacit approval by the Clinton administration. As the conflict intensified through 1994–95, this developed into more or less open encouragement, involving covert US cooperation.

Indeed, the Clinton administration had been publicly arguing for a lifting of the embargo, in conjunction with NATO air strikes on the Bosnian Serb army, and in this was supported by two (non-binding) Senate resolutions.[30] As 1996 Senate inquiries would reveal, Anthony Lake, then national security adviser, admitted US knowledge of the Bosnia arms pipeline – originally in the shape of Iran Air flights to Tuzla airport via Turkey – following a journey to Vienna by the Bosnian prime minister, Haris Silajdzic, to issue bank guarantees for TWRA and Hassanien-Omal-Fathi in 1992.[31] In light of the continuing impasse of the various EC and UN peace proposals, the administration decided on a more proactive role, with the mid-1994 appointment of Richard Holbrooke as assistant secretary of state with direct responsibility for the former Yugoslavia. In April 1994, the US ambassador to Croatia, Peter Galbraith, had been directed that he had 'no instructions' on the arms traffic from Iran – effectively, a statement of US approval.[32] Assistant secretary Holbrooke was to visit Croatia in November 1994, accompanied by then chief of US European Command (EUCOM) intelligence (and later head of the CIA) Michael Hayden. Here, meeting with Prime Minister Silajdzic, Croat President Tudjman and representatives of TWRA, arrangements were made to massively expand the shipments, with the aid of black-painted C130 military transport planes, provided by Turkey.[33]

To the consternation of British and French contingents in the Bosnian UN forces, hundreds of tonnes of arms then continued to flow through the Croatian pipeline, aided by Hayden's EUCOM, which provided the slots in the air-traffic-control schedule. Shipments were further aided by the (UN) Operational Section in Tuzla, which 'consisted almost entirely of Pakistanis' under overall control (the G-3) of a Pakistani lieutenant-colonel.[34] Whilst the arms deliveries were clearly critical in turning the tide of war for Izetbegovic and the Bosnian government, worries of a longer-term legacy were beginning to emerge after the conclusion of the Dayton Peace Accords in November 1995. Senior al-Qaeda defector Jamal al-Fadhl was to detail the establishment of intelligence and financial networks linking Bosnia with the Sudan from late 1992,[35] which would provide crucial support for later al-Qaeda European operations. The network of EIJ, Algerian and Iranian-run training camps was to continue operating for several years, despite US and NATO pressure,[36] and would provide two of the pilots for the plot of 9/11.[37] The Bosnia connection was also to figure strongly in the earlier World Trade Center (WTC) bombing of 1993. US investigators were able to trace a payment of $40,000 – donated by TWRA – smuggled into the USA in January and February 1993, ostensibly to help train volunteers for Bosnia. This was traced by FBI officials to the ringleaders of the WTC plot, notably the courier, Clement Hampton-El, and the 'blind sheikh' Omar Abdul Rahman. Abdul Rahman had been admitted to the USA in 1990, on a CIA-expedited visa from the US embassy in Sudan.[38]

The new doctrine of international community

If the success of Dayton was to convince the re-elected Clinton administration of the efficacy of 'humanitarian intervention', by 1999 the president and secretary of state Madeleine Albright were again engaged in the former Yugoslavia on behalf of another nominally Muslim minority – in Kosovo – but this time with an enthusiastic level of support from a major NATO ally, Tony Blair. Unlike the previous Conservative government of John Major – agnostic on the Balkans conflicts, if not mildly pro-Serbian – Blair was strongly in favour of military intervention in humanitarian crises. Blair's proclaimed 'new doctrine of international community'[39] was to place Britain in the forefront of NATO's most ambitious Balkan intervention to date, involving some 24,000 air sorties and 28,000 ground troops, backed by heavy armour and artillery. From the start, however, the unfolding revolt by the Kosovo Albanians was to embrace a covert component conjoining the same networks of radical Islamists with Western intelligence agencies, as had been established in Bosnia.

Whilst the establishment of permanent bases in the region was to become a major *ex post facto* justification for US actions, the main drivers of policy at the time seem to have been Western public opinion and, above all, maintaining the 'credibility' of NATO, then celebrating its fiftieth anniversary.[40] In October 1998

Richard Holbrooke had issued an ultimatum to Serbian President Milosovic to withdraw Yugoslav forces from Kosovo under the threat of NATO air strikes. With the outbreak of fresh fighting soon after – largely instigated by the insurgent Kosovo Liberation Army (KLA)[41] – Secretary Albright again threatened air strikes, backed by a full NATO ultimatum on 29 January 1999. The KLA, hitherto a marginal force in Kosovar politics, had come to public prominence in late 1997 as a loosely coordinated guerrilla opposition to the increasingly draconian Serb repression in the region. If its initial military successes drew much from the cross-border flood of arms from Albania, where central government had virtually collapsed for some months, the financial support drew mostly from crime – notably narcotics[42] – and the Saudi/Gulf-based Islamist charity network active in Bosnia.

Prominent here again was the Muwafaq Foundation. Although placed under investigation by the US Treasury Department after 9/11, alongside thirty-nine other named organizations and individuals,[43] Muwafaq had shared financial and personal links across a global network of banking and charitable institutions. These extended from such established enterprises as the National Commercial Bank of Saudi Arabia (NCB), the kingdom's largest bank, to oil and diamond interests and big-league US investors, notably the Carlyle Group.[44] In 1998, according to Albanian intelligence chief Fatos Klosi, 'a major network of bin Laden supporters was established in Albania under the cover of various Muslim charities.'[45] Millionaire Saudi industrialist Yassin al-Qadi, Muwafaq's chief executive, had set up a string of legitimate business outlets in Albania and was also owner of Massachusetts-based software firm Ptech, which handled classified US government contracts. Its speciality was the development of risk architecture software for the protection of classified databases, notably the Defense Department's 'Military Architecture Information Framework (MAIF), used to coordinate information traffic throughout the

DoD.[46] Ptech, later sold off by al-Qadi, had also reportedly served as a conduit for covert CIA money-laundering and funding for the KLA and was raided by federal authorities in 2002.[47] Al-Qadi's extensive Albanian portfolio was subject to similar scrutiny, with a construction company seizure in December 2001,[48] and further assets, including land and property holdings, seized by Albanian justice officials in December 2006.[49]

If al-Qadi's key role in Balkan fund-raising – allegedly involving a direct payment of $195,000 to President Izetbegovic[50] and some $10 million distributed in Albania alone[51] – was not unknown to the US intelligence community, mutual interest and links with senior US officials had combined to keep the arrangements running smoothly. Until late 1998 the Clinton administration had been determined to avoid the use of ground troops in either Bosnia or Kosovo. Heretofore, key training and logistics functions had been performed by established US military contractors MPRI, whose aid had been instrumental in turning the tide of war leading up to Dayton. Despite much advocacy by Britain's Tony Blair, however, the ingrained doctrinal preference in the Pentagon for third-party ground forces, backed by air power, had led to a similar US/UK tolerance for radical Islamist fighters in the emerging Kosovo crisis as in Bosnia. And here, British intelligence – and MI6 in particular – were able to draw upon the extensive network of long-established Islamic organizations based across the UK and centred in London.

Kosovo: the London connection

As well as providing a haven for a wide spectrum of Islamist exiles and headquarters for numerous charities, London by the 1980s had become the Arab world's media hub, with major Arabic-language newspapers – *As Sharq al Awsat* and *Al Quds* among many others

– based in the capital. Prominent within the highly fractionated dissident community was a militant Salafist grouping, Al Muhajiroun (AM), which by the mid-1990s had evolved into the central coordinating body for Islamist radicals. Originally launched in Jeddah in 1983 by former activists of Hizb-ut Tahrir and participants in the failed 1979 Saudi coup of Juhaiman al-Utaiba, Al Muhajiroun ('The Emigrants') was formally set up in London in 1996 under Syrian-born Omar Bakri Mohammed, a highly influential, self-declared 'sheikh' who had previously established the UK branch of Hizb-ut and the parent AM in Saudi Arabia. With wide-ranging global links to Hizb-ut and the Muslim Brotherhood,[52] Omar Bakri's proselytizing across university campuses and his takeover of North London's Finsbury Park mosque had drawn the attention of several intelligence agencies, including the CIA and the French DGSE, as well as MI5, MI6 and the Metropolitan Police Special Branch.

However, if some in the intelligence world were concerned about Omar Bakri's calls for global jihad – notably the French DGSE, which, furious at support for Algerian Islamists, mounted active operations against AM affiliates (see Chapter 5) – the Syrian was nevertheless to remain at liberty until retiring into voluntary exile in Lebanon after the 7 July 2005 London bombings. In similar fashion, following the events of 9/11, leading Islamist preacher Abu Qatada had fled his Acton, West London, home with family members in an SUV for what was then claimed as an unknown destination. Qatata – described by Spanish special prosecutor Baltasar Garzón as 'the spiritual head of the mujahideen across Europe'[53] – was imam of the Baker Street mosque in Marylebone and a key figure in the Egyptian-based Takfir wal-Hegira, which had claimed responsibility for the assassination of Anwar Sadat in 1981.

The apparent latitude granted Bakri, Qatada and regular tabloid hate-figure Abu Hamza of the Finsbury Park Mosque had prompted US and Israeli accusations of British 'appeasement' of radical Islamism in the UK[54] and further claims of an at least de facto understanding between Bakri and the other Islamist leaders and elements in British intelligence, in the light of AM's role as a recruitment conduit for British Muslims fighting in the Balkans. In this regard, a network had been established by Pakistan-based militant group Harkat ul-Ansar (HUA), which had dispatched a 200-strong contingent of fighters to Bosnia in 1994 with aid from US intelligence and the government of then prime minister Benazir Bhutto – which was also to provide a training mission under retired Pakistan ISI chief General Hamid Gul.[55] HUA maintained a significant UK presence, in later partnership with Al Muhajiroun, and counted among their British number Omar Saeed Sheikh,[56] a Bosnia veteran later convicted for the murder of *Wall Street Journal* reporter Daniel Pearl (see below). Omar Bakri was later to confirm, in a March 2004 interview, that he 'used to encourage people to go to Bosnia to help their Muslim brothers and sisters, when the UK law permitted that type of intervention'. Bakri was also to stress that 'of course, we do not encourage Muslims in Britain or in any other Western country to copy al-Qaeda, as we are all bound by the "Covenant of Securities" ... I study English law. Therefore, I can tell you when I am right on the edge of the law.'[57]

In January 2005, however, after warning of the 'inevitability' of jihadist attacks on London, Omar Bakri was to renounce comprehensively the 'Covenant of Securities' live on the Internet. Claiming that the agreement had been 'violated' by British anti-terrorist legislation – notably the forthcoming 'Prevention of Terrorism Act', which reinstated the 2001 Act's indefinite detention of foreign nationals[58] – and the arrest under the Act of Abu Hamza, Bakri declared that 'the whole of Britain has become Dar ul-Harb (land of war)' and 'the kuffar (unbeliever) has no sanctity for their own life and property', while further calling for global jihad under the al-Qaeda banner.[59] By coincidence or not, the trial of Abu Hamza had been scheduled to begin on 7 July 2005.

A further leading UK-based Islamist, Haroun Rashid Awsat, has been linked to MI6 operations in the Balkans and to terrorism in the UK itself. Awsat, a close associate of Omar Bakri and 'right-hand man' to Abu Hamza at the Finsbury Park Mosque, was arrested in Pakistan and deported to America in July 2005.[60] According to a former US Justice Department prosecutor, John Loftus, 'we knew about this guy, Awsat ... back in 1999 ... The Justice Department wanted to indict him in Seattle because him and his buddy were trying to set up a terrorist training school in Oregon.'[61] The authorities subsequently were to drop the case, in Loftus's view because 'apparently, Awsat was working for British intelligence ... the US was used by Al Muhajiroun for training of people to send to Kosovo. Believe it or not, British intelligence actually hired some al-Qaeda guys to help defend the Muslim rights in Albania and in Kosovo ... The CIA was funding the operation.' Loftus, then retired from the Justice Department, may well have had his own reasons for retailing the story, but undeniable was the seemingly total freedom of international movement afforded Awsat. He had appeared in South Africa and London and then flew on to Pakistan immediately before the 7/7 London bombings – despite being flagged on both UK and US 'watch lists'.[62] Rashid Awsat was also linked to the network of terrorist plots uncovered by the three-year international police and intelligence campaign, 'Operation Crevice',[63] which, aside from the London tube bombings, included the thwarted 2004 attempt to target UK nightclubs and the Kent Bluewater shopping centre.[64] In the view of many credible analysts, the 'rogue agent' hypothesis brooks little other explanation.[65] Awsat, however, was by no means the only high-profile Islamist militant to profit from the UK/US intelligence war in the Balkans, as we shall see below.

Pakistan, the ISI and the troubled
partnership against terror

As in the case of Afghanistan, the hands-off use of Islamist militant networks in the Balkan wars – and the critical role of Pakistan's Inter-Service Intelligence as the prime facilitator – was to return to haunt their erstwhile Western collaborators. The wide international publicity surrounding the kidnap and murder of Daniel Pearl, later the subject of films and a major 'reconstructive' study by best-selling French author Bernard-Henri Lévy – and the leading role of former public schoolboy and high-flying LSE student Ahmed Omar Saeed Sheikh – has also cast a spotlight on the highly ambivalent relationship between Western intelligence services, the ISI and the War on Terror in general, albeit one most unwelcome for all concerned. Pearl, a leading *Wall Street Journal* reporter and South Asia bureau chief, had been probing possible links between organized crime, elements in the ISI and the bombers of 9/11. One focus of his researches was an armed militant group, Jaish-e-Mohammed,[66] purportedly banned but apparently still operating freely, and a sister organization, Al-Fuqra.

Pearl's *Journal* reporting and his presence on the Karachi Islam-ist circuit had attracted the attention of the formerly London-based Saeed Sheikh, who was by now an established figure among Pakistani militants. Among other activities, Saeed Sheikh had co-founded Jaish-e-Mohammed, drawing in Balkans veterans from Harkat ul-Ansar. Saeed Sheikh had offered to arrange interviews for Daniel Pearl. First of these was to be with Al-Fuqra leader Ali Gilani, a long-term contact and former US resident, who had fled the United States after the failed 1993 World Trade Center bombing. Al-Fuqra, which featured in the State Department's terrorist list from the mid-1990s, was also linked to the US-based Muslims of the Americas – investigated for credit-card fraud and a range of immigration and smuggling offences – and the Al Rashid Trust, an Islamic charity. The latter foundation was among the first sequestered by Federal authorities after 9/11. What had caught Pearl's interest in Al-Fuqra were reports that it had earlier hosted a visit from 'shoe-bomber' Richard Reid.[67]

That Pearl was clearly getting close to something is borne out by a sometime collaborator, intelligence consultant Robert Baer. Baer, a former CIA station chief in Iraq in the early 1990s and later subject of the Oscar-nominated film *Syriana*, notes 'the immediate questions that need to be answered are in Pakistan ... [in] ... the complicated nature of relationships between Muslim extremists and their political and financial sponsors that Danny had stumbled upon.'[68] Chief among these were the links between the ISI, later captured alleged 9/11 mastermind Khalid Sheikh Mohammed – named by some as the actual killer of Daniel Pearl – and Saeed Sheikh.[69]

Omar Saeed Sheikh certainly maintained a striking public profile. In 1994 he had orchestrated the kidnap of four Western tourists (three Britons and an American) outside New Delhi. He had also delivered a ransom note to the BBC's Delhi offices in person. Seized shortly afterwards, following a gunfight, he was given a ten-year prison sentence by the Indian authorities. No moves were made at this time by either the UK or the US government for his extradition. Prior to this, Saeed Sheikh claimed to BBC reporters to have spent two years fighting in Bosnia.[70] Freed by India in December 1999, in a hostage exchange following the hijacking of an Air India flight – widely rumoured to have been arranged by the ISI – Saeed Sheikh returned to live openly at his family home in Lahore. He also made two return visits to relatives in the UK in 2000 and early 2001. These, despite furious protest by the 1994 kidnap victims, were allowed to proceed entirely unhindered. Formal UK interest in the case (legally known as *Letters Rogatory*) was first registered in September 2001. Given Saeed Sheikh's express wish to return to the UK, and a series of prison visits made by UK officials, it is hard not to conclude that there existed some arranged, possibly long-standing, quid pro quo with British intelligence, particularly in the light of the Bosnia connection. Such indeed was claimed in *The Times*[71] and the *Daily Mail*. In response, the Foreign Office was to observe blandly that 'he has not been convicted of any offences [in the UK]. He has not even been brought to trial.'[72]

The eventual issuing of a formal UK request for information on the 1994 events was succeeded by the 2002 release of 'sealed' US indictments, apparently first registered in November 2001. It has never been explained why these were not acted on at the time. One determining factor may have been widespread press allegations – notably in the *Wall Street Journal* – that Saeed Sheikh had been the financial liaison between al-Qaeda and leading 9/11 hijacker Mohammed Atta.[73] The funds, estimated at between $100,000 and $200,000 were said to have been wired to Atta's Florida accounts in stages during August 2001. Also alleged in the *Wall Street Journal*, however, was that the direct instruction had come from the then head of the ISI, General Mahmoud Ahmad. This had been traced through a series of mobile phone conversations tracked, inter alia, by Indian intelligence, which, aside from the kidnap and air-hijack concerns, had focused on Saeed Sheikh's linkages with organized crime in the subcontinent. According to Indian press reports, the Mohammed Atta transfers themselves were drawn from ransom money, extracted from a wealthy Calcutta shoe magnate after his kidnap in Dubai in July 2001. The money was then sent on to Saeed Sheikh via Dubai-based Indian gangster Aftab Ansari, whom Saeed Sheikh had met in New Delhi's Tihar prison.[74] There has been much speculation regarding how much Mahmoud Ahmad – and, indeed, Saeed Sheikh himself – were in the loop of 9/11. Caution would suggest at least some general ignorance of operational detail. General Ahmad was having breakfast in Washington at the time, with members of the House and Senate Intelligence Committee.

What is not in doubt, though, is that both had contact with bin Laden and the Taliban and that Saeed Sheikh enjoyed close links with the ISI.

Responding to strong US and allied pressure, in which deputy secretary of state Richard Armitage had threatened to bomb Pakistan 'back to the stone age', Islamabad's ruler, General Pervez Musharraf, announced on 7 October 2001 a 'quiet' reform of the ISI, replacing Ahmad along with two other ISI leaders, lieutenant generals Mohammed Aziz Khan and Muzaffar Usmani. Aziz Khan had been chief liaison with Jaish-e-Mohammed, co-founded by Saeed Sheikh and Afghan war veteran Maulana Masood Azhar following their release from prison in the Air India swap. The sacking of Mahmoud Ahmad – a particularly painful episode for Musharraf, who had relied on Ahmad during his own 1999 coup – provoked a backlash from militants. On 23 December, Harkat ul-Ansar attacked the Indian Parliament in New Delhi and the Provincial Assembly in Kashmir's capital, Srinigar, amidst a spate of sectarian killings in Pakistan itself. The open challenge to his rule and intense US pressure forced Musharraf to take a public stance condemning terrorism, which he did on 12 January 2002, and order the arrest of some 2,000 militants. Left at liberty, however, was Omar Saeed Sheikh. And on 22 January 2002 he was to organize an attack on the American Cultural Center in Calcutta, in conjunction with the now officially banned Jaish-e-Mohammed. On the next day, Daniel Pearl was kidnapped by a group calling itself the 'National Youth Movement for Restoration of Pakistan Sovereignty'.

The somewhat incoherent demands levelled by the hitherto unheard-of National Youth Movement – which included the resumption of sales of F-16 fighter aircraft – and the attention of a multitude of intelligence services, soon led investigators to Saeed Sheikh, who publicly surfaced when Pearl's video beheading was released after a month of captivity. Saeed Sheikh, however, surrendered to a provincial official, Ijaz Shah, his reputed ISI handler, and was only handed over to civil authorities after a week incommunicado and much pressure on family members in Lahore by Musharraf loyalists. As veteran *Washington Post* columnist Jim Hoagland surmises, Saeed Sheikh's whereabouts were no secret, as he was 'contacting the intelligence service as part of a long-standing relationship'.[75] After three transfers of location, a trial was finally held in camera in a bunker beneath the Karachi High Court. Saeed Sheikh had been confidently expecting just a four-year jail term, but in fact the death sentence was pronounced in July 2002. This, however, was subject to appeal. To date, forty appeals have been lodged, in direct contravention of Pakistan's civil code, which stipulates a maximum of two. There has been a total silence from all parties in London and Washington.

Saeed Sheikh's central role in coordinating Islamist and insurgent networks with state actors in Gulf/Saudi security services and the ISI was proving a huge embarrassment to the divided British security establishment, notably in highlighting the far more radical divisions in the security forces of Pakistan. In September 2006 a leaked report from the MOD-sponsored Defence Academy observed:

> The Army's dual role in combating terrorism and at the same time promoting the MMA [Muttahida Majlis-e-Amal – a six-party Islamist coalition] and so indirectly supporting the Taliban ... is coming under closer and closer international scrutiny ... Pakistan (through the ISI) has been supporting terrorism and extremism – whether in London on 7/7 or in Afghanistan or Iraq.

The trenchant analysis from the Defence Academy, compiled by a senior naval commander 'linked to MI6', was similarly to condemn the 'blind eye towards existing instability [in Pakistan]' and hold that 'The US/UK cannot begin to turn the tide until they identify the real enemies from attacking ideas tactically – and seek to put in place a more just vision.' Any progress along these lines would require 'Pakistan to move away from Army rule and for the ISI to be dismantled and, more significantly, something to be put in its place.' The paper was also to offer a more immediate prognosis, that 'Musharraf knows that time is running out for him … at some point the US is likely to withdraw funding (and possibly even protection) of him – estimated at $70–80 million a month … Without US funding his position will become increasingly tenuous.'[76]

The Defence Academy's essay in South Asian realpolitik was, perhaps not uncoincidentally, brought into public view at the time of the Old Bailey trial over the Operation Crevice-linked plots. On 18 September 2006, the alleged ringleader, British Pakistani Omar Khyam, withdrew from giving testimony, on the grounds that

> the ISI in Pakistan has had words with my family relating to what I have been saying about them … I think they are worried I might reveal more about them, so right now, as much as I want to clarify matters, the priority for me has to be the safety of my family so I am going to stop. I am not going to discuss anything related to the ISI any more or the evidence.[77]

Omar Khyam had previously admitted to undergoing training in explosives use and urban warfare in Pakistan whilst 'working for the cause'. But more rationalist elements in Pakistan's military–industrial and intelligence complex were clearly opposed to unleashing random jihadism among their main backers in the West. In a diplomatic counteroffensive in Britain and the USA, Pervez Musharraf was to mount a robust defence of his policies. In a London television interview on 27 September 2006, Musharraf declared, 'You will be brought down to your knees if Pakistan doesn't cooperate with you … And if the ISI is not with you, you will fail.' And elsewhere, not inaccurately, blaming the West for the rise of the Taliban, he declared, 'we fought the Soviet Union for you. We won the Cold War for you … We don't like anyone telling us to dismantle the ISI, least of all the British Ministry of Defence.'[78] While in his autobiography – released to coincide with the image-boosting tour – Musharraf was to suggest that, indeed,

> It is believed in some quarters that while Omar Sheikh was at the LSE he was recruited by the British intelligence agency MI6. It is said that MI6 persuaded him to take an active part in demonstrations against Serbian aggression in Bosnia and even sent him to Kosovo to join the jihad. At some point he probably became a rogue or double agent.[79]

The apparent confirmation of Saeed Sheikh's relations with British and, possibly, US intelligence, was, in the first instance, a repost to internal critics still smarting at the dismissal of Mahmoud Ahmad and the tentative attempts at reining in the ISI. The link between Saeed Sheikh and the ISI itself had been publicly denied by Colin Powell on 2 March 2002, at the height of press interest in the Pearl affair. It had also, however, been inadvertently confirmed the previous week in off-camera remarks by Donald Rumsfeld.[80] Four years on, though, General Musharraf was to make much of the '680 terrorists' handed over to the allies to date, notably the loquacious alleged 9/11 planner Khalid Sheikh Mohammed. He was to claim further that British interrogation of 'an associate of KSM' captured in February 2004 had revealed the link between al-Qaeda and the London suicide bombers, Mohammed Siddique Khan and Shehzad Tanweer, albeit with the complaint that 'this information … was not shared with us until 28 July 2005, three weeks after the attacks in London.'[81] To its discomfort, British intelligence had been forced to acknowledge that Khan and Tanwer had indeed been under close MI5/Special Branch surveillance throughout this period, the initial 'cleanskin' line having been quietly dropped after newspaper exposure. The surveillance level had apparently been downgraded some three weeks before the attacks of 7 July.[82]

In early 2008, General Musharraf was again visiting London, in attempts to shore up the growing doubts in the West about his grip on power. Here, escalating guerrilla conflict in the Frontier provinces and mass civil disobedience were serving to spotlight a multilayered crisis of legitimacy. The scale of the crisis was thrown into stark relief with the December 2007 assassination of Benazir Bhutto. Bhutto – a long-term opponent of army rule and the ISI in particular – was killed at a closely policed rally in the garrison town of Rawalpindi. While many in Bhutto's PPP were quick to accuse Musharraf himself of involvement, the general was in fact set to be the main loser. His remaining hopes of Western support rested on concluding a deal with Bhutto, whom he had recently let back into the country.

At a 28 January 2008 Downing Street press conference, Musharraf was to claim that the UK itself was lacking a long-term counterterrorism strategy, registering the spread of endogenous radicalism and pointing out that, unlike Britain, Pakistan had banned Hizb ut-Tahrir.[83] But Pervez Musharraf's 'So why blame us?' plea was issued against a further high-profile instance of the volatility of the rule of law back in Pakistan. This was brought out by the disappearance from police custody of alleged 'terror mastermind' Rashid Rauf, while en route to court from Islamabad's Adiala prison. Rauf's mysterious escape, on 14 December 2007, took place after the courts had agreed his extradition to Britain on (non-terrorist) murder charges. (These stemmed from the death, four years earlier, of an uncle in Birmingham.) But what had first sparked Rashid Rauf's arrest in Pakistan on 9 August 2006 was his alleged involvement in an attempt simultaneously to bomb ten transatlantic airliners in mid-flight from Britain to America. The 'Airlines Plot' – which had led to chaos at Heathrow and at airports across the western hemisphere – was part of a global network of conspiracies uncovered in the wide-ranging 'Operation Crevice' investigations. To the apparent dismay of MI5, these investigations had been rolled up at an early stage under US pressure.[84]

Despite the operational differences between the approaches of MI5 and the CIA, there was agreement on the central importance of the insurgent matrix of Rashid Rauf. A close family relation of Rauf, Jaish-e-Mohammed co-founder Maulana Massod Azhar also runs Darul Uloom Madina, a well-known radical madrassa in his hometown of Bahwalapour, 450 miles south of Islamabad.[85] After Rauf's own arrest in Bahwalapour, British, US and the competing Pakistan agencies wrangled for access. This was selectively forthcoming. But, again, nothing was said (at least publicly) to link the Rauf investigations with the activities of Omar Saeed Sheikh.[86]

In the lengthy official Report of the 9/11 Commission,[87] the role of Pakistan in training, financing and providing safe haven for terrorists was widely covered, but only in the most general terms. The efforts of President Clinton to gain the cooperation of Pervez Musharraf are noted, although 'Clinton did not want to press the bin Laden issue too heavily at the main meeting [in April 2000] because ISI members were present.'[88] There are two passing mentions of Mahmoud Ahmad, both in the context of post 9/11 diplomacy. Omar Saeed Sheikh gets no reference at all. Interviewed on the American CBC network in August 2006, Commission vice chair Lee Hamilton (formerly chair of the House Intelligence Committee) stated 'I don't know anything about it', when questioned on the Saeed Sheikh money transfer allegations published in the *Wall Street Journal*. And when further asked about Commission probing of any more general ISI connections, Hamilton replied: 'They may have; I do not recall us writing anything about it in the report. We may have, but I don't recall it.'[89]

Iran–Contra redux: promoting the 'arc of moderation'

Despite much recent rhetoric on the supposed 'clash of civilizations', the Western response to the rise of political Islam has, as we have seen, taken a consistent path of expediency. During and after the Cold War, Islamist populism has been taken up as a ready corrective to both socialism and the sort of nationalist currents that could promote genuine independence in decision-making. Here, Islamism's claimed compatibility with free-market principles has been viewed as the touchstone, with massive involvement by major US and European institutions such as Citibank, Chase Manhattan and Goldman Sachs in setting up an 'Islamic' banking system after the petrodollar boom of the mid-1970s.[90] Indeed, this approach has been embraced by even the most avowedly radical of Islamists, such as the Algerian Front Islamique (FIS) – whose 1990 election programme strongly backed the IMF – and al-Turabi's Sudan, where finance minister Abdul Rahim Hamdi was a declared disciple of Milton Friedman. Within successive US administrations, influential oil and banking interests have promoted the mutual interests of Islamism and capitalism, from the early days of Aramco in Saudi Arabia to Unocal's courtship of the Taliban under Bill Clinton.[91] In a major 2003 study, former CIA and RAND consultant Graham Fuller noted: 'Classical Islamic theory envisages the role of the state as limited to facilitating the well-being of markets ... Islamists have always powerfully objected to socialism and communism ... Islam has never had problems with the idea that wealth is unevenly distributed.'[92]

US support for Islamists against the Soviet Union and the sporadically influential view of an innately conservative and pro-market force had been tempered, however, by a growing awareness of the differing currents within Islamism itself. The 1979 Iranian Revolution had brought the Shi'a–Sunni division into US political discourse, conjoined with the geopolitical rivalry between Iran and Saudi Arabia. Riyadh was waging a proxy war against the Shi'ite ayatollas and backed Sunni-dominated Iraq in Saddam's 1980 invasion. A further factor in the Reagan/Bush administration's calculations were the views of Israel and the growing US neoconservative lobby, which saw the Iraq–Saudi Sunni axis as the greater long-term threat and advocated a modus vivendi with Tehran. Israel had, indeed, been covertly shipping US-supplied materiel to Iran from the start of the conflict and had hopes of enlisting the Iranian-backed Shi'a minority in Lebanon against the PLO.

The series of covert negotiations between Iran, Israel and the USA – culminating in the sale of 1,508 TOW and eighteen Hawk missiles and much ancillary equipment – collectively known as 'Iran–Contra' were revealed by the Iranians themselves on 4 November 1986, amidst much embarrassment for the administration. Many of the indicted (and later pardoned) US officials involved, however, would remain influential in US policy circles and resume office under George W. Bush. Notable here were then assistant secretary of state Eliot Abrams and former NSC consultant Michael Ledeen. Abrams, named deputy national security adviser in February 2005 and later appointed Baghdad ambassador, had line responsibility for 'Global Democracy and Strategy', a concept embracing some ambiguity in the Bush administration. Whilst the personnel associated with Iran–Contra have remained in government, however, the focus in policy had shifted to regarding Iran and Shi'ism in general as the main enemy.

There have, in fact, been two contending strands in US policy since the 1980s concerning the relative merits of Sunni and Shi'a Islamism. What remains common ground, however, is a willingness to embrace the most reactionary social and political currents in the Middle East in order to secure continued US ascendancy. The 2003 invasion of Iraq saw the USA seeking allies among the principal Shi'ite opposition, the Supreme Council for Islamic Revolution in Iraq (SCIRI) and the Islamic Call (al-Dawa), whilst some in the neocon lobby advocated Shi'a secession in Saudi Arabia's (oil-rich) Eastern provinces. 'Independence for the Eastern Province would clearly be catastrophic for the Saudi state', observed Richard Perle in his 2003 book *An End to Evil*, 'But it might be a good outcome for the United States.'[93] With the ending of any perceived threat from Iraq, however, and the departure from the US administration of some of the more vocal critics of Saudi Arabia, the focus again shifted to Iran and its close ally Hizbollah, the increasingly assertive Shi'ite movement in Lebanon.

Indeed, a consensus view emerging in Washington and among its allies is that Iran, despite being a part of US President Bush's 'axis of evil', has been the 'chief beneficiary of the war on terror in the Middle East'. An August 2006 Chatham House report notes that

> The United States, with Coalition support, has eliminated two of Iran's regional rival governments – the Taliban in Afghanistan in November 2001 and Saddam Hussein's regime in Iraq in April 2003 – but has failed to replace either with coherent and stable political structures … Consequently, Iran has moved to fill the regional void with an apparent ease that has disturbed both regional players and the United States and its European allies. Iran is one of the most significant and powerful states in the region and its influence spreads well beyond its critical location at the nexus of the Middle East, Turkey, the Caucasus, Central Asia and South Asia.[94]

In 2006, the Bush administration asked congress for $75 million to promote 'democratic change' in Iran, disbursed by Abrams's NSC office. Concurrently, a Washington conference organized by the American Enterprise Institute (AEI) called for a federated Iran, with autonomy for Kurdish, Azeri and Turkmen areas.[95] In the less public realm, it was reported that Bush had signed a 'non-lethal Presidential finding' in early 2007, authorizing 'propaganda, disinformation and manipulation of Iran's currency and international financial transactions'.[96] In a further echo of the build-up to war in Iraq, Michael Ledeen founded the 'Coalition for Democracy in Iran', sponsored by AEI. Ledeen, back in the Pentagon at Douglas Feith's Office of Special Plans, had teamed up with fellow Iran–Contra veteran, arms dealer and alleged Mossad agent, Manicur Ghobanifar, to funnel supposed intelligence on

Iran's nuclear programme to the wider US government and the media.[97]

Aside from the coordinated 'non-lethal' campaign against Iran by the USA and its allies, there has also been much evidence of a more sanguinary programme. The Iraq-based Mujahideen-e Khalq (MEK) – former Marxist guerrilla fighters in the 1979 Iranian Revolution, later sponsored by Saddam Hussein – had been allowed to retain its bases, structure and light weaponry after the US invasion of 2003. Although subject to official US repudiation and listed as a terrorist organization by the State Department, the MEK conducted a series of attacks in southern Iran throughout 2006.[98] Also based in Iraq, the Party for a Free Life in Kurdistan (PJAK) – linked to the insurgent Kurdistan Workers' Party (PKK) and, in some accounts, 'trained and equipped by Israel' – has mounted a series of cross-border raids of increasing sophistication.[99]

If focusing ethnic and separatist tendencies has constituted one pole of the Bush administration's Middle East policy – with a major Pentagon study on the subject commissioned from defence contractor Hicks & Associates in 2005[100] – there has been a more controversial approach to the ostensible targets of the War on Terror itself, militant Islamist jihadis. In Iranian Baluchistan, a Sunni extremist group Jundulla (Brigade of Allah) has engaged in assassinations and car-bombings, including a major assault on a Revolutionary Guards barracks in the city of Zahidan – with reported support from the USA and Pakistan's ISI.[101] The emerging front line, however, has been in Syria and the Lebanon. Here, a portion of the $200 million US military aid package to the embattled Lebanese government of Fouad Siniora has reportedly been passed on to militant Salafist groups, along with a significantly greater amount of Saudi 'black' funding.[102] And in Syria, the main beneficiary of US/Saudi funding has been the Syrian National Salvation Front, dominated by the Syrian Muslim Brotherhood. Following Israel's disastrous thirty-day invasion of Lebanon in

July–August 2006, Vice President Dick Cheney had visited Saudi Arabia at the invitation of King Abdullah and national security adviser Prince Bandar for emergency talks on Iran and Hizbollah. Hizbollah, its position strengthened throughout the Middle East after resisting Israeli forces, were viewed as the cutting edge of a renascent Shi'ism and as such to be tackled at all costs by the Sunni-fundamentalist al-Saud regime.

What was to emerge as the new US policy was sketched out by Secretary of State Condoleezza Rice before a January 2007 Senate Foreign Relations Hearing. Depicting a 'new strategic alignment' in the Middle East, Rice characterized the major Sunni states as 'centres of moderation' in contrast to Iran, Hizbollah and Syria, 'on the other side of that divide'. The Sunni 'arc of moderation' theme had earlier been put forward, in December 2006, by close Bush ally Tony Blair at a speech in Dubai. Blair had strongly backed the Israeli invasion of Lebanon and stressed the need to 'pin back' Iran's advances in the Middle East. Blair had earlier caused controversy by halting an investigation into Saudi-linked bribery allegations by UK defence contractors BAE Systems, on the grounds of 'national security'. The main beneficiary of the $1 billion largesse was allegedly Saudi Prince Bandar.[103]

Prince Bandar, long-serving Washington ambassador and confidant of the Bush family, had been a major player in funding both the Afghan mujahideen and Iran–Contra – a relationship renewed in a series of autumn 2006 meetings with Eliot Abrams and Dick Cheney in which the shift in Middle East policy was finalized. An early and perhaps unlikely victim of the change was Bandar's replacement as ambassador, former intelligence chief Prince Turki. Turki's sudden resignation on 15 December had come after his advocacy of the 'inclusive' approach to Iran and Syria found in the bipartisan 2006 Report on Iraq by the Baker Commission.[104]

In a post-invasion interview with leading US commentator Seymour Hersh, Hizbollah leader Sheikh Nasrallah observed that

Bush's goal would seem to be 'the drawing of a new map of the region' so that 'Israel will be the most important and the strongest state in a region that has been partitioned into ethnic and confessional states.'[105] Clearly, such an outcome – whether intended or not – remains well within the bounds of possibility. But the advent of such a 'perfect storm' warned of in CIA assessments of the Iraq invasion[106] might also be not unwelcome to some sections of the Washington policy community. Writing in 2002, influential US neoconservative Michael Ledeen was to propose that

> The radical transformation of several Middle East countries … is entirely in keeping with the American tradition … Creative destruction is our middle name … Our enemies have always hated this whirlwind of energy and creativity … They must attack us in order to survive, just as we must destroy them to advance our historical mission.[107]

Ledeen's 'creative destruction' advocacy had been much in vogue in the run-up to the 2003 Iraq invasion. In the next chapter we consider how this first instalment of what was to be a highly ambitious plan was at once a marketing triumph and an intelligence disaster – and how the response was sought in an equally radical transformation of public discourse into a new theatre of warfare.

2

Faith and lies

The absolute cynical manipulation, deliberately cynical manipulation, to shape American public opinion ... it worked; they said
'we want to go to war', including me. (Senator Jay Rockefeller, CBS
News, September 2006)

A convenient truth: the 'state of war' and mass mobilization

As we have seen, there have been long and sometimes intimate
relations between Western interests and radical Islamism. Across
the Middle East and South Asia, intelligence has often formed
the focal point. Throughout, the policy assumption was that the
Western powers were able to balance individual, issue-based arrangements with sections of the Islamist networks against wider
concerns. The US-led invasion of Iraq, however, served to highlight
how a new, asymmetric power struggle – and pattern of power
distribution – had already taken on its own distinctive identity for
the twenty-first century. The new front line was to be found on
what had hitherto served as safe Western patrimony – the terrain
of globalized media. In this chapter, we track the concepts, conflicts and players behind the US/allied attempts to maintain media

domination in the course of War on Terror. And we consider how the target of these efforts, militant Islamism, was perhaps emerging as the main beneficiary.

The launch of the Iraq War in March 2003 was conceived in some Washington quarters as not merely the chance to remove a running sore that had troubled US policy since Bush senior, nor simply a fortuitous move on the world's third largest oil reserves,[1] but as a conclusive repost to 9/11. 'Afghanistan wasn't enough', veteran US statesman Henry Kissinger declared, 'We need to humiliate them.' The events of 9/11 needed a US response, 'essentially more than proportionate'. It was necessary 'in order to make the point that we're not going to live in this world that they want for us'.[2] Kissinger, whose voice carried weight in the Bush inner circle,[3] was also the author of 'madman theory' – the deliberate cultivation of an image of irrationalism as a politico-military tool.[4] This was, at the time, very much of a piece with the neocons' 'creative destruction' advocacy and the use of demonstrative war to bring it about. In the wider public arena, however, this was not an obvious point-of-sale advantage in moving mass opinion. As such, the Bush administration had decided, in close consultation with Tony Blair, to craft a coordinated, rolling campaign stressing conventional public concerns and justified by supposedly unimpeachable – but, naturally, unreleasable – intelligence information. This was to be deployed across a wide media spectrum, using the formidable resources of mass-marketing and public relations technology built up over decades.

The role of what former NSC consultant and Harvard professor Joseph S. Nye has called 'soft power' – the possession of market lead in both the production and content of cultural artefacts – has long been seen as part of the furniture for US policymakers.[5] What is now termed 'strategic communication' has long played a prominent role in US policy. The massive effort expended during the Cold War on acknowledged US government media outlets like Voice of America and more covert manipulation of ostensibly

independent news and broadcast media[6] seemingly (
in the collapse of the Soviet Union. From the o
a parallel programme was set in train aimed at
'scientific' basis for perception management at both the individual
level – brainwashing – and that of mass manipulation.

The search for a set of formulas for moulding mass opinion
was cast in the governing 'behaviourist' methodology of the US
social sciences, in which both individual and mass actions are
construed as subject to a near-infinite malleability. As one analyst
has observed, 'Modern attitude theory is a branch of behaviourism
which views the higher mental functions as explainable in terms
of stimuli and response ... Psycholinguists have long believed that
the grammatical and semantic features of a given language shape
the world view of its speakers.'[7] Often at a level employing a simple
repertoire of dumbing-down tabloid techniques based on word-
association, juxtaposition and repetition, the approach has been
crude but undeniably effective in a host of instances, notably in
swaying electorates in such Cold War flashpoints as Italy and Chile
– although in the latter instance a multi-million dollar campaign,
including radio/television broadcasts, economic sabotage and the
covert takeover of the hitherto moderate mass daily *El Mercurio*,[8]
had to be supplemented by more traditional methods. At a darker
level was the conducting of a series of experiments by the CIA, on
often unsuspecting individuals, whose latter incarnations were to
surface at Abu Ghraib.

The information aspect of the 'full spectrum dominance'[9] sought
by US strategy in 1992 was subject to growing attention, particularly
after the perceived successes of US media coverage during the first
(1991) Gulf War. The existing Cold War structure involving 'public
diplomacy' was to remain essentially unaltered, however, until the
advent of Presidential Decision Directive (PDD) 68 of 1999. This
merged the hitherto departmentally independent US Information
Agency (USIA)[10] with the State Department – deleteriously, for

some observers[11] – and handed over the agency's broadcasting empire (Voice of America, Radio Free Europe/Liberty, Radio Free Asia, Radio/TV Marti, Arabic-language Radio Sawa and Al-Hurra satellite station and the Persian-language Radio Farda) to an independent governing board.

With an annual $1.2 billion budget, the whole spectrum of public diplomacy has been subject to intense bureaucratic turf battles between the various agencies and attracted over fifteen government and independent inquiries since 9/11.[12] In the immediate aftermath of the attack, US government agencies struggled to shape a co-ordinated response. In October 2001, the State Department set up a wholly new 24-hour public diplomacy coordination group, linking the Defense Department (DoD), US embassies, US regional commands and the White House. A Counter Terrorism Strategy Policy Coordinating Committee was established in the National Security Council (NSC). In addition, the Defense Department's established Information Warfare sections went into high gear, with the hiring of PR professionals and consultancies, such as the Rendon Group, and constant appearances in the media by officials and military leaders. Amidst the flurry of ad hoc crisis response teams linking defence, intelligence and the NSC, the White House created a network of 'Coalition Information Centers' (CICs), crossing time zones for simultaneous global coverage. Using a whole battery of techniques – focus groups, opinion polling, attitudinal research – honed in US and British electioneering and political marketing, and by NATO in the Kosovo campaign, the CICs aimed to present above all a unified front for maintaining the 'message of the day' within the current news cycle. As then Secretary of State Colin Powell declared, 'Those who abet terror by spreading distortion and hate and inciting others take full advantage of the global news cycle. We must use the same cycle.'[13]

Unfortunately for the administration, it was the *content* of the global news cycle rather than its presentation that was and remains the burning issue. And here, the State Department's own polling statistics confirmed an increasingly bleak picture. In surveys conducted in July 2004 by Zogby International, opinion in six targeted Arab countries was virtually in freefall, with those of the population 'favourable' to the USA overall dropping over a two-year period from a pre-Iraq figure of 38 per cent to 11 per cent in the case of Morocco, the most supportive of the group; in Jordan, a country with a modicum of regime legitimacy by Middle East standards, and underwritten by US security guarantees for decades, the drop was from 34 per cent to 15 per cent; in Egypt, the second largest recipient of US foreign aid, the decline was from 15 per cent to an alarming 2 per cent. On the question of support for the US War on Terror, Iraq and Middle East policy in general, the 1 or 2 per cent actually in favour was a figure below the statistical error margin.[14]

Faced with such a 'fundamental problem of credibility' – reflected in the 82.5 per cent of negative media coverage in a March 2003 State Department (INR) 72-country survey[15] – an exhaustive 2004 report for the president's Defense Science Policy Board (DSPB) concluded that 'simply, there is none'.[16] And, indeed, that 'al-Qaeda clearly outflanks the US in the war of information.'[17]

The DSPB – a reclusive but highly influential body – advanced an equally forthright analysis of US strategy across the board. 'Worldwide anger and discontent are directed at America's tarnished credibility and ways the US pursues its goals',[18] they observed. Identifying the overall strategic context as 'acutely uncomfortable',[19] the Board further noted that 'American direct intervention in the Muslim world has paradoxically elevated the stature of and support for radical Islamists, while diminishing support for the United States to single-digits in some Arab societies … *in the eyes of Muslims*, American occupation of Afghanistan and Iraq has not led to democracy there, but only more chaos and suffering',[20] given that 'the dramatic narrative since 9/11 has essentially borne out the entire radical Islamist bill of particulars'.[21] And, moreover, 'there is no yearning-to-be-liberated-by-the-US groundswell in Muslim societies – *except to be liberated perhaps from what they see as apostate tyrannies that the US so energetically promotes and defends*' (emphasis in original).[22]

In the face of the Board's gloomy estimate that 'It will take decades to counter extremist terrorist recruiters and fully restore US global standing and credibility',[23] and plausible sociological analysis of 'the generational and global struggle about ideas'[24] – widely shared across Washington, as the neoconservative bandwagon began to derail – the USA and its junior allies were, nevertheless forced to forge a fresh approach. Confronting the resurgent 'realists' in the State Department, the Bob Gates Pentagon and Michael Hayden's hectically reforming CIA – if not the still-unreformed White House – was, however, the unpalatable fact that, in 'an environment of free and open information flows',[25] the gains of asymmetry had entirely accrued to 'an enemy of tiny proportions and relatively meagre resources', which was left 'clearly in control of the political dialogue in the war on terror'.[26] And, furthermore, the previous US media strategy – consistently revealed in press and congressional reports as lies and disinformation – had contributed to this state almost as much as the administration's heavy-handed diplomacy and bungled military offensives in Iraq and Afghanistan.

Spinning the war: the Rumsfeld legacy

Notwithstanding such bleak assessments, US and allied efforts in the field of strategic communication, Psyops and 'managed information dissemination'[27] have, in the course of the Bush wars, eclipsed even the levels of the Reagan era and Vietnam. In the wake of 9/11, the NSC created an Office for Combating Terrorism, with a lead role for a senior director for Strategic Communication and Information. In parallel, a Counter Terrorism Strategy Policy

Coordinating Committee was established by National Security Adviser Condoleezza Rice to 'coordinate interagency activities ... [and] develop and disseminate the President's messages across the globe'.[28] More controversially, on 30 October 2001 the Pentagon established the Office of Strategic Influence (OSI) to serve as a 'focal point' for the 'strategic information campaign in support of the war on terror'.[29] Aiming to 'develop a full-spectrum influence that would result in greater foreign support of US goals and repudiation of terrorists and their methods', the OSI met fierce opposition from more traditionally minded government officials, concerned at the placement of 'news items, possibly even false ones, to foreign news organizations'[30] and much of the mainstream US media. Given that the US government is, in theory at least, legally prohibited from overt domestic propagandizing, the Pentagon was compelled to close down the OSI in February 2002. But in offering 'the corpse' of the OSI to his critics, Donald Rumsfeld averred to 'keep doing every single thing that needs to be done'[31] and moved many of the same functions to a more covert unit, the Information Operations Task Force (IOTF). Here, DoD concerns for 'leveraging private sector competencies' were to find a fuller expression in partnership with the Rendon Group, a multi-million-dollar Washington communications consultancy.

Formed in 1981 by ex-Democratic National Committee director and self-proclaimed 'information warrior' John Rendon, the Rendon Group was to establish a formidable record in US electioneering for such presidential hopefuls as John Kerry and Walter Mondale. Increasingly, however, the firm's main client base had become the State Department and the DoD, with Rendon providing 'media guidance' for a succession of US military campaigns throughout the 1990s. 'Going all the way back to Panama', the rarely interviewed John Rendon observed, 'we've been involved in every war, with the exception of Somalia.'[32] After securing massive global media coverage for the December 1989 Panama campaign – successfully drawing a veil over prior US support for the regime and demonizing erstwhile US client General Noriega – Rendon's next target was a further lapsed US ally, Iraqi dictator Saddam Hussein. Saddam's August 1990 invasion of Kuwait had brought Rendon a further tranche of lucrative PR contracts from the grateful Kuwaiti government and an enhanced profile in the Middle East. Following President George H.W. Bush's intelligence 'finding' of May 1991 authorizing the removal of Saddam, the CIA approached Rendon with a $20 million budget and a putative leader in waiting – former banker and University of Chicago alumnus Ahmad Chalabi.[33]

Operating from an extensive suite in Catherine Place, London SW1, John Rendon was to craft a seemingly credible international profile for the Iraqi dissidents grouped under his own choice of name, the 'Iraqi National Congress' (INC). And if success in the field had remained elusive, solid gains were forthcoming on Capitol Hill, with Congress voting $58 million in direct aid for the organization and a further $97 million to come with the passage of the Iraq Liberation Act on 31 October 1998.[34]

By February 2002, Rendon – by now out of favour with the CIA on the grounds of Ahmad Chalabi's financial dealings[35] – was a natural choice to coordinate media strategy at the IOTF. The first act was the setting up of a 24-hour 'Information War Room' to monitor global media and offer instant rebuttal in standard US/UK election campaign style. In parallel with an initial $16 million Pentagon contract, Rendon was closely involved from the outset with the White House Office of Global Communications, responsible for promoting the 'message of the day' among government departments and media briefers. And yet a further front in the info-war was opened by Rendon, with the establishment of the White House Iraq Information Group (WHIG).

Drawing on a combination of Bush's political and NSC staffers, the WHIG was to become the central all-media clearing house, soon nicknamed 'the mighty Wurlitzer'.[36] Chaired by the president's chief political adviser Karl Rove – 'Bush's brain' – the group was to merit the ultra-secure White House situation room for its weekly meetings. A who's who of the administration's inner circle participated, including seasoned Republican campaign manager Mary Matalin, deputy director of communications James Wilkinson, legislative liaison (i.e. lobbyist in chief) Nicholas Calio, Condoleezza Rice, deputy national security adviser Stephen Hadley and Vice President Cheney's deputy, Lewis 'Scooter' Libby. Although the existence of the WHIG was publicly acknowledged in August 2002, operations were not to begin in earnest until September, since, as White House chief of staff Andrew Card observed, 'from a marketing point of view, … you don't introduce new products in August'.[37]

Central to the administration's point-of-sale strategy were two key dates at this juncture, the forthcoming 11 October congressional vote on military action and the November mid-term elections. Accordingly, the end of the summer vacation season would see a full-spectrum media assault by the entire Bush war cabinet, with support from leading military figures and sympathetic commentators and academics. Following Andrew Card's candid *New York Times* observations of 6 September, Bush himself used a joint press conference with visiting British prime minister Tony Blair to air 'new' evidence on Iraq's pursuit of nuclear weapons – based, in fact, on a routine IAEA report, issued in July, which noted merely sporadic construction activity at some industrial sites – a claim given further 'legs' by leaked information on Iraq's attempted procurement of aluminium composite tubes, with a possible nuclear role in building gas centrifuges.

The 3,000 precision tubes had been ordered from China in 2000 and tracked by the CIA's Weapons Intelligence and Arms Control Center (WINPAC). In July 2001 the consignment was seized on Jordanian territory. Suppressed at the time, however, was the overwhelming (and later vindicated) inter-agency view that the tubes were conventional battlefield artillery rocket vehicles.[38] Allowing a day's news cycle for the leaks to circulate, the centrifuge story appeared in full in an 8 September *New York Times* report by much-favoured administration outlet Judith Miller. The Miller piece – one of many alarmist Iraq stories later found to be baseless – was central to further 'smoking gun' Iraqi nuclear weapons claims by Vice President Dick Cheney, Condoleezza Rice, Donald Rumsfeld, Colin Powell and General Richard Myers, chairman of the Joint Chiefs, on television talk shows that same day. 'We don't want the smoking gun', Rice intoned gravely on CNN's midday news slot, 'to become a mushroom cloud'.

The coordinated launch of apparent intelligence leaks followed by the simultaneous appearance of leading administration figures 'in a choreographed performance worthy of Riverdance'[39] was central to the WHIG's rolling information management campaign. In marketing terms, the aim was to construct a message aimed at a 'soft support' target audience.[40] Securing at least acquiescence from undecided opinion – the 'swing vote' usually seen as key to election victory – required a reiteration of narrative at once dramatic and directly connected to public concerns. Hence the focus on nuclear weapons, chemical/biological weapons of mass destruction (WMD) in general, and supposed Iraqi links with al-Qaeda. Here, as the DFPB freely admits, 'information saturation means attention, not information, becomes a scarce resource.'[41]

As is well known, the $200 million media blitz was, in the short term, a resounding success. A Republican majority was duly returned to Congress and few dissenting voices were heard in the October War Powers resolution. Congressional waverers were undoubtedly swayed by a CIA White Paper, released on 2 October. Drawing a stark picture of 'Iraq's Weapons of Mass Destruction Programes'[42] the report makes much of the supposed nuclear centrifuge endeavours and launches unequivocal claims on resumed chemical and nerve agent production. However, in the ninety-page classified version – a somewhat rushed National

Intelligence Estimate (NIE), uniquely demanded from the Agency by Congress itself – much qualification is in evidence, with State Department Intelligence (INR) and the Department of Energy dissenting altogether on the nuclear issue. Prior to the October White Paper, and in close consultation, Bush's allies in Whitehall had delivered a now-notorious report in September,[43] aimed as much at the USA as at Blair's own increasingly sceptical constituency. The critical role of PR, 'sensitizing the public',[44] and the US elections in particular are frankly discussed in a series of leaked British cabinet documents for the March–July period, known as the 'Downing Street Minutes'.[45] Here, a 23 July cabinet memo records that, whilst no final date had been settled for the Iraq invasion, in defence minister Geoff Hoon's view 'the most likely timing in US minds for military action to begin was January, with the timeline beginning 30 days before the US congressional elections'.[46]

It had been clear from the outset – the 6–7 April Blair visit to the Bush ranch in Crawford, Texas, had finalized the plan – that, particularly from Britain's perspective, 'For Iraq, "regime change" does not stack up. It sounds like a grudge between Bush and Saddam. Much better ... to make the objective ending the threat ... from Iraqi [WMD] before Saddam uses it or gives it to terrorists.' This was at once easier to justify in terms of international law, 'but also more demanding'.[47] The unique selling proposition (USP) for the Iraq War was thus the conjunction between nuclear weapons and 'terrorism'. Facing target audiences in both the Washington establishment and the wider public, deputy defense secretary Paul Wolfowitz was characteristically candid: 'for bureaucratic reasons, we settled on one issue, weapons of mass destruction ... because it was the one reason everyone could agree on.'[48] And, as another 'senior administration official' was later to admit, 'the administration took what looked like the path of least resistance in making its public case for war: WMD and the intelligence links with al-Qaeda. If the public read too much into those links and thought Saddam had a hand in September 11, so much the better.'[49] A December 2002 Pew poll for the Council on Foreign Relations revealed that two-thirds of US citizens interviewed did indeed so believe.

If public opinion at large was inclined to give the administration the benefit of the doubt on national security matters, the policy community – and intelligence professionals in particular – on both sides of the Atlantic would require more radical measures. In moves unprecedented from any previous administration, Vice President Dick Cheney and his national security assistant Lewis Libby made a series of personal visits to the CIA's Langley headquarters, to corral mid-level analysts on message. Reportedly, a January 2003 meeting of fifty Joint Iraq Task Force (JITF) officials in the CIA's WINPAC was told, 'You know what, if Bush wants to go to war, it's your job to give him a reason to do so.'[50]

In the face of such intense pressure, the 'self-reinforcing and risk-averse culture'[51] of the CIA and other agencies duly buckled, as reflected in the October White Paper. It was glaringly apparent, however, that there could be no avoiding the palpable lack of any actual intelligence to support the administration's claims. Bob Woodward reports that when CIA deputy director John McLaughlin arrived at the White House to brief Bush on WMD evidence in December 2002, the president remarked, 'Nice try, but that isn't gonna sell Joe Public … This is the best we've got?'[52] The problem was, though, viewed as merely presentational. And, again, the lead would come from the Office of the Secretary for Defense and the Pentagon. Thus, in parallel with the short-lived Office of Strategic Influence and its more clandestine successor, Donald Rumsfeld ordered the creation of a highly secret Pentagon unit to evaluate all available raw intelligence traffic and report directly to undersecretary Douglas Feith.

Set up in late September 2001 under close Feith associate David Wurmser and former RAND specialist Abram Shulsky, the Policy Counter Terrorism Evaluation Group (PCTE) had the leading role in promoting the claims of linkage between Iraq and al-Qaeda. An initial product came in the form of a large flow chart or 'sociometric diagram' purporting to confirm a loose-knit cooperative network of Islamist terror organizations and 'rogue states' – principally Iraq. Given the near-total dearth of reliable field reporting from Iraq by any of the US agencies,[53] the mass of intelligence input was drawn from Iraqi exiles, mostly provided by the well-oiled 'Information Collection Programme' run by Ahmad Chalabi's Iraqi National Congress. Chalabi, a long-standing associate of inter alios Douglas Feith, Richard Perle and deputy defense secretary Paul Wolfowitz, was working closely with John Rendon, whose organization helped place some 108 Iraq-related articles and broadcasts in leading world media outlets (including 50 in the USA) between October 2001 and May 2002.[54]

As the INC's stable of between 75 and 100 informants continued to 'stovepipe' untested intelligence reports directly into administration – and presidential – statements and speeches via the PCTE[55] group, the Pentagon cell itself was expanded in October 2002. Renamed the Office of Special Plans, the shop remained under Abram Shulsky's direction and reported to Deputy Undersecretary William Lutti of the DoD's Near East and South Asia Directorate. A former Senate Intelligence Committee aide and author, Shulsky was known in intelligence circles for his innovative approach to intelligence analysis. Drawing as much on anthropology and Weberian sociology as the traditional empiricism of intelligence tradecraft, Shulsky stressed the importance of psychological profiling or 'Red Teaming' an opponent's operational code and a form of hypothesis-driven analysis known as heuristic prediction by approximation. This novel methodological mandate – effectively, a reversal of the burden of proof – was given free rein in promoting the adminstration's terrorism and WMD claims, all of which were subsequently discredited. A March 2004 report to the House

Committee on Government Reform was to detail in all 237 'specific misleading statements' by administration officials in 125 public appearances in the run-up to war.[56]

Prior to the OSP's full-tilt media offensive of September 2002, the key target for Feith and the Shulsky cell was – as we have seen – the still largely sceptical CIA. Thus, in addition to Dick Cheney's in-person arm-twisting at Langley, a high-powered Pentagon team led by Douglas Feith himself was to confront senior CIA analysts and director George Tenet in August, drawing a further, if somewhat hedged, concurrence from the Agency, which would set the ground for the forthcoming NIE. With the US intelligence community at least publicly on board, the WHIG was to open yet a further front in the PR battle with the formation of the Committee for the Liberation of Iraq (CLI).[57] Timed to coincide with Bush's most forthright attack on Iraq to date – the 7 October speech in Cincinnati, which flatly asserted an Iraqi WMD 'arsenal of terror' and 'high level contacts' with al-Qaeda 'going back a decade'[58] – the CLI drew much from established conservative Washington think-tanks in terms of expertise and personnel. Having on its board leading Washington luminaries such as former CIA director James Woolsey, ex-UN ambassador Jeane Kirkpatrick and the ubiquitous Richard Perle, its major sponsor was the Project for the New American Century (PNAC).

'Leveraging the private sector': the rise of the think-tanks

Even among the panoply of right-wing institutes and lobby groups, PNAC occupies a unique position in the Washington communications hierarchy. Cast in one report as 'consisting mainly of conservative Jews and heavy-hitters from the Christian Right', the Project's prescriptions on fighting 'terrorism' in general and unqualified US support for Israel 'have anticipated to a remarkable degree the (Bush) administration's own policy course'.[59] This was, perhaps, hardly surprising. Of the many PNAC alumni to hold senior posts in the administration, the most prominent included Vice President Dick Cheney, Lewis Libby, Paul Wolfowitz, Douglas Feith, UN ambassador John Bolton, Afghanistan and Iraq Ambassador Zalmay Khalilzad and Richard Perle. All had, over the years, authored a slew of reports and articles advocating US/Israeli pre-emptive war in the Middle East against Iran and a range of Arab countries. Founded in 1997 by leading conservatives Robert Kagan and William Kristol, with seed money from the Wisconsin-based Lynde & Harry Bradley Foundation, PNAC had, from the outset, a primary aim of influencing US Middle East policy. Its immediate genesis was in a 1996 task force set up by Perle, Feith and David Wurmser at the Jerusalem-based Institute of Advanced Strategic and Political Studies, where Wurmser was visiting fellow at the time. Set up to advise incoming Israeli prime minister Benyamin Netanyahu, the trio were to advocate invading Lebanon, drawing in Syria and, finally, ousting Saddam Hussein. This, in turn, would allow the 'neutralizing' of Iran and, overall, Israel to 'shape its strategic environment'.[60] The pretext to be used was WMD. Yet more forthright on the question of pre-emptive war or 'anticipatory self-defense' in the Middle East for the USA itself was a September 2000 report from the now-ascendant PNAC, entitled *Rebuilding America's Defenses*. Here, overturning embedded public reluctance to fund endless wars would perhaps require 'a catastrophic and catalysing event', in PNAC's view, 'like a new Pearl Harbor'.[61]

With the Committee for the Liberation of Iraq up and running, and sister organizations such as PNAC, the American Enterprise Institute, the Hudson Institute, the Washington Institute for Near East Policy, the Middle East Forum and veteran right-wing lobbyists the Heritage Foundation providing message coordination, the administration had built up a seemingly unstoppable momentum.

An October 2001 report on *Managed Information Dissemination* from the Defence Science Board Task Force had stressed the importance 'not only in leveraging private sector competencies but in new structures and *a degree of distance* that attracts credible messengers with non-government resumes, creative thinkers and talented communicators'.[62] A major player here was Washington PR firm Benador Associates. Benador maintained an 'International Speakers Bureau' of thirty-four names from a client list including Richard Perle, James Woolsey, former secretary Alexander Haig and conservative columnist Charles Krauthammer. They had indeed been successful in obtaining 'maximum exposure on talking-head television programs and … op-ed pieces in a number of the nation's major newspapers'.[63] Whilst the ostensibly independent lobby network was maintaining its degree of distance, close de facto relations were maintained with the Pentagon's Office of Special Plans (OSP) and the newly established White House Office of Global Communications (OGC). Formally established by Executive Order 13283 in January 2003 the OGC was to absorb the existing Coalition Information Centre and 'coordinate the formulation amongst appropriate agencies that reflect the strategic communications framework and priorities of the United States.'[64] The closely involved John Rendon would take responsibility for the 9.30 morning cross-media conference call to set the 'message of the day'. As the military clock ticked away and the administration prepared for the key events of Bush's 28 January State of the Union Address and Secretary Powell's UN presentation on 5 February, the OGC offered its first publication, entitled – apparently without irony – *Apparatus of Lies: Saddam's Disinformation and Propaganda, 1990–2003.*

Apparatus of Lies drew much from earlier proto-OGC publications, in particular *Iraq: Denial and Deception*, put out on 12 September to coincide with Bush's appearance at the UN. And, in similar fashion, the guiding hand was John Rendon. The centrepiece here were claims from defecting Iraqi civil engineer Adnan al-Haideri that he had personally overseen the construction of covert CBW facilities at twenty named sites throughout Iraq, including villas, bunkers and the Baghdad General hospital. Al-Haideri, provided by the INC to Rendon associate Paul Moran, had previously been extensively interviewed by the *New York Times*'s Judith Miller, whose front-page splash appeared on 20 December 2001.[65] Three days before, al-Haideri had been polygraphed by the CIA, giving a strong negative finding. This would not, however, affect the defector's standing with the Pentagon and Rendon, who continued to promote the story even after the end of hostilities.[66] Another prominent administration claim, the bogus aluminium centrifuge tubes referred to above, had also emerged from the INC/Rendon axis, duly publicized, as we have seen, by Judith Miller. This was timed to give substance to the later (and equally bogus) 'Niger uranium' claim and was featured in a host of statements by leading Bush officials and the 2003 State of the Union Address. The story's apparent origin was in a July 2002 meeting between Paul Wolfowitz and dissident Iraqi scientist Khidir Hamza, facilitated by INC PR adviser (and former Rendon consultant) Francis Brooke.[67] Although seemingly qualified on account of his former role in Saddam's nuclear programme, Hamza was closely following the INC script, and was a Benador regular on the 'International Speaker's Bureau'.

Spinning the peace: the threat of 'revisionist history'

The total discrediting of the administration's WMD claims by the US Army's 75th Exploitation Task Force and 1,200-strong Iraq Survey Group – in the face of Colin Powell's assertion of 'facts and conclusions based on solid intelligence'[68] – was, by mid-2003, coming home to haunt the administration. Equally damning was the utter failure to reveal any meaningful links between Saddam's defeated regime and al-Qaeda. Bush, uncharacteristically, was forced on the defensive. 'This nation acted to a threat from the dictator of Iraq ... Now there are some who would like to rewrite history – revisionist historians is what I like to call them.'[69] Indeed, as a series of Senate and other reports were to confirm, far from the 'secret, Iraqi high-level intelligence contacts with al-Qaeda ... offering chemical or biological weapons training' of Powell's UN presentation,[70] the Ba'athists were waging a concerted campaign against the several hundred Wahhabi al-Qaeda militants who had infiltrated Iraq after the 2002 US defeat of the Taliban, and 'had issued a decree aggressively outlawing Wahhabism and threatening offenders with execution'.[71] And, moreover, Secretary Powell's centrepiece claim, that 'Iraq today harbors a deadly terrorist network headed by Abu Musab al-Zarqawi'[72] and had declined information from a 'friendly intelligence service' (in some accounts, Germany's BND)[73] that could have led to the arrest of the high-profile Jordanian, was again somewhat short of the facts. As the Senate Intelligence Committee records, 'IIS (Iraqi intelligence) did respond to a foreign request for assistance in finding and extraditing al-Zarqawi ... in spring 2002, the IIS formed a "special committee" to track down al-Zarqawi, but were unable to locate him.'[74]

The dramatic unravelling of Bush and Cheney's own 'apparatus of lies' in the face of the seemingly unstoppable descent of Iraq into chaos and insurgency had prompted a hectic information warfare counteroffensive by the administration and its private-sector outriders. In the Pentagon, a massive info-war reorganization had produced the *Information Operations Roadmap*,[75] approved in October 2003. Aimed at avoiding the PR own-goals that attended the somewhat ad hoc OSI arrangements of 2001, the *Roadmap* sought to establish more clear-cut 'lanes in the road' between often con-flicting departmental priorities in public diplomacy, public affairs and psychological operations (psyops). As ever in the Donald Rumsfeld Pentagon, the more proactive information warfare element was taking clear precedence over more traditional 'soft power' public diplomacy concerns. A $205 million supplemental[76] was granted to Special Operations Command (SOCOM) psyop forces, designated as one of five 'core elements' in Information Operations (IO) (alongside military deception, computer network operations, electronic warfare and operational security). With US Strategic Command (STRATCOM) as the overall umbrella, the civilian direction was taken by the undersecretary of defense for intelligence (USD/I), a newly created post occupied by Rumsfeld protégé Stephen Cambone.

Along with the expanded USD/I arrangements, the *Roadmap* marked a further stage in Donald Rumsfeld's ongoing ambition to secure Pentagon dominance in the intelligence field. Although of a piece with the defense secretary's far-reaching military reorganization, the document itself reveals much about overall US strategic thinking in the aftermath of the Iraq invasion. Aiming to 'advance the goal of I/Ops as a core military competency' and 'begin the process of developing IO into a war-fighting capability',[77] the study outlines a sweeping programme of 'full-spectrum IO'. This would stretch from the use of US-sponsored websites, strict media supervision and 'rapid rebuttal truth-squads' to the development of 'miniaturized, scatterable public address-systems'[78] to propagandize 'denied areas' and – ultimately – to exert 'maximum control over the entire electromagnetic spectrum'.[79] However, though the undertaking to 'fight the net as it would an enemy weapons system'[80] was perhaps unsurprising, given the often stated US goal to achieve military hegemony, it was the more subtle mix of 'commercial quality psyop product proto-types' that drew attention as the *Roadmap* leaked into public. As with the disbanded Office of Strategic Influence, the Pentagon envisaged overcoming acknowledged US strictures on domestic psyops by simply feeding from foreign sources. 'Psyop messages disseminated to any audience', the *Roadmap* notes, 'will often be replayed for much larger audiences, including the American public'.[81]

Clearly unnerved by the sheer intensity of opposition to the Iraq occupation and US policies in general, the Pentagon was to confront the Iraqi insurgency with an 'insurgent' propaganda offensive. The response was outlined by the Defense Science Policy Board. Drawing on the latest in business school and marketing theory, they contended that, as opposed to 'incumbents' – characteristically 'bloated, slow … change-resistant' – 'insurgent' brands 'invariably harbor today an attitude of difference, move faster and welcome change as an opportunity'.[82] Given the comprehensive status of the USA as a world, and local occupying, power, the bid to alter public perception in these respects would seem an uphill struggle. Commenting a year after the *Roadmap*, the DSPB maintained that the way forward lay in lending a gloss of differentiation to specific US programmes. And here, the key could be found in 'greater private sector initiatives that contain a built-in agility, credibility and even deniability that will be missing from government-sponsored initiatives'.[83]

The Rendon Group had specialized in precisely this field since the beginning of the Bush administration, winning thirty-five Pentagon contracts worth some $100 million between 2000 and 2004. The post-Saddam era in Iraq, however, was to yield an ever-expanding market for 'credible messengers with non-government résumés' and soon saw the entry of a significant new player, the Lincoln Group. Whilst Rendon's lack of public profile was an undoubted asset to the ambitious start-up company, Lincoln, founded in mid-2004 by British-born entrepreneur Christian Bailey, worked a clear inside track from the outset. In April 2003, Bailey's then hedge fund, Lincoln Asset Management, launched $100 million investment in defence and security-related companies.[84] A subsidiary, Lincoln Alliance Corp, was then formed to provide 'tailored intelligence services for government clients faced with critical intelligence challenges'. By 2004, Lincoln Alliance had transformed into Iraqex, with a Baghdad office and a presence at the December 'Baghdad Expo' trade fair.

It had also formed a partnership with Rendon, which would be short-lived, and more enduring links with Ahmad Chalabi's INC. It had also, moreover, secured a $6 million Pentagon contract to 'accurately inform the Iraqi people of the coalition's goals and gain their support'.[85] The October 2004 deal with the Information Operations Task Force – a part of 'Multi-National Corps–Iraq' in the alliance command structure – involved efforts to convince audiences of the 'strength, integrity and reliability' of Iraqi forces in the inconclusive US-led battle for the militant stronghold of Falluja.

In contrast to the chaos on the Falluja battlefield, Iraqex's 'aggressive advertising and PR campaign' proved a successful prelude to further lucrative deals with the US military. With a further name change to the Lincoln Group, the company entered into a $100 million arrangement with the Joint Psychological Operations Support Element in association with established Washington PR insiders Science Applications International Corp (SAIC). The June 2005 deal was, however, increasingly controversial as it transpired that Lincoln teams based at 'Camp Victory' in Iraq and the Tampa, Florida, headquarters of Special Operations Command were engaged in planting 'good news' items in the Iraqi media on a massive scale. According to reports in the *Los Angeles Times* – later confirmed in Congress and by the Pentagon inspector general – Lincoln had placed over 1,000 articles in some fifteen Arab and Iraqi newspapers during late 2005, along with Arabic-language web content and videos.[86] Controversially, the basic 'storyboards' were prepared by serving military personnel before editing by Lincoln – under such titles as 'More money goes to Iraq's development'[87] – and placement in friendly outlets such as *Al-Mutamar*, Ahmad Chalabi's Baghdad daily. With some Iraqi journalists on a regular $500 monthly stipend, delivery of Lincoln's own completed product was usually by email or courier. For a typical piece, credited to the untraceable 'Media Services' and 'International Information Center', papers would be paid between $50 and $2,000, although, as one leading editor observed, had the US provenance been clear he would have charged 'much, much more'.[88]

'Creating message authority': the coalition of the willing

Although US neocons had been arguing for regime change in Iraq since the first Gulf War in 1991, the wider Washington policy community had remained sceptical. But, as the changing climate soon became apparent after 9/11, it was clear that a crucial element in the administration's forging of a domestic consensus was at least some measure of international collaboration. Three US allies became critical in this: Israel, Australia and the UK.

As we have seen from the Downing Street minutes, the British government of Tony Blair had been closely involved in Iraq War planning from the outset. But perhaps more important than the UK's valued military support was the degree of diplomatic credibility offered by London to the administration's aims – and, more vital yet, the unique ability of the prime minister to sway US domestic opinion. That Blair was able to place his full weight behind the Bush administration delivered critical mass in the drive to war.

The close media and propaganda collaboration between Whitehall and Washington took on much of its institutional form during the later Clinton administration. As we have seen, joint military actions in Iraq and Kosovo possessed a parallel communications component managed from Coalition Information Centres (CICs) – reputedly set up at the initiative of Blair communications chief Alastair Campbell.[89] With planning under way for the invasion of Afghanistan, the CICs were re-established, with offices co-ordinating across time zones in London, Washington and Islamabad. Structures became more developed for the campaign against Iraq. The White House OGC 9.30 morning conference call between Bush communications director Dan Bartlett, State Department spokesman Richard Boucher, Torie Clarke for the Pentagon, and John Rendon always included much input from Alastair Campbell.[90] This call established the day's themes, packaged with talking points and ready-to-use quotes. The OGC's mass 'Global Messenger' email bulletin was then dispatched, providing an evening focal point for US and allied media operations across the 24-hour news cycle.

At the London end, there were two communications groups, both chaired by Alastair Campbell. The UK Iraq Communications Group (ICG) was based at the Foreign Office Information Directorate, with a parallel (if confusingly named) Iraq Communications Group run from Downing Street itself. Although later claims that Campbell 'chaired' intelligence committees were somewhat misleading, the Downing street communications director was clearly directing Whitehall meetings with intelligence officers present,[91] notably his new 'friend' John Scarlett, chair of the Joint Intelligence Committee. It was the ICG in particular that was responsible for the now-discredited 'dossiers' of September 2002 and February 2003. The familiar saga of the supposedly intelligence-based accounts of Iraqi WMD[92] efforts and 'Infrastructure of Concealment, Deception and Intimidation'[93] has been widely covered elsewhere – the latter's crude plagiarism exposed within hours by Cambridge academic Glen Rangwala.[94] What remains of interest is the degree of 'groupthink' mutual dependency between the media operations in Whitehall and Washington. As the Downing Street minutes reveal, the March 2002 period saw a frenetic pace of meetings between Bush cabinet officials and senior Blair aides. A 14 March memo from foreign policy adviser Sir David Manning, reporting a lunch with Condoleezza Rice, observes: 'I said you [Blair] would not budge in your support for regime change, but you had to manage a press, a parliament and a public opinion that was very different from anything in the States.'[95] Manning further notes that 'there is a real risk that the administration underestimates the difficulties.'[96] The latter point was reiterated by UK ambassador Sir Christopher Meyer to Manning, in a follow-up meeting with Paul Wolfowitz: 'we backed regime change, but the plan had to be clever and failure was not an option ... there had to be strategy for building support for military action against Saddam.'[97]

A central part of the strategy, overseen as ever by the industrious Campbell, was 'the establishment of an ad hoc group of officials under Cabinet Office Chairmanship, to consider the development of an information campaign to be agreed with the US'.[98] This, as we have seen, became the Iraq Communications Group, whose two most notorious products sprang from a newly created position of 'Head of Story Development'.[99] Despite opposition from the CIA, the inclusion of the WMD dossier's spurious Niger uranium claim in the Bush 2003 State of the Union Address drew much of its effect from its supposed endorsement by the British government. It was also, according to one NSC staff member, left in to avoid leaving 'the British flapping in the wind'.[100]

As closely connected as Tony Blair was with Bush's war advocacy in the wider public arena, perhaps more important in swaying congressional opinion in the USA was pressure from Israel. In a political system where lobbies and interest groups wield immense power, the multitude of pro-Israel organizations – such as the Jewish Institute for National Security Affairs (JINSA) and the American Israel Public Affairs Committee (AIPAC) – are the acknowledged market leaders. Pioneering current lobbying techniques such as mailshots, databasing and instant rebuttal, and hosting a massive membership overlap with the organized neocon network, AIPAC and its sister foundations have, in the words of one recent study, 'no serious opponents in the lobbying world'.[101] Unfortunately for the largely liberal-leaning and Democrat-voting US Jewish population – a majority of whom were opposed to the Iraq War[102] – these organized bodies have overwhelmingly taken a hard-right stand on Israeli policies, broadly supportive of Likud and its allies. And here a purely military approach to politics in the Middle East has been accepted without question.

As we have seen, the AIPAC/neocon nexus had long advocated the overthrow of Saddam Hussein, and with its dominating influence within the Bush administration policy machinery had worked energetically to bring this about.[103] With 9/11 providing the 'new Pearl Harbor' catalyst for policy, prominent Israeli politicians and conservative commentators in the USA unleashed a torrent of pro-war speeches and articles in the public arena.[104] A more covert Israeli intelligence campaign was emerging in parallel, with close links to operations in London and Washington. Operating from Prime Minister Sharon's private office, the Israeli cell deliberately bypassed established Mossad channels – long sceptical, like the CIA, of an actually existing Iraqi WMD threat[105] – and fed directly into Douglas Feith's office in the Pentagon.[106] Here, a steady stream of alarmist reports were constructed with the Policy Counter Terrorism Evaluation Group (Iraq and al-Qaeda) and Abram Shulsky's Office of Special Plans (Iraqi WMD) and duly circulated by the OGC and the Rendon Organization.[107] Israeli military intelligence (AMAN) had previously briefed the specialist monthly *Jane's Foreign Report* on an Iraqi role in 9/11,[108] whilst a closed June 2002 NATO Council meeting had heard much graphic detail of alleged Iraqi nuclear devices[109] from Mossad chief and Sharon insider Ephraim Halevy – information directly contrary to that in the assessments of his own agency.[110]

Whilst the Sharon government, with much public support,[111] was intent on reducing the perceived threat from *any* conceivable future Iraqi regime, Tel Aviv, along with the Bush team, were acutely aware of the need for circumspection regarding the actual *casus belli*. As senior Bush NSC aide Philip Zelikow was candidly to put it,

> Why would Iraq attack America or use nuclear weapons against us? I'll tell you what I think the real threat [is] and actually has been since 1990 – it's the threat against Israel ... And this is the threat that dare

not speak its name, because the Europeans don't care deeply about that threat, I will tell you frankly. And the American government doesn't want to lean too hard on it rhetorically, because it is not a popular sell.[112]

If the UK and Israel were to provide the indispensable element in Bush's propaganda war, a subsidiary but not unimportant contribution was to come from the third ranking power in the 'coalition of the willing' – Australia. Although sharing the private scepticism of CIA and SIS mid-level officials regarding the Bush administration's claims,[113] Australia's agencies were rarely invited to comment on the Canberra government's Iraq line – and the five major speeches by Prime Minister John Howard in particular – on the grounds that, with some 97 per cent reliance on 'allied' (US/UK) intelligence sources,[114] there was much that was unknown to these agencies.[115] For Howard himself, though, the case was unequivocal. 'The Australian government', the prime minister declared, 'knows that Iraq has chemical and biological weapons and that Iraq wants to develop nuclear weapons.'[116] The assertion was grounded, inevitably, on the, 'compelling evidence within the published detailed dossiers of British and American intelligence'. Welcome diplomatic and military support notwithstanding, Australia's central importance perhaps was as a world media hub. Rupert Murdoch's News International – owners of the trenchantly pro-war US network Fox News – maintains a virtual stranglehold on the Australian media, as it does in the UK. And it was a senior Australian Rendon Group associate, broadcaster Paul Moran, who was the first choice of Ahmad Chalabi to launch the fabricated 'buried WMD' claims of Iraqi defector Adnan al-Haideri.[117]

'A core military competency'

Despite decidedly ambiguous results in the field for the US/allied Global War on Terror (GWOT), the Pentagon has remained intent on 'the process of developing I/OPs into a war-fighting capability'.

The militarization of public discourse here was, however, not without consequences for the very values that the alliance had taken issue on. At the height of conventional Iraq hostilities, Rendon Group contractors operating from the Pentagon's IOTF deployed an in-house 24-hour newswire collection service, known as 'Livewire', able to secure international copy at the point of a story being filed. The advantages in this for achieving information dominance were plain. As John Rendon himself observed, 'We functioned twenty-four hours a day … We were doing 195 newspapers and 43 countries in fourteen or fifteen languages … I can tell you what's on the evening news tonight in a country before it happens.'[118]

A further advantage of the 'Livewire' system was in 'media analysis'. A conventional PR tool, described blandly in the DFPB report as 'Identifying daily influences on audiences including content analysis, agenda and biases, relevance and credibility, structure and control',[119] it could also, in the hands of Pentagon info-warriors, take on a more proactive role. On 8 March 2003, veteran BBC correspondent Kate Adie reported a senior Pentagon official as threatening to 'take down' any non-accredited journalists working in the campaign theatre – a threat all too credible after US assaults on the BBC's own Kabul studio in November 2001 and a same-day strike on neighbouring Arab satellite channel Al Jazeera. And on 8 April 2003, US tank fire hit the prominently displayed media centre in Baghdad's Hotel Palestine, killing a further Al Jazeera staff member, a Reuters reporter and camera operator from Spanish television. Many were to wonder if the term 'information battle-space' had perhaps assumed a somewhat literal meaning.

3

Spies, 'enemy combatants' and the long war

In the first war of the twenty-first century, one of the most critical battlefronts is the home front. (George W. Bush, remarks of 17 December 2005)

The new exceptionalism: pre-emptive war and global doctrine

The use of public outrage after 9/11 to advance an ambitious drive for US military dominance in the Middle East – and, in parallel, to promote Bush's political agenda – was to rest on two corresponding moves in domestic governance and strategic doctrine. On a day-to-day basis, the administration had, with great precision, coordinated the march to war with the political and electoral timetable. But Bush's keenly taken decision to 'run on the war' in seeking re-election was also drawn from more far-reaching aims for assuming ultimate authority for the executive, with the president's powers as 'commander in chief' as the final sanction.

In this chapter, we take up what can arguably be termed the 'organic' linkage between the dynamics of the War on Terror and doctrines of pre-emptive war abroad and unlimited executive power domestically. The whole grand project, however, had roots grounded in the same industrial/lobby interests, conceptual frameworks and, frequently, personnel, established in the long-running debates within the US policy community on Cold War planning – and nuclear planning in particular. Common ground was taken, above all, in the adoption of black-and-white, zero-sum policy choices, or 'with us or against us', in Bush's own frequent assertion. But if nuclear scenarios had provided a ready template for both the 'state of war' and unquestioned presidential powers therein, the translation of this in the event was to prove more problematical.

The post-9/11 efforts to roll out US military power as an instrument for world transformation – and the concept of perpetual struggle to be packaged and sold to global opinion – have, as we have seen, had decidedly mixed results for the George W. Bush administration and its allies in the Global War on Terror. It should be emphasized, however, that unlike previous interventions – for example, in Vietnam (lost, though there had been a recognizable, if unattainable, military end) and, indeed, the 1991 'Desert Storm' campaign ('won', but with an attainable military end undone by consequences) – the sheer opportunism of the Iraq War had broken step not only with previous US doctrine but, in significant measure, with established strategic thinking across the board. For some protagonists of the War on Terror, this was, perhaps, precisely the point. 'Stability is an unworthy American mission', wrote leading US neoconservative Michael Ledeen; 'we do not want stability in Iran, Iraq, Syria, Lebanon and even Saudi Arabia. The real issue is not whether, but how best to destabilize.'[1] If the views of Ledeen, a former Iran–Contra kingpin and sometime consultant to the Pentagon and NSC, have been considered somewhat maverick even in neocon circles – if only for their unvarnished expression – the overall strategic cast was one becoming inexorably mainstream.

George Bush's *National Security Strategy for the United States*, set forth in September 2002, was conceived as the definitive statement of US policy after 9/11. In it, the president declared that American status as the sole superpower after the Cold War would be, if anything, conclusively reinforced by the same factors of market economics and military superiority that were seen as securing triumph over the Soviet Union. 'The great struggles of the twentieth century between liberty and totalitarianism ended with a decisive victory for the forces of freedom', Bush had declared, 'and a single sustainable model for national success.' These assertions, however, were decidedly not up for debate, as the president laid down a blueprint for a renewed period of US singularity in the world system – and one where potential opponents could expect to be brought into line.

The idea that US policy should eschew a long-entrenched pursuit of 'stability' in the international system in favour of 'a single sustainable model' and 'a distinctively American internationalism' found in Bush's National Security Strategy in fact appeared to mark the conclusion of a decades-long conflict within the US policy community. The distinction between 'status quo' and 'revolutionary' powers, long axiomatic in US statecraft and elaborated in its fullest form by then secretary of state and national security adviser Henry Kissinger,[2] had it seems been finally turned on its head.

To be sure, proclamations of US 'leadership' in world affairs – and the construction of the global military infrastructure to support them – have been central to American strategy since the time of Harry Truman, as have also the statements of intent featured in a series of presidential 'doctrines'. In a further continuity, these, with some exception for the Nixon Doctrine of 1969, have all concerned, in one way or another, the status of the Middle East. Thus, from declarations by presidents Truman and Eisenhower to the 1980 assertion of 'vital US national interest' in the Gulf, under Jimmy Carter, the unique significance of the region to US strategy was made clear. In similar fashion, the establishment of a

US military presence in the Middle East had been long considered, with moves to secure a permanent base – the British-owned island of Diego Garcia in the Indian Ocean – set in train from 1964. What was to represent the truly radical turn in the Bush–Cheney administration, however, was the concept of open-ended military occupation – carried through in Iraq – allied to a blunt assertion that any perceived threat to the USA in the region could provoke pre-emptive action.

Like much of the policy platform to see fruition under Bush and Cheney, the assertion that 'To forestall or prevent … hostile acts by our adversaries, the United States will, if necessary, act pre-emptively'[3] has long – if not uncontested – provenance in the formulation of US strategy.[4] Indeed, it was the prospect of nuclear pre-emption against Russia, much discussed in the 1950s, that provided a strong, if unpublicized, rationale for Britain developing its own nuclear weapon, with a view to exercising leverage on US decision-making.[5] And if the concept went into abeyance after the 1962 Cuban Missile Crisis, Israel's successful pre-emptive military offensive in the 1967 Six-Day War – one covertly encouraged by then president Lyndon Johnson and his close advisers[6] – was to bring 'anticipatory self-defence' back into contention. The Israeli victory in 1967 was also to give rise to what later became known as the neoconservatives, who originally were Democratic supporters of Israel. With the departure of President Johnson and the acceptance by Kissinger and Nixon of strategic 'rough parity' with the Soviet Union as stated US policy, the nascent neocons took on an increasingly public profile and organizational base in opposition to arms control treaties and 'détente' in general. But a particular preoccupation was the promotion of Israel as a US strategic outpost in the Middle East – a concept without, at that time, the bedrock status it was to take on subsequently. This theme, along with many of its leading exponents, was to assume growing prominence in shaping the direction of US policy.

Israel aside, the original touchstone issue for the neocons was strategic superiority and ballistic missile defence (BMD) – an essential prerequisite for establishing a pre-emptive 'first strike' capability. Here, the leading proponent of BMD during the first (1969) Nixon administration was the highly influential Democratic senator Henry 'Scoop' Jackson, leader of the Senate Armed Services Committee. Prominent on the staff of 'the Senator for Boeing' were two analysts who would become increasingly well known: Paul Wolfowitz and Richard Perle.[7] The willingness of Nixon to bargain away BMD in the 1972 SALT treaty, coupled with Kissinger's pressure on Israel to cease hostilities in the 1973 Yom Kippur War, was to consolidate the increasingly powerful right-wing challenge.[8] The new realignment became clear in the closing stages of the (1974–76) Ford administration. In a move to accommodate the rising forces of conservatism (both neo- and traditional) represented by Ronald Reagan, Kissinger and US-Soviet détente were increasingly marginalized by new hard-line defense secretary Donald Rumsfeld and his close associate, White House chief of staff Dick Cheney.

Although the 1976 elections brought to office the initially liberal-sounding Democrat Jimmy Carter, what was now generally known as the 'neoconservative' caucus was essentially succeeding in moving the terms of debate on defence and US foreign policy. A controversial study, known as 'Team B', had been set up by President Ford in 1976 to challenge the CIA's annual National Intelligence Estimates of Soviet capability. Team B, also known as the Pipes Report after chairman Harvard professor Richard Pipes, was largely drafted by Paul Wolfowitz, seconded from the Arms Control and Disarmament Agency. Its conclusions, released in January 1977, painted a stark picture of rising Soviet superiority and corresponding US decline. As is well known, the estimates of supposed Russian military strength, yielding 'superiority in all indices of capability',[9] were revealed as wildly inaccurate. Nonetheless, as a contemporary *Washington Post* editorial pointed out, it would still 'serve as a reference for policy makers across the top echelon of government'[10] – a prediction to be substantially borne out, as the Carter administration took on an increasing hard line in its policies and finally itself embraced strategic superiority in confronting the Soviet Union.

As the Carter administration moved its defence posture away from 'essential equivalence' with the Soviets, the 'countervailing strategy', outlined in the final Defense Department Annual Report[11] from Secretary Harold Brown, contained a further new development. The redrafted US nuclear doctrine, Presidential Directive (PD) 59 of July 1980, placed a new emphasis on 'counterforce' – that is, nuclear war-fighting – and, under certain circumstances, pre-emption. As Secretary Brown observed, 'many of our forces can be moved upon strategic warning, and some on receipt of even very early and ambiguous indicators'.[12] In addition to the fresh emphasis on war-fighting, the 'Carter Doctrine' made clear the emerging geopolitical front in US strategy – the Gulf and South Asia. In this, the groundwork had again been laid in a Pentagon report by Paul Wolfowitz – then deputy assistant secretary for regional programs – on *Capabilities for Limited Contingencies in the Persian Gulf*.[13] The classified study had recommended an enhanced US force structure in the region, early consideration of the nuclear option and action against 'non Soviet' contingencies, notably Iraq. It was presented in June 1979 – preceding both the Russian intervention in Afghanistan and the Iranian Revolution.

The Reagan–Bush years of the 1980s saw many of the emergent neocons in office – Richard Perle at the Pentagon, Paul Wolfowitz in a variety of posts in defense and state – and what influential defence analyst Colin Gray was to term 'a case for a theory of victory'[14] increasingly emerging as strategic orthodoxy. We have seen a graphic uptake of this logic in the 'by any means necessary' presidential directive in the 1980s' Afghan war.

Even this course, however, would necessarily labour under the constraints of alliance-building against the still powerful Soviet Union. With the latter's comprehensive demise in 1991, however, the view took hold that 'victory' had indeed been attained and the requirement was now to 'preclude any hostile power from dominating a region critical to our interests'.[15] The latter statement – taken from the George H.W. Bush administration's final Defense Review and enthusiastically promoted by departing secretary Dick Cheney – represented a public statement of more forthright policy contained in the Defense Policy Guidance, set under Paul Wolfowitz's auspices in 1991. The Policy Guidance, a classified paper presented every two years to Congress, covers both the conceptual framework for US military strategy and the range of weapons systems to follow through. As ever, the Pentagon's main eye was on shielding favoured programmes from prospective budget cuts. This risk was seen as particularly acute at the end of the Cold War, with senators such as Edward Kennedy calling for massive cutbacks in military spending to realize the anticipated 'peace dividend'.[16]

The unipolar moment

As defense undersecretary for policy, Wolfowitz had delegated the drafting of the Guidance paper to deputy Lewis Libby and Zalmay Khalilzad – both of whom would come to execute the strategy under Bush Junior. But, although in keeping with the general Washington climate of post-Cold War triumphalism, the measures proposed to perpetuate the 'unipolar moment'[17] of US power in the world aroused much controversy when leaked in early 1992. Notable here was the assertion that 'we must maintain the mechanisms for deterring potential competitors from *even aspiring to a larger regional or global role*'[18] (emphasis added). Additional background suggested this prescription applied as much to erstwhile allies

– Germany and Japan – as to established great powers such as China and Russia.[19] Less contentious, at least in the USA itself, was a further aim: 'In the Middle East and South West Asia, our overall objective is to remain the predominant outside power in the region and preserve US and Western access to the region's oil.'[20] If US 'predominance' had replaced untrammelled hegemony as the guiding theme when the unclassified version of the Defense Policy Guidance was released two months later, the base assumption would remain essentially the same: that US standing in the international system be underpinned by a military establishment – and matching budget – so extensive that no possible combination of powers could indeed 'even aspire' to mount a challenge. And, moreover, that in the event 'We will … not ignore the need to … protect our critical interests … with only limited additional help, or even alone, if necessary.'[21]

Writing in early 2000, Paul Wolfowitz was – with some reason – to reflect on how 'a draft memo prepared by my office at the Pentagon' had influenced debate to the extent that 'there is today a remarkable degree of agreement on a number of central points of foreign policy.'[22] To be sure, the Clinton administration had continually emphasized alliance-building and international consensus in its diplomacy. It also, however, maintained military budgets at approximately Cold War levels,[23] mounted near-unilateral military action in Iraq and the Balkans, and embraced 'full spectrum dominance' as a strategic goal. No less than Ronald Reagan, officials were wont to stress the exceptionalism of 'the indispensible nation'. For Wolfowitz and the neocons, however, despite such actions, 'today's consensus is facile and complacent, reflecting a lack of concern about the possibility of another major war, let alone agreement about how to prevent one.' Wolfowitz, along with Donald Rumsfeld, had been closely involved in drafting the foreign policy platform of the Bob Dole presidential challenge to Clinton in 1996. Here, a central concern was the perennial neocon drive for ballistic missile defence. Unsuccessful though the Dole campaign was, a Republican Congress was instrumental in setting up a commission, headed by Rumsfeld, to review the issue again. With echoes of the 'Team B' report of twelve years earlier, the commission findings were to contradict directly a National Intelligence Estimate of 1995 (which saw no pressing case for BMD)[24] and fuel an ultimately successful effort to develop the system, culminating in the Bush administration's unilateral withdrawal from the existing Anti-Ballistic Missile Treaty in December 2001.

The scrapping of the hallmark 1972 agreement on restricting missile defence, 'written in a different era' as President Bush was to put it,[25] was integral to a wide range of military innovations designed to bolster US unilateral capability. Of central importance here was the aim to achieve superiority in space – the 'High Frontier' of much Reagan-era lobbying. In July 2001 the recently established US Space Command issued a mission statement, *Vision for 2020*. In it, the need to 'dominate the space dimension to military operations' is clearly spelt out, with 'denying other countries access to space' as an explicit corollary.[26] Of a piece with the US using, in the words of defense undersecretary Peter Teets, 'our space supremacy ... to achieve warfighting success',[27] the DoD was to seek congressional funding for a new range of 'sub-strategic' nuclear weapons, outlined in the March 2002 Nuclear Posture Review. Along with the request for 'robust earth penetration' weapons of below one kiloton yield and a resumption of nuclear tests, the administration was to outline a list of likely opponents and possible targeting contingencies involving 'an Iraqi attack on Israel or its neighbours, or a North Korean attack on the South, or a military confrontation over the status of Taiwan'.[28] To be sure, the inclusion of the familiar roll call of 'axis of evil' states – Iraq, Iran and North Korea – in the administration's sights was perhaps unsurprising. What was new, however, was the explicit consideration given to possible Great Power confrontation – with

Taiwan as a long-established conservative talisman – and the implict interest in limited nuclear war-fighting.

'Unwarranted influence':
the rise and rise of the Pentagon

On departing office in January 1961, Dwight D. Eisenhower issued his often-cited warning to 'guard against the acquisition of unwarranted influence, whether sought or unsought, by the Military Industrial Complex' and that 'We must never let the weight of this combination endanger our liberties or democratic processes.' Strongly influenced, to be sure, by a conservative fiscal aversion towards the 'military Keynesianism' of his predecessor, Harry Truman, the president's strictures identified two enduring traits in the American state's relations to the military. First, the military–industrial complex is an established fact of political life. Second, though, 'sought or unsought', unwarranted influence and misplaced power have surely proliferated in abundance, to the clear detriment of liberties and democratic process. Historically, as Eisenhower well knew, defence spending has been the one accept-able path for US government intervention in the economy. Under George W. Bush, this has reached heights unheard of outside full mobilization. With a projected bill of $424.4 billion for FY 2006–7, the level exceeded that of the next fifteen nations combined.[29]

In its determination to 'keep military strengths beyond chal-lenge, thereby making the destabilizing arms races of other eras pointless',[30] as George Bush declared in his address to West Point military academy graduates in June 2002, the administration has produced a defence establishment that could be ranked as the world's seventeenth largest economy. It is the largest oil consumer in the USA and thirty-first in the world, with an outlay of 395,000 barrels per day,[31] slightly below the total daily energy usage of Greece. It is also, according to the Pentagon's *Base Structure Report* for FY 2005, 'one of the world's largest landlords with a physical plant consisting of more than 571 facilities (buildings, structures and utilities) located on more than 3,740 sites, on nearly 30 million acres'.[32] This overall figure is an underestimate, however, as bases under 10 acres are discounted, as are leased foreign facilities and covert 'black' sites (reflecting host nation sensitivity). On the books, however, are listed 725 overseas sites deploying 254,788 personnel in 153 countries.[33]

In addition to its expanding global reach, the Pentagon's domestic footprint has also enlarged to take on a raft of new roles and responsibilities. In 2002, the Bush administration set up a new regional military command with responsibilities for North America, Canada and Mexico. The Northern Command – NORTHCOM – essentially completes the US global military network, in tandem with commands for Europe (EUCOM), Asia /Pacific (PACOM), the Middle East (CENTCOM), Latin America (SOUTHCOM) and the new AFRICOM, set up in January 2007. Along with the Department of Homeland Security, established in 2003, NORTHCOM represents a radical and conscious attempt at 'horizontal'[34] integration of civilian and military agencies. Featuring joint command and control, the new arrangements seek to 'improve the [Defense] Department's capabilities by sharing information, expertise and technology as appropriate across military and civilian boundaries'[35] and to 'standardizing operational concepts, developing compatible technology solutions and coordinating planning'.[36]

Whilst a clear need to address the glaring incompatibility between the US federal agencies was laid bare in the aftermath of 9/11, a wider agenda is also in view. Since the 1878 Posse Comitatus Act, US military personnel have been expressly excluded from policing functions on US soil (with the partial exception of border patrols and in a 'national emergency'), and previous attempts at domestic military involvement were resisted by the Church and the Pike congressional commissions of the 1970s. However, in the

DoD's view, 'Authorities, procedures and practices must permit the seamless integration of Federal, state and local capabilities at home and among allies, partners and non-governmental organizations.'[37] This position was further expanded on by the first NORTHCOM combatant commander, General Ralph Eberhart, when he observed that 'We should always be reviewing things like Posse Comitatus and other laws if we think it ties our hands in protecting the American people.'[38]

What this would mean in practice was to become increasingly clear. From the outset of the Bush administration, Secretary Rumsfeld was determined on a radical transformation of the sprawling US defence establishment away from a 'static' reliance on large field armies and conventional heavy weapons systems such as tanks and aircraft carriers to a more hi-tech, flexible 'effects based' organization, stressing mobility and Special Forces. As we have seen, an initial move created the new post of undersecretary of defense for intelligence – aiming to secure Pentagon control over the overall intelligence process. Announcing the appointment of Rumsfeld loyalist Stephen Cambone on 8 May 2003, deputy secretary Paul Wolfowitz noted: 'the new office is in charge of all intelligence and intelligence-related oversight and policy guidance functions.'[39] This, in practice, meant control over the Defense Intelligence Agency, the Defense Security Service, the National Imagery and Mapping Agency, the National Reconnaissance Office and the National Security Agency – thus thwarting efforts by the 2002 Scowcroft Commission to transfer the last three agencies to the director of Central Intelligence and effectively sidelining the CIA.[40] In tandem, Rumsfeld established a wholly new agency – the Counterintelligence Field Activity (CIFA) – to conduct domestic intelligence operations.

Although precise details remain classified, CIFA, in its initial form, was organized under nine directorates with 1,000 full-time staff under the deputy undersecretary of defense for counter intelligence and security and able to call upon some 4,000 personnel from the service agencies.[41] In keeping with the overall approach of the Rumsfeld Pentagon, CIFA had a global as well as a domestic remit, with one directorate, Field Activities (DX), tasked for 'preserving the most critical defense assets, disrupting adversaries and helping control the intelligence domain', in conjunction with 'Grey Fox' covert operations teams, transferred from military (SOCOM) control to Cambone's office in April 2003.[42] Another directorate, Behavioral Sciences, began with a staff of psychologists under a former chief psychologist of the CIA's counterterrorism centre, S. Scott Shumate, with responsibilities for 'offensive and defensive counterintelligence efforts', including risk assessment (i.e. interrogation) of detainees in Guantánamo Bay. Given formal authorization to conduct domestic investigations in December 2003, CIFA's aims to become the central coordinating body for counterintelligence within the USA were not without controversy. In late 2005, reports appeared of a massive surveillance campaign directed at US citizens. Particularly targeted were anti-war protesters, whose details were collated on the DoD's TALON (Threat and Local Observation Notice)[43] database, in apparent breach of the Defense Department's own legal restrictions of 1982. The programme was also held to break the established Foreign Intelligence Surveillance Act (FISA) of 1978, prohibiting the bugging of domestic activities without a court order.

Apart from the sheer scale of surveillance undertaken – with more than 12,000 reports logged over a two-year period[44] – what caused concern was their speculative nature. TALON data, collated by CIFA's Counterintelligence and Law Enforcement Center, provides 'non-validated domestic threat information' against military bases or personnel. While the Pentagon itself was to admit 'irregularities' on a scale of one in every hundred reports, it was further to appear that the uncorroborated entries on such groups as the Quakers, whose meetings were classed as 'suspicious incidents', were to be retained under a 2003 Bush administration ruling and distributed across a range of federal databases, reversing previous policy on the destruction of files after an investigation's closure. Whilst congressional and media pressure forced a public retraction by the administration, it had further emerged that a parallel and much larger surveillance programme was also under way by the NSA, which had carried out a blanket monitoring of US calls and emails to numbers overseas. 'The whole idea of the NSA is intercepting huge streams of communication, taking two million communications an hour', observed NSA expert and author James Bamford.[45] The NSA's 'special collection program' began shortly after 9/11, with a partial briefing of selected congressmen in October and November 2001. While some in Congress were later to claim that there was 'no discussion about expanding [NSA eavesdropping] to include conversations of US citizens',[46] the administration was adamant that the briefings – held by then CIA director George Tenet and Michael Hayden of the NSA – were, in fact, 'very, very comprehensive', and provided full justification for the policy under the Patriot Act and presidential executive authority.

Presidential power and 'all necessary and appropriate force'

The issue of 'plenary' executive power, presumed under the president's role as commander-in-chief, is at the heart of the burgeoning growth of the Pentagon and the military–industrial complex in general. Congress's authorizing of the president to 'use all necessary and appropriate force'[47] in resolutions passed after 9/11 was taken as a sanction for unlimited authority – 'full', 'complete', and 'absolute', in the words of White House legal opinion. In the first instance, such powers were taken by the vice president's office to include indefinite detention without trial and a wide latitude in conducting prisoner interrogation. Whilst both actions were,

quite unambiguously, in breach of both the 1996 US War Crimes
Act and the internationally binding Geneva Conventions, legal
opinion drafted by Vice President Cheney's general counsel, David
Addington, was to hold that existing law only applied 'to the extent
appropriate and consistent with military necessity'.[48] The issue of
presidential prerogative was further codified in a classified legal
opinion of 1 August 2002. In this, David Addington, then White
House counsel Alberto Gonzales and John Yoo of the Justice
Department had declared that Congress 'may no more regulate
the President's ability to detain and interrogate enemy combatants
than it may regulate his ability to direct troop movements on the
battlefield'. The definition of 'enemy combatants' – including those
claiming American citizenship – had been left wholly open-ended
in an earlier ruling of 19 June 2002, which contended that 'the
court[s] may not second guess the military's enemy combatant
determination'.[49]

Following the John Yoo 'torture memo' of 1 August, Donald
Rumsfeld issued new formal guidelines in a classified finding of
2 December 2002. The Secretary's authorization of a 'package' of
permitted techniques, including hooding, 'deprivation of light and
auditory stimuli', stress positions and 'exploitation of phobias' drew
strong dissent from senior Pentagon lawyers.[50] It was, however,
seized upon by army and CIA interrogators stymied by the low
volume of meaningful intelligence obtained from the thousands
'processed' in the increasingly global detainee programme. That the
vast majority of these were either low-level, peripheral insurgents
or, in one former officer's view, 'just dirt farmers in Afghanistan'
picked up at random (or for paid bounty) was secondary to the need
for recordable 'results', as demanded by those such as Guantánamo
and later Abu Ghraib commander General Geoffrey Miller.[51] But
for Miller and some in the growing behavioural science branch
of the US military, results were seen as anyway beneficial in
terms of refinement of technique – or, in General Miller's own

words, 'developing integrated interrogation strategies and assessing interrogation intelligence production'. Notable here were the efforts at 'reverse engineering' the all-service 'Survival, Evasion, Resistance, Escape' (SERE) course, designed to help captured US POWs and taught at Fort Bragg Special Warfare Center.[52] The range of exercises involving mock interrogations – prolonged noise, nakedness, sleep deprivation, and so on – have now been carried out for real on a massive scale.

If the use of Guantánamo and the host of other 'black site' facilities as a global laboratory for probing the outer limits of behaviourism recalls the discredited, government-sponsored 'mind control' progammes of the 1950s and 1960s, exposed in the 1976 Pike Report on the CIA, the actual intelligence yield was hardly more forthcoming. An early 'high value' US detainee, al-Qaeda camp commander Ibn Sheikh al-Libbi, provided the subsequently much-cited account of supposed Iraqi chemical/biological weapons training for al-Qaeda, after interrogation in Egypt and Afghanistan. Sheikh al-Libbi, seized in Pakistan in November 2001, was the 'senior terrorist operative' featured in Colin Powell's UN presentation of 5 February 2003. Following the Iraq War, however, al-Libbi was to recant comprehensively; moreover, he had apparently previously outlined the false WMD claims to al-Qaeda leaders as a deliberate disinformation strategy. The aim, according to later al-Qaeda defector Omar Nasiri, was to provoke a US invasion of Iraq, because it was 'the weakest Muslim country'.[53]

The battle in Congress: the McCain amendment and 'implicit legal consent'

The assumption of presidential fiat to conduct carte blanche interrogations was, as we have seen, not the only area where the proceeding demands of wartime emergency were to extend government authority across the board. In a legal finding of 25

September 2002, then attorney general John Ashcroft asserted that 'The constitution vests in the President inherent authority to conduct warrantless intelligence surveillance (electronic or otherwise) of foreign powers and their agents and Congress cannot by statute extinguish that constitutional authority.'[54]

The assumption of such 'extravagant, monarchical' claims, in the words of a former Reagan deputy attorney general, made under the 14 September 2001 Joint Congressional Resolution, was to be contested by both Congress and the judiciary. On 5 October 2005, the Senate passed Senator John McCain's Detainee Treatment Act, which reinstated the provisions on 'humane' treatment of prisoners and due legal process from Geneva Convention Common Article Three.[55] This was, though, to be circumscribed in the final version by the insertion of a qualifying clause vesting authority again in presidential privilege, stemming from the role of commander-in-chief. On 29 June 2006 the US Supreme Court led a further attempt to rein in Bush's prerogative, ruling that Geneva Article Three did indeed apply to 'unlawful enemy combatants' and that these provisions were enforceable by courts within the United States. The judgment also rejected White House arguments of 'implicit' legal consent for warrantless surveillance and wire-tapping.[56] In the wake of the Abu Ghraib scandal, the return of Article Three was taken up by the Pentagon's uniformed legal staff as a welcome clarification and the prohibition on 'cruel, inhuman or degrading treatment or punishment' was incorporated verbatim in the army's new *Field Manual*.[57]

However, further pressure from Dick Cheney's office produced the compromise 'Military Commissions Act' (MCA) of September 2006. Here, in the shadow of mid-term elections and 'hurried through Congress with only a few hours of debate',[58] the Act was to exempt CIA officers and government personnel in general from prosecution for past war crimes or torture, albeit without formally repealing the existing 1996 War Crimes Act. Furthermore, it reaffirmed presidential authority over the Supreme Court in deciding standards of treatment where 'enemy combatants' were concerned.

Following the passage of the September MCA and new attorney general Alberto Gonzales's assertions that detention of any designated 'enemy' was authorized by Congress as pursuant to 'a fundamental incident of waging war',[59] some wider implications of the president's executive licence were becoming apparent. 'In the first war of the twenty-first century', Bush had declared, 'one of the most critical battlefronts is the home front.'[60] On 24 January 2006, Halliburton subsidiary Kellogg, Brown & Root announced a $385 million Department of Homeland Security contract to build a network of detention centres. The plan, part of a $400 million programme set up by homeland security secretary Michael Chertoff, aimed at a 32 per cent increase in detention capacity for FY 2007, adding an additional 6,700 places in purpose-built facilities.[61] Ostensibly aimed at 'all removable aliens' – notably illegal economic immigrants and 'potential terrorists' – the Halliburton contract forms the first instalment in a ten-year Homeland Security strategy, codenamed ENDGAME, authorized in 2003. ENDGAME itself, however, represents an updating of earlier plans for 'Continuity in Government' (COG), first proposed under the Nixon administration and given formal sanction in the early 1980s by Ronald Reagan. Part of the Reagan administration's overall preparation for nuclear war-fighting, COG provides for some one hundred top government officials to evacuate to mountain bunker complexes in Virginia and Pennsylvania, near Camp David.[62]

Whilst the relocation part of COG planning was actually implemented in the hours after 9/11, the more covert measures envisaged for 'national emergency' were similarly placed under fresh consideration. These included mass detentions, warrantless eavesdropping, martial law and suspension of the US Constitution. Working under then vice president George H.W. Bush and the blandly named National Program Office, the senior 'action officer' for continuity on the Reagan NSC was Colonel Oliver North.[63] Before North's removal in 1986 over Iran–Contra, he had supervised a 1984 'readiness exercise' – codenamed Rex 84 – in which the detention of up to 400,000 supposed 'refugees' would take place by the Federal Emergency Management Agency (FEMA). Regulars among the designated 'team leaders' for the annual COG preparations in the 1980s were Donald Rumsfeld and Dick Cheney.

Bugging wars, data-mining and 'Total Information Awareness'

With the reluctant departure of Donald Rumsfeld as secretary of defense in mid-2006, there were some expectations of a change of emphasis in the Pentagon's intelligence strategy. 'More than a few CIA veterans', declared incoming secretary Robert Gates (himself a former CIA director), 'are unhappy about the dominance of the Defense Department in the intelligence arena and the decline in the CIA's central role.'[64] Perhaps more important at an organizational level, Rumsfeld's exit had also brought about the replacement of Stephen Cambone, 'Rumsfeld's enforcer', as defense undersecretary for intelligence. Cambone had directed the generalized expansion of Pentagon intelligence, both foreign and domestic, and had introduced a routine procedure for issuing 'National Security Letters' permitting the viewing of domestic personal and financial records.[65] In addition to opposition from the CIA, Cambone had also clashed with the FBI after authorizing the direct liaison of military officers with local police – bypassing established Bureau channels – but at the same time restricting the transfer of FBI personnel to other agencies.[66]

Although the tempo of bureaucratic infighting had lessened somewhat with the Gates appointment at DoD and the replacement of Porter Goss – George Tenet's short-lived successor at the

CIA – by the experienced former NSA chief Michael Hayden, fresh controversy was emerging over the Pentagon's domestic intelligence role. In August 2007, hearings opened in lawsuits against US communications conglomerate AT&T. The legal class actions, brought by privacy campaign group the Electronic Frontier Foundation, suggest that the NSA had installed a massive server array in a restricted room at AT&T's main West Coast telephone and Internet hub in San Francisco.[67] Along with similar installations in sixteen other Bay Area centres and exchanges in Seattle, San José, Los Angeles and San Diego, this enabled the Agency to assemble an estimated 150 terabytes of call records between 2001 and May 2006, when it was exposed in a *USA Today* report.[68] The ultimate aim behind access to 'every call ever made', as one source was to put it, was to trawl through the unit data in search of underlying patterns and connections. This was based on the controversial emerging technology of 'data-mining' (a technique for mass database correlation) and a sub-methodology known as 'link analysis'. Here, a survey by the US Government Accountability Office (GAO) listed 199 admitted data-mining projects by federal agencies, including 122 involving personal data.[69]

The furore surrounding the AT&T case, which surfaced during confirmation hearings for CIA director Michael Hayden, were to highlight Hayden's then NSA role in administering the programme. What had also become apparent, however, was that the NSA itself was only a component of the wider Pentagon effort at domestic (and global) surveillance, which had emerged in 2002 as 'Total Information Awareness' (TIA). Launched publicly on the website of Rumsfeld's newly established Information Awareness Office, TIA sought the open-ended gathering of 'transactional data' on every aspect of social activity – with 'financial, education, travel, medical, veterinary, country entry, place/event entry, transportation, housing, critical resources, government, communications' records being declared targets[70] – in order to establish an 'electronic footprint' for cross-referencing. When combined with the growing capability to amass biometric data – with DNA, iris scans and fingerprinting all increasingly required to be on record – the prospect of a potentially limitless global information bank arose, one whose only foreseen limitations were purely technical. To be sure, the egregious presentation of TIA – which featured a comic-book eye-and-pyramid logo and the Latin motto *scientia est potentia* (knowledge is power) and the choice of convicted Iran–Contra overseer John Poindexter as director – were to see the programme officially dropped in the face of widespread public opposition. However, like the related and similarly ill-starred Office of Strategic Influence, and much else in the Rumsfeld Pentagon, the main thrust of Total Information Awareness would continue, unpublicized and under another name.

Some detail on TIA's current status was to become at least partially public in the AT&T hearings and the row over Bush's forced acknowledgement of warrantless wiretapping, in December 2005. Although congressional reform of the FISA statutes was, in August 2007, to provide some future sanction to unimpeded NSA surveillance of communications with others, 'reasonably believed to be outside the United States',[71] a February 2006 grilling of attorney general Alberto Gonzales before the Senate Judiciary Committee had revealed outlines of much wider NSA intelligence gathering, known as the 'Terrorist Surveillance Program' (TSP). Here, Gonzales's obfuscation on the data-mining issue – subsumed under a general rubric of activities, 'that the President has con- firmed' – was to lead to perjury accusations as further evidence of intense inter-agency conflict and resignation threats began to leak to the Senate Intelligence Committee in July 2007.[72] Further probing by senators prompted the admission by Mike McConnell, newly installed director of national intelligence, that the TSP itself is 'the only aspect of the NSA activities that can be discussed publicly', whilst Alberto Gonzales himself was to acknowledge that earlier statements 'may have created confusion, particularly for those knowledgeable about the NSA activities authorized by the presidential order'.[73]

Whilst the full extent of Pentagon intelligence activity in the Bush administration is heavily concealed under black budgets and the assertion of 'state secrets privilege', argued for in the AT&T case, informed speculation suggests at least three major domestic programmes, involving mass wiretapping, collating call and email records from customer databases, and data-mining across the board.[74] In one example, the DoD's 'Pathfinder', the aim is analysing government and private-sector databases and searching multiple large databases simultaneously.[75] Another development is the fast-evolving ADVISE (Analysis, Dissemination, Visualization, Insight and Semantic Enhancement)[76] software, developed jointly by the NSA and the Department of Homeland Security, with the intention of overall database correlation.

Following the 4 August 2007 congressional ruling, the NSA was granted unimpeded legal access to the 38 per cent of world telephone, data and Internet traffic transiting the US.[77] Data-mining technology is used to correlate with the estimated 190,000 names on the CIA's international terrorist watch list and the admitted 325,000 records kept by the National Counterterrorism Center (NCTC), the majority supplied by the NSA.[78]

However, despite the massive efforts in data-mining, the sheer scope of the programme has flaws in its dependence on human subjectivity. Like the aborted TIA, its direct, though unacknowledged, predecessor, ADVISE depends critically on finding correlation between public and corporate information – including financial records, news reports, blogs and even library records – and classified databases. And here the scope for 'false positives' is exponential. As we have seen in the TALON controversy, much classified (and thus unaccountable) data is subjective, unverified and possibly sheer fabrication. There exists no effective recourse to removing false data, a danger which is, in any event, further complicated by pooling among the twenty-six classified government data networks.[79] Once TALON data is logged on the CIFA's 'Cornerstone' network, for example, it is most likely to remain there, or somewhere else, for ever.

The dark glass – the Pentagon and 'shaping the future'

To be sure, funding constraints, public pressure and the more conventional approach to security issues brought to the Pentagon by Robert Gates have all had some effects on the Rumsfeld-era vision of limitless surveillance. ADVISE was officially suspended in August 2007 after a critical congressional report by the Privacy Office condemned the programme for using 'live' (real world) data in its testing procedures[80] and, more importantly, performing worse than commercial software available off the shelf. And TALON, the brainchild of – perhaps unsurprisingly – Paul Wolfowitz, was officially shut down on 17 September 2007, 'because reporting to the system had declined significantly', as a closing Pentagon press release was to put it.[81] This, though, clearly begs a wider question: the extent of the actual threat itself. Although the Bush White House has made much of breaking up ten domestic terror cells, it is the absence of any significant terrorist outbreak since 9/11 that is arguably more telling – particularly as Bush's own ten plots include the thwarting of the Richard Reid 'shoe bombing' (by ordinary airline passengers) and other events triggered by routine police action. 'If we're recording thousands of people and secretly collecting documents regarding tens of thousands of people', former FBI undercover agent Mike German observes, 'why aren't thousands of people going to jail?'[82]

As former NSC counterterrorism chief Richard Clarke recalls, the central piece of advice from staffers to George W. Bush in the 2004 elections was 'run on the war'.[83]

The president clearly needed no prompting. And, as we have seen, the claims to unlimited executive power by the Bush White House have been mirrored by a wholesale expansion of the Pentagon's domestic role as well as near dominance in moulding foreign and security policy in general. But if the 'long war' has provided the pretext for launching a raft of long-sought repressive policies (and weapons-system bonanzas) by what Eisenhower first dubbed the 'military–industrial complex' and their congressional and media allies, the actual military component itself has been constantly undone, not least by a roller-coaster of unforeseen consequences and vicious government feuding. The ambitions in Donald Rumsfeld's 2006 *Quadrennial Review* of moving 'From conducting war against nations – to conducting war in countries we are not at war with' (presumably not excluding the USA itself) and 'From threat-based planning – to capabilities-based planning' have been widely read globally as a blueprint for unlimited licence, whose only limitation is the Pentagon budget bottom line. Whilst another Rumsfeld CEO bullet point, 'From crisis response – to shaping the future',[84] was already severely compromised by the grip of a past – the Cold War in the Islamic world – whose unresolved tensions, as we have seen, were threatening to spin way beyond the reach of the most elaborate capabilities-based planning scenarios.

In an extended 2007 essay on international legal obligations and the War on Terror, NSC consultant and director of the 2004 9/11 Commission, Philip Zelikow, observed: 'It is ... striking ... that the United States has not persuaded most states, including many of our allies, to agree that a policy of armed conflict is appropriate.'[85] Zelikow had overseen the wide-ranging, if selective, investigation into the background to 9/11 and was arguing against the 'original pre-9/11 paradigm – criminal justice plus diplomacy'. But if Zelikow was surely correct in identifying the path from policy decision to *ex post facto* legal justification in the

USA, 'responding to some informal guidance from the White House', he was also conceding the ground for overall policy failure. The admission that 'Many governments, including practically all of Western Europe, have never accepted any change from the pre-9/11 criminal justice/diplomacy approach' and believe that 'armed conflict is rarely, if ever, a solution to a problem' points, if inadvertently, to the intrusion of reality that began to be observable in the latter half of the second Bush administration. The further admission that 'the United States made careful, deliberate choices to place extreme physical pressure on captives' after 2002 perhaps also points out, in an indirect way, the reason for this divergence. But where Zelikow is surely accurate in observing the temptation on the part of some 'local governments' to 'let the Americans do the distasteful things', the pattern adopted by practically all of Western Europe – the EU and NATO countries – has also been, as we shall see, one of freeriding on US excesses to promote their own agendas on governmental/bureaucratic empire-building and bolstering of unaccountable power. The next chapter examines the one stand-out case in Western Europe where the 'armed conflict paradigm' has indeed been accepted without question in government, if certainly not elsewhere: the United Kingdom.

4

Liberty: the casualty of lies

Truth is the first casualty of war. The second has to be civil liberties. (Philip Knightley)

'Shoulder to shoulder': the UK and the retreat from civil liberties

On Tony Blair's first visit to the Bush White House, the almost instant affinity manifest between the two leaders came as something of a surprise to both.[1] Perhaps less surprising, however, the virtually unconditional embrace of heavy-handed US international moves in the War on Terror was to find an echo in the Blair government's domestic agenda. Like his new soulmate in the Oval Office, Blair combined a talent for lobby pleasing and tabloid opportunism with an almost unshakeable belief in his own convictions. And, as would soon become clear, the torrent of new legislation rushed through Parliament in the wake of 9/11 and the London bombings of July 2005 was constantly tailored for signing off many a Whitehall wish-list as well as feeding media support for the Iraq War in particular and outflanking any sort of dissent from government policies in general.

Despite consistent objection to the renewal of the 1989 Prevention of Terrorism Act and other (largely Irish Republican-related)
bills while in opposition, the Blair government has (in figures
collated by the Rowntree Reform Trust) itself enacted more than
200 pieces of specified 'anti-terrorist' legislation when in power,
quite apart from related offences in criminal law.[2] Here, many
of the more contentious aspects of the (then temporary) 1980s'
provisions – detention, movement restrictions, block surveillance
– have been substantially expanded and placed on a permanent
footing. The foundation for counterterrorism policy under New
Labour was the Terrorism Act 2000. Covering three broad areas
of legislation, the 2000 Act extended the powers of the home
secretary on the proscription of terrorist organizations, with new
offences concerning membership, financing and associated activity,
and created additional specific offences of terrorist fundraising and
training in the use of firearms. It provided greater police powers
to cordon areas, access information, stop and search and detain
without charge – increased from 24 to 48 hours – extendable by
warrant to seven days, with provision for a further seven days.
More controversially, the Act empowered a police officer to arrest
anybody, 'whom he reasonably suspects to be a terrorist', unrelated
to any specific offence. This extension of the right to arrest set
the point of departure for future policy, an erosion of liberty
based on heavy-handed intelligence and the spinning of policy.
Here we look at the ways in which this was done and consider its
far-reaching consequences.

The immediate aftermath of 9/11 in the UK produced the
Anti-Terrorism, Crime and Security Act (ATCSA) of December
2001. Bundled through parliament with little dissent from Labour's
168-seat majority, the Act's 125 clauses contained new provisions on
asset disclosure and the immediate seizure of financial assets at the
start of investigation; extended powers for the British Transport
Police, Ministry of Defence Police and UK Atomic Energy Police;

and powers to order the disclosure of telephone, email and other communications records and flight passenger data. To the satisfaction of many in Whitehall, it also allowed, by means of the designation 'secondary legislation' (thus avoiding prior parliamentary scrutiny), the incorporation within UK law of a raft of pending EU criminal legislation and inter-European police and intelligence harmonization measures. If further measures for generalized access to confidential records from 81 government bodies, from the NHS to the BBC, drew disquiet from even the opposition Conservative Party,[3] Part 4 of the Act, covering indefinite detention for designated foreign nationals, raised opposition across the board, notably from the judiciary and the legal profession at large.

The reintroduction of, in effect, 1970s-style internment for foreign UK residents deemed (with no published supporting evidence) 'threats to national security' was presented by home secretary David Blunkett as a response to a public emergency. Unlike the 1970s and 1980s, however, where 'political status' was explicitly denied, detainees under ATCSA were to be held precisely on the grounds of 'the use or threat of action where the action is designed to influence the government or advance a political, religious or ideological cause'.[4] As human rights groups such as Amnesty International and much legal opinion have pointed out, this provision breaks entirely with habeas corpus and the fundamental presumption of innocence, in that imputed motivation – rather than commission – has become the basis for arrest and detention.[5]

The deportation option – routine in criminal cases involving foreign nationals – was ruled out for many countries by the 1998 incorporation of the European Convention on Human Rights (ECHR) into their law. This precluded deportation to states where there was a credible risk of torture or, 'cruel, degrading or inhumane treatment', a provision legally classed as non-refoulement. In Britain, David Blunkett and the Blair government had taken the unprecedented step of 'derogation' from the relevant passage of ECHR[6] – the only member of the Council of Europe nations to do so. Here, concerns for the potential abuse of process were soon amply borne out. On 19 December 2001, nine mostly Algerian foreign nationals were arrested overnight, under conditions of total secrecy, and taken straight to Belmarsh and Woodhill high-security prisons.

Aside from the blanket security clampdown surrounding these arrests, neither the detainees nor their families were informed in any way of either potential charges or their destination. Legal representation was not provided, and a solicitor only became involved due to a chance encounter with fellow (non-ATCSA) prisoners in Belmarsh.[7] In all, seventeen Muslim men have been detained for up to three years under ATCSA. However, though this did indeed include a notional framework for legal process – the right of appeal to a 'Special Immigration Appeals Commission' (SIAC) – the latter proceedings were conducted entirely in closed session, with neither the defendant nor lawyers being allowed to view charges or any evidence. The defence was allocated a security-vetted Special Advocate to act on their behalf, but still prohibited from examining what the intelligence-based evidence comprised. Of ten such appeals monitored by Amnesty International in 2003, all had been rejected, leading the chairman of the UK parliamentary Constitutional Affairs Committee to conclude very reasonably that 'The Special Advocate system lacks the most basic features that make for a fair trial.'[8]

Aside from the total lack of legal accountability surrounding the ATCSA detentions, concern has also mounted regarding the nature of evidence presented, even under the supposed 'public emergency' imperative of the Act's own terms. Whilst the presentation of intelligence evidence has long been circumscribed in open court – for example, in Northern Ireland terrorism trials – the blanket non-disclosure of evidence in ATCSA cases raises new issues, not only of provenance but, on a basic level, of reliability. And these factors are fundamentally linked. For beyond the need to protect conventional intelligence methods (infiltration, surveillance etc.) in given instances of operational security, the secrecy attending ATCSA suggests a less defensible reliance on hearsay. Sourced either from informants (sometimes paid or otherwise motivated) or from foreign intelligence services whose true interests are also far from clear, such information – as independent scrutiny of individual cases has made clear – has often emerged under torture.

Ducking the ECHR: control orders and 'reasonable suspicion'

Despite being party to the long-standing UN Convention Against Torture and the European Convention on Human Rights – where the absolute ban on torture and inhumane treatment of Article 3 has been incorporated into UK law since 1998 – the Blair and Brown government's record on the issue has been decidedly ambivalent in practice. According to the March 2005 report of the parliamentary Intelligence and Security Committee (ISC), British intelligence officials have been present in a variety of roles at over 2,000 interrogations in Afghanistan, Iraq and Guantánamo Bay.[9] With regard to the last, all nine of the UK nationals released between March 2004 and January 2005 reported consistent maltreatment during US interrogations, including instances where UK officials were present when they were threatened with guns.[10] For detained UK (non-citizen) residents, the position is even worse. Denial of even notional consular representation in such cases has not prevented the presence of MI5 and MI6 officers. In one case, Ethiopian refugee Benyam Mohammed al-Habashi alleges being forced to sign 'confessions' whilst under US/UK questioning at the notorious 'Salt Pit' facility at Bagram Airbase in Afghanistan, before being shipped to the harsh Camp V section of Guantánamo. A more publicized case concerns British-educated long-term London resident Bisher al-Rawi, arrested with others in Gambia after a UK tip-off and transferred to US custody in Afghanistan and Guantánamo Bay. Al-Rawi's claims to have worked (unpaid) as an MI5 intermediary and translator over a period of years[11] – and subsequently visited by the same handlers in Guantánamo – were neither 'confirmed nor denied' in subsequent parliamentary ISC reporting.[12] Refusal to detail the 'exact nature' of al-Rawi's relations with the security service and the admission of a 'fact-specific' claim in this case are suggestive of the existence of a more widespread intelligence-gathering pattern among Islamists. This is further borne out by al-Rawi's eventual release in March 2007 after the personal intervention of then foreign secretary Margaret Beckett, 'somewhat late in the day'.[13]

With the December 2004 House of Lords ruling that indefinite detention under ATCSA Part 4 was 'incompatible with the right to liberty' under ECHR, the Blair government was to push through an additional set of countermeasures – the Prevention of Terrorism Act (PTA) of March 2005. Far from responding to the widespread concerns of the Lords' judgment, the effect of PTA/05 was to extend the powers of ministerial fiat to UK as well as non-British nationals, with indefinite detention replaced by 'control orders' – effectively, house arrest – and a range of restrictions on personal contact and communication. As with the ATCSA legislation, the grounds were a 'reasonable suspicion' of terrorist links by the home secretary, with non-disclosure of evidence in open court and detention of potentially infinite duration. These strictures were immediately applied to the remaining non-UK detainees, as the government sought diplomatic assurances from the home countries on maltreatment, which could then be used to justify deportation.

The London bombings of 7 July 2005 and failed 21 July plot were to prompt a further spate of anti-terrorism legislation. The

Terrorism Bill of October 2005 – the Blair government's fou[r?]
five years – created new offences of 'inciting terrorist acts' (directl[y?]
or indirectly), attending a terrorist training camp, preparing terrorist acts and involvement in terrorist acts abroad. The Bill's
centrepiece, extension of pre-trial detention from 14 to 90 days,
was, however, cut down to 28 days after fierce opposition in the
Lords and a rare rebellion from Labour's now reduced majority.
Similarly watered down were other provisions on a loosely drawn
offence of 'glorifying terrorism' and the proscription of designated
terrorist organizations.

The controversy stirred by Blair's efforts to secure 90-day detention – by far the longest period without charge in any Western
democracy – stemmed not only from legal concern but from perceptions of blatant government politicking across the board. As the
Iraq War marketing roll-out has shown, this was nothing new in the
Blair government's approach to national security. The succession
of terrorism bills have been – seamlessly – taken up for further
tabloid grandstanding. 'The shame will lie with the conservatives',
Blair had declared in the March 2005 PTA debate; 'If they want
to vote against it, let them. We will be content ultimately to have
the verdict of the country on it.'[14] As often with Blair's statements,
there was a revealing political bottom line. The PTA Bill had
been hastily cobbled together after the not-unexpected Lord's
ECHR ruling, after decisions taken to hold a May election. And,
throughout, the underlying narrative was clear. In former maverick
and now firmly on-message Leader of the Commons Peter Hain's
exposition, 'Britain will be safer under Labour.'[15]

If headline-friendly populism had perhaps reached an apogee
under David Blunkett's tenure as home secretary (a career undone
ironically by media revelations of impropriety), with attacks on
the judiciary as a regular feature, there were some hopes for de-
politicized consensus under his more emollient successor, Charles
Clarke. And in the fraught political climate after 7/7, Clarke was

out to opposite numbers on the Tory and
ıt benches. On 5 August 2005, however, Tony
nounced a new and unheralded '12-point plan'
Bypassing the Charles Clarke negotiations and
ırprise of Home Office officials and junior min-
ıst.   ırs, Blair went on to outline a range of measures
on prosc.   ın, detention (albeit without specific timing) and,
critically, 'a new approach to deportation orders ... if necessary,
amending the Human Rights Act in respect to the European
Convention on Human Rights.'[16] 'What I am trying to do here',
Blair declared, 'is to send a clear signal out that the rules of the
game have changed.'

Appropriate guarantees and 'practices well below the line'

The government's 'new approach' to foreign detainees represented
yet another effort to get round the intractable international legal
obligations – notably, EHCR Article 3 – prohibiting deportation
to states where there was a likelihood of maltreatment or torture.
Like much else in Blair's rolling legislative programme, deportation
to some ten mostly Middle Eastern 'key countries', under what
were termed 'appropriate guarantees', had been under increasing
consideration for some time.[17] Reversing earlier Foreign Office
opinion, active negotiations had begun from late 2002 with the
first 'Memoranda of Understanding' (MoUs) signed with Libya
and Jordan in August 2005. Immediately, ten men were arrested,
including the nine Algerians released under the December 2004
Lords ruling and placed under control orders pending deportation.
The conditions imposed, including an eighteen-hour curfew, movement and social restrictions and constant surveillance, were close
to constituting 'cruel and inhuman treatment' in themselves. Lord
Carlisle QC, appointed as an independent reviewer, observed that

'On any view, these obligations are extremely restrictive ... They fall not very short of house arrest, and certainly inhibit normal life considerably.'[18]

That both the (secret) evidence behind the control and deportation orders and the likely fate of the deportees were bound up almost inevitably with torture were not decisive factors in the Blair government's view. 'There are certainly circumstances where we get intelligence from a liaison partner where we know ... that their practices are well below the line', then foreign secretary Jack Straw declared; 'it does not follow that if it is extracted under torture, it is automatically untrue.'[19] Similarly unacknowledged was the wider threat opened by the MoU policy to the whole basis of international human rights legislation built up since 1945. The UN Convention Against Torture states unequivocally that 'any statement which is established to have been made as a result of torture shall not be invoked as evidence in any proceedings.' Furthermore, as noted by the UN Special Rapporteur on torture, 'the very fact that such diplomatic assurances are sought is an acknowledgement that the requested state, in the opinion of the requesting state, is practising torture.'[20] As the legal battle over torture evidence unfolded, the government was finally defeated in a unanimous Lords judgment of December 2005, with Lord Bingham (the leading opinion) ruling that 'the principles of common law standing alone ... compel the exclusion of third party torture evidence as unreliable, unfair, offensive to ordinary standards of humanity and decency and incompatible with the principles that should animate a tribunal seeking to administer justice.'[21]

The Blair government's clashes with the judiciary throughout 2005 had coincided, not fortuitously, with campaigning for the May 2005 elections. Aside from successfully outflanking the opposition Conservative Party under right-wing populist former home secretary Michael Howard, the main target was the British tabloid press, whose appetite for ever more draconian measures was to be assiduously cultivated. Blair's sudden 5 August '12-point plan' was a case in point, with its release attended by a 'Downing Street whispering campaign'[22] against the consensus-seeking Charles Clarke at the Home Office. Headlines in Rupert Murdoch's *Sun* newspaper provide a telling commentary, from the 3 August 'Let's Hope the Bombers Are on Holiday Too' banner accusing MPs of inaction, to the triumphal 6 August claim of 'Victory for the Sun over New Terror Laws'.[23]

If Blair's 'new terror laws' had gained some at least notional legal palliative from the MoUs with Jordan and Libya, even this fig leaf of legitimacy was absent in the home nation of the great majority of foreign detainees, Algeria. Despite repeated government assurances that a memorandum and an 'appropriate' monitoring system would soon be in place, this was denied by the Algerian authorities themselves in an official statement of March 2006.[24] UK government lawyers then immediately changed tack, claiming that any new formal mechanism was now unnecessary, on account of Algeria's own February 2006 decree on amnesty and 'national reconciliation' – a stance strongly disputed by human rights groups and most legal observers. Beyond dispute, however, was Algeria's past record on torture, detention and arbitrary execution. A military coup against the January 1992 elections (looked to be won by the Islamist populist Front Islamique du Salut) launched a decade of civil conflict in which some 150,000 were killed, with government forces vying with Islamist guerrillas in episodes of brutality.[25] However, while most Western governments, including the UK, were to grant tacit support to the generals' ruling junta, much evidence was emerging of collusion and outright manipulation of the leading militant Groupe Islamique Armé (GIA) by the Algerian army and intelligence services.[26]

The direct participation of Algerian counter-intelligence (the DRS) and the army Securité Militaire in 'torture, disappearances and extra-judicial executions'[27] as detailed by Amnesty International and many others, had not escaped the notice of the UK government either. In March 2000, a three-year Old Bailey terrorist trial collapsed when a key prosecution witness and MI5 informant withdrew from giving testimony. This followed the production, on the judge's orders, of a range of classified FCO and intelligence assessments stating that 'Sources have privately said that some of the killings of civilians were the responsibility of the Algerian security services' and that 'military security would have … no scruples about killing civilians … my instincts are that parts of the Algerian government would stop at nothing.' Whitehall's circumspection on the potential diplomatic and PR fallout from its intelligence was also made clear. 'If revealed … [it] could open us up to detailed questioning from NGOs and journalists.'[28]

From Wood Green to Washington: Colin Powell and the phantom ricin

If the ruling military junta in Algiers had indeed 'no scruples' about using an undoubted Islamist insurgency to serve its own ends – notably, in garnering Western support and suppressing any stripe of potential opposition – a key permissive factor was the similarly expedient compliance of Paris, London and Washington. This enduring feature in the politics of the War on Terror was to come together in a remarkable way in the London 'ricin plot' of early 2003. On 6 January the Metropolitan Police announced that seven suspected terrorists (six of whom were Algerian) had been arrested in raids across North and East London. The joint Anti-Terrorist Branch, Special Branch and MI5 'Operation Springbourne', carried out 'on receipt of intelligence', had seized 'a quantity of material' at a Wood Green, London, flat, 'a small amount' of which, the press release was to claim, 'has tested positive for the presence of ricin poison'.[29]

In the build-up to the Iraq War, this apparently major anti-terrorist breakthrough was seized upon by the Blair government as further proof of an imminent WMD danger, with home secretary David Blunkett and health secretary John Reid confirming, in a 7 January joint statement, that traces of ricin had indeed been found. These claims were further reinforced by Tony Blair in a speech to foreign diplomats the same day.[30] Despite the fact that the suspects had no discernible Iraqi connection and that ricin itself has never been weaponized (and would presumably require a large research facility to do so), the 'huge potential' highlighted by Blair was immediately given prominence in the general case for war against Saddam. In a keystone section of Colin Powell's 5 February UN presentation, the supposed Wood Green ricin factory was linked to an 'explosives and poison training center camp' in Iraqi Kurdistan, run by the Ansar al-Islam insurgent group and (declared, if fractious, al-Qaeda associate) Abu Musab al-Zarqawi. There was a 'sinister nexus', Powell had declared, 'between Iraq and the al-Qaeda terrorist network ... that combines classic terrorist organizations with modern methods of murder'.[31]

Powell's unhesitating identification of the London 'cell' with 'al-Zarqawi and his network' was seemingly uncompromised by his further commendation of the 'fine paper' issued in tandem by Downing Street, soon known as the 'dodgy dossier' (see Chapter 1). And on 30 March the head of the US joint chiefs, General Richard Myers, again made the connection between 'a site in north-eastern Iraq, where the Ansar al-Islam and al-Qaeda had been working on poisons ... that's probably where the ricin found in London came from'.[32] Conclusive tests carried out at the UK chemical weapons establishment at Porton Down had soon established, however, that although the raided flat contained some rudimentary ingredients (dried castor-oil beans), ricin itself was definitively not present. This inconvenient truth was suppressed by government for over two years – supposedly because it was *sub judice* – whilst the original allegations were continually cited by both government and the police as grounds for ever stronger anti-terrorist legislation.

As the ricin trial finally concluded, it transpired that the original intelligence for 'Operation Springbourne' had come from an Algerian illegal immigrant, Mohammed Meguerba, arrested in London on fraud and immigration charges in September 2002. Released on police bail, he fled to back to Algeria, to be promptly rounded up in a swoop on organized people-smugglers. Once under questioning, Meguerba provided details of his circle of contacts in the North London Islamist exile community, the commonly used Wood Green apartments and a number of the alleged conspirators. As the trial proceeded, however, the emerging picture was of a petty criminal/fantasist milieu, rather than a base for serious terrorist operations. This led to the jury acquitting four of the defendants and issuing an unprecedented public statement protesting their proposed deportation.[33] In the case of one of the acquitted, Algerian refugee Mustapha Taleb, three of the jurors wrote an open letter to Amnesty International, expressing 'shock' that exactly the same evidence rejected in the seven-month trial was being used to justify his being deported to face the 'real risk' of torture. Observing that 'we have had our eyes opened to such an unfair and unjust sequence of events orchestrated by the authorities that we feel compelled to speak out', the jurors were to declare the government's 'persecution' of Taleb 'contrary to anything we thought could be possible in a democratic and free society'.[34]

Most unusually, the trial judge also issued a public warning against comment on the proceedings by the home secretary. And whilst the 'ringleader', Kamal Bourgass, was undoubtedly a violent criminal, convicted for murder and attempted murder, the charge filed in connection with the ricin was 'conspiracy to commit a public nuisance'.

If we cannot entirely banish the suspicion that Meguerba – possessing an obvious suspect profile – was simply *allowed* to abscond to Algeria, in the hope that robust interrogation by the DRS might yield a quick result, the initial UK response was certainly indicative of established institutional cooperation between Algiers and Scotland Yard. A signed deposition to the Lords by MI5 head Eliza Manningham-Buller notes that 'Meguerba was already known to the Security Service and the police' and that the Meguerba case 'provides an example of full cooperation with our Algerian partners'. The reciprocity at issue was also made clear: 'no inquiries were made of Algerian liaison about the precise circumstances that attended their questioning of Meguerba.'[35] Some indication of the latter were to appear in *The Times* in May 2005. As reporters present at the Algiers court record, 'Meguerba looked frail and had many of his teeth missing.'[36]

A corporate media strategy:
the press, the Met and 'Scotland Yard sources'

Wittingly or unwittingly, the police and security services have become highly attuned to the need for strategic communications, after years of exposure to management consultant reviews and business school methodology. The role of senior police officers in backstopping Blair's propagandizing efforts has also stretched boundaries in the politicization of civil liberties. Metropolitan police commissioner Sir Ian Blair was quick to push for control orders and for the failed 90-day detention policy and slow to deny the circulation of demonstrated falsehoods, as in the ricin case and the shooting of Jean Charles de Menezes. And as late as October 2005, assistant commissioner Andy Hayman was citing the escape of Mohammed Meguerba as grounds for the 90 days' detention, despite his being released after only 3 days of the possible 7 to 14 then allowed at the time.[37] To be sure, police and security forces have an important voice in the debate. What has been insidious, however, is the nexus of police and security spokesmen proactively calling for specific measures in concert with Blair government policy launches and organized media campaigning.

Indeed, in several high-profile cases, 'sources' have seemingly deliberately fuelled lurid media speculation on grounds later found to be wholly baseless. Notoriously, the Greater Manchester police allowed weeks of national headlines to continue on a supposed April 2004 plot for suicide bombers to target Old Trafford football ground, only to concede finally that the entirely innocent Kurdish refugee suspects had no case to answer. Presumably the combination of potential terror bombings, 'asylum seekers' and Premier League football was proving too attractive for the press to be distracted by issues of accuracy. Whilst newspaper accounts came replete with supposed detail, the suspects themselves were 'never told why it was' they had been arrested, 'or [given] any of the particulars relating to the offence that was under investigation'.[38] A further headline-grabbing but subsequently abortive mass police action was to take place in Forest Gate, East London, in 2006. Here, a dawn swoop by 250 officers on 2 June had raided two houses, arresting two terrorist suspects and cordoning off neighbouring streets. Immediately, press reports of a 'Hunt for the "Poison Bomb"'[39] and a 'lethal chemical suicide vest' appeared, attributed to 'Scotland Yard sources' and dominating news headlines with increasing detail for the next ten days. However, despite police partially demolishing the two houses (and nearly shooting dead one of the suspects), no evidence of any indictable terrorist activity was uncovered, and the two arrested brothers were subsequently released without charge.

Clearly, the nature of the supposed intelligence prompting the Forest Gate raid is not in the public domain – although one anonymous police source cited in the *Sunday Telegraph* was to claim 'a tip-off to the Met's anti-terrorist hotline' as responsible, possibly involving a grudge against the families concerned.[40] However, what antagonized local residents – and was the subject of a highly critical report to the Metropolitan Police Authority (MPA) by the Newham Monitoring Project – was the almost total denial of information to neighbourhood forums, coupled with a stream of misleading leaks to the national press about anthrax and cyanide vests. Even after police had reluctantly conceded the parties' innocence, the *Sun* was provided with details of £38,000 in family savings (disclosed to police at the outset), in order, so the Newham Monitoring Report surmises, 'to create the impression that the money implied some degree of guilt'.[41] The report observes that, at best, the Metropolitan Police Service condoned selective briefings and leaks, 'but, at worst, was responsible for orchestrating them ... The strategy directly fuelled a process of character assassination of the two brothers that were arrested and by implication other family members.' And, moreover, in the Monitoring Group's view, the 'corporate' media strategy rolled out from the start, by 'members of the senior management team' in New Scotland Yard, 'appeared to focus on reducing or eliminating any cause for members of the public to pass informed and perhaps even critical comment on police performance or its operational priorities'.[42]

The rise of 'an organized and consistent practice of disinformation' in Sir Ian Blair's Met and 'a media strategy that is seemingly out of control', identified in the Forest Gate report, was becoming an all too familiar complement to his namesake's conduct of national security strategy. Amidst the intense lobbying for the 2005 Prevention of Terrorism Act, Tony Blair was to insist repeatedly on being given the powers to take on the 'several hundred' terrorists 'out there, determined to destroy our way of life'.[43] In the government's own published figures, however, post-9/11 and up to the end of 2004, there were 701 arrests under the 2000 Terrorism Act. Of these, 119 were charged under the Act but only 17 were convicted. Of these convictions, moreover, 7 related to Ulster Loyalist and dissident Republican terrorism, 2 involved

Sikh separatists and 1 was a member of the Tamil Tigers. Only 3
stemmed from any form of radical Islamism.[44]

Renditions, ghost flights and a
'shadow system of justice'

If the actual figures for convicted terrorists – and, indeed, those
held under control orders – were to give cause for serious reserva-
tion regarding government claims for the need for ever greater
powers, what was beyond dispute were the effects of anti-terrorist
policy under existing legislation. Given the latitude of 'reasonable
suspicion' and a fast-spreading targets culture pushed by government, the parliamentary Joint Committee on Human Rights was
to note that 'there is mounting evidence that the powers under the
terrorism act are being used disproportionately against members
of the Muslim community.' According to the Met's own data, the
stop-and-search rates for Asian people in London increased by 41
per cent in the period 2001–02, whereas for white people it increased
only 8 per cent.[45] And in British Transport Police figures, people
of Asian appearance were five times more likely to be stopped and
searched than white Caucasians. However, out of 8,120 uses of stop-
and-search in so-called 'designated areas' (i.e. at individual police
discretion) in 2003–04, there were only five arrests for offences
connected with terrorism, all of white people.[46]

Even after the rushed-through 2001 Anti-Terrorism Act, many
in government still favoured an approach treating terrorism as
essentially a criminal rather than a special-category offence. The
December 2003 Newton Report,[47] commissioned to review the
workings of ATCSA, took the view that, in so far as possible,
terrorists should be dealt with specifically as criminals under the
criminal law, noting that nobody had suggested that it has been
'impossible' to prosecute suspected terrorists because of a lack
of available offences[48] and that 'most of the reported uses of the

(ATCSA) Part 10 powers (on search, photographing, fingerprinting
and DNA sampling at police stations) have not been related to
counterterrorism.' The increasingly dominant view at the Home
Office, however, and in Downing Street, was that it was entirely
'appropriate' to be pursuing criminals under anti-terrorist legislation, rather than under criminal law. A February 2007 report
by Interception of Communications commissioner Sir Swinton
Thomas revealed that 439,000 intercept orders had been issued
against UK residents over the past year, including over 4,000
admitted errors – a level described as 'unacceptably high'. Meanwhile, Prime Minister Tony Blair admitted that it was proposed
to collate this data with fingerprints and other information to be
collected under the forthcoming government ID scheme to conduct
a sweep for unsolved crimes.[49] If these measures were successful,
Britain would have achieved a level of surveillance akin to that of
many a totalitarian state. And, as again made clear by Tony Blair,
it was this very reversal of established legal order that was the
developing trend in policy.

After a 2005 Labour Party conference characterized by over
600 stop-and-searches under the Anti-Terrorism Act – and an 82-
year-old party delegate and Holocaust survivor, Walter Wolfgang,
manhandled from the conference hall – Tony Blair declared, 'If
people want us to tackle the new types of crime today, international
terrorism, this very brutal violent organized crime, antisocial
behaviour … you can't do it by the rules of the game we have at
the moment … the only way you deal with it is [to] put the duty
to protect the law abiding citizen at the centre of this system, and
that comes first.'[50]

The inexorable advance of what Amnesty International was to
term a 'shadow system of justice'[51] was brought into further relief
with the emerging revelations that some 200–400 CIA-operated
flights had transited UK airspace over a three-year period, en
route or returning from countries involved in secret detentions.[52]

The existence of a large-scale programme of 'rendition' led to the establishment of an all-party House of Commons committee and was extensively documented by an EU Parliament special committee.[53] The January 2007 EU report established that at least 170 stopovers at UK airports took place, 'deplored' the manner in which UK government ministers cooperated with the EU investigation, and was 'outraged' by legal opinion from FCO adviser Michael Wood holding that possessing or receiving information extracted under torture is not per se illegal under the UN Convention Against Torture. The EU's forthright critique of British government policies found further reinforcement with the exposure of a secret FCO memo of December 2005, which stated: 'In certain circumstances [rendition] could be legal', albeit, 'difficult, and likely to be confined to those countries not signed up to [e.g.] the ICCPR (International Convention on Civil and Political Rights)'.[54] For Blair's government, though, as for Washington, this was precisely the point. As had now become clear, most of the known countries hosting rendition sites were, in effect, in that category.

The tide of concern on both sides of the Atlantic about black sites and rendition was finally to force a public admission from the Bush administration in April 2006. And, as we have seen, pressure from the US Congress had pushed through the Detainee Treatment Act (or McCain Amendment) of December 2005. At that time, Secretary of State Condoleezza Rice was to declare that 'The United States does not transport, and has not transported, detainees from one country to another for the purpose of interrogation using torture.'[55] As we have also seen, however, this seeming clarity was somewhat undermined by the exposure of the notorious 'torture memo' of legal opinion from US Justice Department official John Yoo, which held that a whole battery of coercive techniques – stress enforcement, sleep/sensory deprivation, 'waterboarding' and 'mild slapping' among them – did not constitute torture at all. In the UK, similar government equivocation had clashed repeatedly with senior Law Lords, with Lord Bingham declaring that not only was torture or 'cruel, inhuman or degrading treatment' illegal under any circumstances, but that 'the prohibition on torture requires member states [of ICCPR and other conventions] to do more than eschew the practice of torture'; they 'must immediately set in motion all those procedures ... that may make it possible ... to forestall any act of torture or expeditiously put an end to any torture that is occurring'.[56]

In the House of Commons, the publicity surrounding rendition led the Intelligence and Security Committee (ISC) to consider the whole basis of the 'special relationship' in the intelligence field with Washington. Here, albeit carefully skirting round the 'allegations that the UK Government has not done enough to ensure that the UK is not involved in such operations', the ISC was to admit that, particularly following the al-Rawi and al-Banna cases (outlined above), 'the UK now has some ethical dilemmas with our closest ally'.[57]

If the ISC's contention that UK knowledge of the rendition programme and accompanying network of 'black sites' for detention and torture had only emerged 'gradually' is somewhat hard to square with widespread reports of British security personnel present at interrogations and in admitted receipt of intelligence, the committee's overall findings point to a clear tension between institutional opinion in FCO and MI5/MI6 and US actions after 9/11. Although quick to declare it 'unimaginable' that intelligence cooperation with the Americans should cease, adding 'nor is it in the national interest for UK agencies to carry out [counterterrorism] work independently of US efforts',[58] intelligence and Foreign Office witnesses were also to claim that, from the outset, 'This has been an impenetrable subject ... there was no give at the edges, almost uniquely.'[59] And whilst at the highest level, Foreign Secretary Jack Straw declared himself satisfied with the US 'assurances' of detainee treatment according to international law – as with the later MoU policy – testimony reveals a mounting unease among the lower ranks, if only for fear of entering a potential legal minefield. After the 2004 Abu Ghraib revelations in particular, one FCO official observed: 'Back in 2003 we were concerned about secret facilities but we did not, at that stage … make an automatic connection between secret facilities and mistreatment. That sort of connection grew as more allegations came to light or … things like Abu Ghraib came to light, which led you to believe, just a minute, if that is happening there, what might be happening in secret facilities?'[60] Or, as a further SIS witness was to put it: 'it never crossed my mind that [intelligence] was coming from torture. We are talking about the Americans, our closest ally. This now, with hindsight, may look naive, but all I can say is, this is what we thought at the time.'[61]

The notion that a whole body of experienced intelligence and foreign policy professionals were apparently out of the loop on the US renditions programme – and its UK operational component in particular – should perhaps be treated with some caution. In a major legal action launched in November 2007, lawyers for six former Guantánamo inmates, including Benyam Mohammed and Bisher al-Rawi, have claimed that a significant proportion of CIA flights transiting Western Europe were planned by a Boeing subsidiary, Jeppersen Dataplan, from their eastern hemisphere HQ in Crawley, West Sussex, a few miles from Gatwick airport.[62] Jeppersen, 'the aviation services provider customarily used by the CIA', has been extensively documented in Dick Marty's EU Parliament report (see above) as organizing renditions under false flight plans to a former KGB facility at Syzmany airport in northern Poland.[63] It is further alleged that these arrangements were agreed in a secret protocol between Tony Blair and Polish prime minister Leszek Miller, after a series of London meetings hosted by MI6 director Sir John Scarlett.[64] Jeppersen's connections to the Agency date back many years and are freely admitted. 'We do all the extraordinary rendition flights', the managing director is quoted as telling the *New Yorker*, 'you know, the torture flights. Let's face it, some of them do end up that way.'[65] The EU report further claimed 'concurring confirmations' of the presence of detainees at the 'British Indian Ocean Territory' US base on Diego Garcia[66] – a claim again carefully denied with 'firm [US] assurances'. This was later to rebound, with much government embarrassment, when two years later, as foreign secretary, David Miliband was forced to concede the presence of at least two CIA flights on the island during 2002.[67] Nonetheless, the concerted efforts by government agencies – if clearly not their political masters – to distance themselves from the 'surprising and concerning' aspects of UK/US intelligence cooperation are not without a certain resonance. 'Although the US may take note of UK protests and concerns', the ISC report concludes, 'this does not appear materially to affect its strategy on renditions.'[68]

Blair, 'belief' and the dilemmas of a pillion passenger

However, if the Commons' Intelligence Committee was to make clear that 'secret detention without legal or other representation is itself mistreatment', and that 'approval must never be given',[69] Tony Blair himself and his close associates remained unerringly wedded to being 'shoulder to shoulder' with the twisting course of US policy. 'I did so out of belief', Blair declared in a May 2007 valedictory speech at his Sedgefield constituency, 'So Afghanistan and then Iraq. The latter, bitterly controversial.'[70] Blair's constant invocation of 'belief' in presenting his own policies put a case that was, in the final analysis, always unanswerable. And with an unshakeable parliamentary majority and the entrenched position of any British prime minister (bolstered by the unreformed Royal Prerogative) in what has long been termed an 'elective dictatorship', has led to a succession of subjectively biased initiatives, wherein the burden of empirical proof has been reversed in the legal realm in conjunction with its demotion as the declared basis of political decision-making. Relentlessly pursued, as we have seen, in the build-up to the Iraq War, the 'test of will and belief' line remained the stock response in the face of mounting terrorist outrages. And with, as before, the accompanying flight from historical causation.

The connection between the Iraq War and terrorism in the UK (and in general) is undoubted, and is widely acknowledged in intelligence analysis. In April 2003 the Joint Intelligence Committee assessed that al-Qaeda and associated groups represented 'by far the greatest terrorist threat', which 'would be heightened by military action against Iraq'. And in line with the gloomy 'perfect storm' predictions issuing at the same time from the CIA it was known that 'any collapse of the Iraqi regime would increase the risk of chemical and biological warfare technology or agents finding their way into the hands of terrorists.'[71] Blair had, of course, flatly denied seeking regime change in Iraq in his 18 March 2003 Commons speech, declaring 'that is not the purpose of our action; our purpose is to disarm Iraq of weapons of mass destruction.' The May 2007 Sedgefield farewell address, however, and indeed every other public utterance by Blair on Iraq in recent years have studiously avoided any mention whatsoever of the supposed WMD *casus belli*. Instead, the invasion of Iraq and its consequences have been constantly conflated with the seemingly endless War on Terror. After the 20 November 2003 bombings of the British consulate and the HSBC headquarters in Istanbul, Blair stated: 'what this latest terrorist outrage shows us is this is war, its main battlefield is Iraq.' And on resigning the Labour leadership, he went further: 'this is a struggle that will last a generation and more ... this terrorism is not our fault ... It's not the consequence of foreign policy. Its an attack on our way of life.'[72]

Tony Blair's denial of any consequential linkage between Muslim radicalization and his policies has faithfully echoed the 'they hate our freedoms' line taken by George Bush. As has the invocation of past terrorist actions – the US embassy bombings of 1998, the first (1993) attack on the World Trade Center – to 'prove' the absence of any connection. But for many, it was Blair's own sustained assault on civil liberties that represented the more profound attack on the very 'way of life' at issue. In the 16 December 2004 House of Lords ECHR judgment (see above), Lord Hoffman observed that 'The real threat to the life of the nation, in the sense of a people living in accordance with its traditional laws and political values, comes not from terrorism but from laws such as these. That is the true measure of what terrorism may achieve. It is for Parliament to decide whether to give the terrorists such a victory.'

Blair's sidestepping of his own intelligence advice before the Iraq War and of later JIC/JTAC assessments that 'the conflict in Iraq has exacerbated the threat from international terrorism' and that 'Iraq is likely to be an important motivating factor for some time to come in the radicalization of British Muslims and for those extremists who view attacks against the UK as legitimate'[73] has not prevented the prompting of intelligence spokesmen in the drive for ever greater curbs on civil liberties. In the run-up to the November 2006 Queen's speech, MI5 head Eliza Manningham-Buller was to warn of some thirty 'priority one' terrorist plots, involving over 1,600 individuals. Ever on cue, Sir Ian Blair was the same week to condemn the 'reluctance' of some in the UK Muslim community to cooperate with Met anti-terrorist measures, coupled with renewed calls for 90-day detention.[74]

Ian Blair's observations that gaining Muslim cooperation will be a 'slow and delicate process' were to sit somewhat uncomfortably with his own department's media strategies in the wake of the Forest Gate affair and the uncorrected spin of the July 2005 de Menezes shooting. And on 2 September 2005 Metropolitan Police anti-terrorist officers (with local backup) mounted a further highly publicized raid, on an established Islamic school, Crowborough

Hall in East Sussex, apparently in response to a tabloid campaign alleging what proved to be entirely non-existent terrorist training.[75] Tony Blair's contention that Muslim opponents of his anti-terror policies betray a 'false grievance against the West', made at the time of not-so-tacit US, EU and UK support for the Israeli invasion of Lebanon – was clearly of a piece with Bush's assertion that the 'same people on the streets of Baghdad' were responsible for 9/11, in the promotion of an all-embracing narrative. But unlike the Bush administration, Blair had been explicitly advised not to 'run on the war'. To revisit Sir David Manning's now-notorious April 2002 memo, Tony Blair needed no prompting on management of a press, a Parliament and public opinion 'that was very different than anything in the States'.

Quite aside from the inescapable event-driven dissonance in the Blair government's presentation, 'A key problem', in the view of authoritative London think-tank Chatham House, 'is that the UK government has been conducting counterterrorism policy "shoulder to shoulder" with the US, not in the sense of being an equal decision-maker, but rather as pillion passenger compelled to leave the steering to the ally in the driving seat.'[76] If the Chatham House assessment – appearing, by coincidence, on 18 June 2005, in the wake of the 7/7 London bombings – reflected no more than mainstream establishment opinion, or indeed simple common sense, it was not one the Blair government wanted to hear. Nor were the think-tank's further observations that 'the situation over Iraq has imposed particular difficulties for the UK … It gave a boost to the al-Qaeda network's propaganda, recruitment and fundraising, caused a major split in the coalition, provided an ideal targeting and training area for al-Qaeda-linked terrorists.'

The Downing Street response to Chatham House, following the earlier – and quite unprecedented – public criticism of the government line by fifty-two retired senior diplomats and civil servants,[77] was to slip into default mode. 'I'm astonished if Chatham House is now saying that we should not have stood shoulder to shoulder with our long-standing allies in the United States', Jack Straw declared, 'But let me also say this: *the time for excuses for terrorism are over* (emphasis added).'[78] The then foreign secretary's instant rebuttal on BBC News 24 was again rehearsing the argument that opposition to the Bush/Blair narrative comes from either fools or knaves. At a 19 July joint press conference with visiting Afghan president Hamid Karzai, Tony Blair was to repeat the 'excuses for terrorism' line: 'They will use whatever is going on in foreign policy to justify what they do ... what you have got to be careful of is getting into their perverted logic, which says even if people abhor the bombings in London, well nonetheless we understand why it has happened because of what has happened in Iraq.' Blair's conflation of Islamist polemic with domestic critics of his policies was to be, perhaps inadvertently, unpacked by close associate and twice-resigned cabinet minister Peter Mandelson. Speaking on the BBC's *Question Time* on the same day as Blair's resignation, Mandelson averred,

> I don't think the prime minister was wrong in sticking with the United States in the decision they took. It was primarily a decision and a judgement formed by President Bush and the US administration. The British prime minister then had to decide: are the Americans to be forced to go into Iraq, they having made up their mind that that is what they were going to do, alone, with all the damage I think that would do to the transatlantic alliance but also to the international community as a whole, or were we going to stick by the United States because we were their ally. ... That's why I think he [Blair] took the decision, that's why he took, actually, the only decision that was available to him.[79]

Here we have the complete catalogue: the retailing of the 'entire Islamist bill of particulars' so identified in the US Defense Science Policy Board report of September 2004. Almost unquestioning, like many an architect of the New Labour project, of the principle that UK support for America rests on some free-standing 'historical necessity', regardless of the empirical merit of any twists and turns of individual policy, Mandelson's acceptance – indeed, advocacy – of an essentially unlimited US licence in world affairs surely also concedes the argument on the very plane of radical abstraction employed by al-Qaeda.

Elsewhere among the Western powers, reactions to the post-9/11 world were equally profound, if perhaps not as clear-cut. In the next chapter, we look to what might be termed 'the coalition of the unwilling' – the states of the European Union. Despite overwhelming public opposition in Europe to the war in Iraq, EU governments and agencies were, however, not disinclined to sign up to other aspects of the War on Terror, for reasons of trans-European bureaucratic integration, domestic social control, US inducement, and – as we have already seen – the minority but active presence of radical Islamist cells that were more or less tolerated in previous times. The uptake of these agendas will be considered below.

5

Europe and the War on Terror

> In Europe, we talk about the four freedoms of the Union ... But there is a fifth freedom – intelligence. Nations want to retain the freedom to spy. (Unidentified EU Commission official, October 1998)[1]

Framing the threat

In this final chapter, we look at the War on Terror in a European context. Although the Bush administration would undoubtedly have preferred to prosecute the war themselves, allied support was essential to the project – not least to assuage American public opinion. In previous chapters we have shown how Pakistan, with its critical geographical position and pivotal role in the Islamic world, was cajoled into supporting the War on Terror. The other vital participant – providing crucial diplomatic, economic, logistic and, most of all, intelligence support – was Europe, and especially the so-called 'G6'. This group of six nations – Britain, France, Germany, Italy, Poland and Spain – is the EU's engine room: together they account for three-quarters of the EU's population, 80 per cent of its economic output and the bulk of its diplomatic and intelligence muscle. Despite misgivings, the G6 and their fellow European states have all signed up to the War on Terror in one way or another, even if they sometimes pretend otherwise and are driven by ulterior motives. However, Europe's role in the War on Terror has thrown up a set of dilemmas and contradictions whose resolution is as yet uncertain and which will have profound consequences, not only for the conduct and progress of the war, but for the future of Europe itself. For the sake of convenience, we use the term 'Europe' fairly loosely here to represent the overlap of the European Union and the European component of NATO, which, as we will see, played a vital role in locking in Europe's engagement in the War on Terror. Of NATO's 26 nations, 24 are European, while the EU now has 27 members; 21 countries belong to both organizations.[2]

One immediate result, reinforcing an already disturbing trend, has been the exploitation of the EU's opaque decision-making structures to push through contentious and illiberal measures without debate or democratic scrutiny.

More generally, involvement in the War on Terror will have a major effect upon Europe's nascent foreign policy. The EU's initial, tentative forays into the international arena have achieved moderate but tangible results. The 2007 Lisbon Treaty could, if fully ratified, inaugurate a more assertive, distinctly European presence on the world stage in which Europe would start to exercise the political muscle to match its undisputed economic clout.

Europe's strength derives from a willingness to remove borders between nations and allow as much free movement as possible. The War on Terror immediately presents a problem. As in the Cold War, from which the War on Terror evolved, the principal actors are the intelligence and security services. Europe's own intelligence set-up is basically an analytical capability. Although this situation is changing post-9/11, for the time being the EU, like NATO, relies on its member states' national intelligence services for operational resources and raw material. However, at a very fundamental level, these national agencies owe their principal loyalties to their own governments and so conduct their affairs in accordance with perceptions of their own national interests. Furthermore, as Western nations have steadily and remorselessly divested themselves of ever more functions through privatization, national security has assumed greater relative importance (although even the intelligence complex is not wholly immune from privatization mania).

That said, the EU's panoply of intelligence and policing agencies have come to realize that their battle against militant Islam depends upon mutual support and collaboration, especially the sharing of intelligence. Cross-border cooperation has undoubtedly increased since the attacks of 9/11 (USA, September 2001), M-11 (Madrid, March 2004)[3] and 7/7 (London, July 2005) but intelligence liaison is a carefully managed, calibrated process, carrying with it 'the sanctity of the Bible'.[4]

The initial task for European intelligence agencies was to identify the nature and extent of the threat posed by militant Islam. There is now broad agreement that it represents the single most serious challenge to national security, but approaches to dealing with it have been far from uniform. The presence of large Muslim populations within the EU demands a more subtle approach than the American solution of blanket border surveillance and control. Discussing the 7/7 attacks in London, the German security service, the Bundesamt für Verfassungsschutz (BfV), identified

> a clear indication of a new type of group that is emerging in Europe. Members of these groups have no experience of the jihad themselves … [nor] links to the global mujahideen network. Rather, members of these 'home-grown networks' are second- or third-generation immigrants who were born and raised in Western societies … Those involved in such groups – although they appear to be fully integrated – are willing to take part in violent jihad after undergoing a process of Islamic radicalization.[5]

Earlier we also showed how the 'blowback' of militant Islam into Europe occurred, beginning in Afghanistan and arriving in stages via Somalia, Bosnia and Kosovo. The arrival of the jihadis among existing Muslim communities, compounded by the conduct of Western foreign policy in the Muslim world, fuelled the rise of Islamist militancy throughout the continent. Not all jihadis followed the trail to Europe and other militants found their way to other conflicts. Among the forty different nationalities represented by the Guantánamo detainees are veterans of conflicts in the transcaucasian regions of Russia, principally Chechnya. There are also fighters from the former Soviet Central Asian republics of Uzbekistan, Kazakhstan and Tajikistan; Filipino separatists fighting for a Muslim republic in the southern islands; ethnic Uighurs, predominately Muslim, from the Xinjiang region of north-west China; along with Maldive Islanders, Somalis and Chadians.[6] In fact, there are individuals from every part of the globe bar Latin America.

As for Europe, the Americans appear to view it as part of the problem as much as part of the solution, Michael Chertoff, secretary for homeland security in the Bush administration, opined that 'We are increasingly worried about Europe [which] is becoming both a target and a platform for terrorists.'[7]

The uniform reaction throughout the EU has been to boost the anti-terrorism resources of the police and the intelligence services to unprecedented levels, while introducing new laws to remove as many obstacles as possible to their operational and strategic demands. Attempts to deal with the underlying social, political and economic causes have spawned innumerable official committees, working parties and 'initiatives', to little effect. Dick Marty, the Swiss rapporteur who assembled a report on the European role in 'extraordinary rendition' (this is one of the most important documents in the ever-growing War on Terror catalogue), expresses it thus: 'The fact is that there is no real international strategy against terrorism, and Europe appears to have been tragically passive in this regard.'[8]

Many of the Western European intelligence services have considerable experience of counterterrorist operations, based variously on counter-insurgency wars in soon-to-be ex-colonies, domestic regional/ethnic struggles and left/right-wing ideological campaigns. They know that accurate intelligence is the *sine qua non* of counterterrorist operations. Their perception of militant Islam, however, is of a new phenomenon. The recently retired MI5 head Eliza Manningham-Buller pronounced that 'al-Qaeda represents the first truly global terrorist threat. The extremist ideology it sponsors has spread around the world and seeped into and infected individuals and groups almost everywhere.'[9]

The irony of this observation is that only recently had Manningham-Buller and her fellow securocrats realized that the nature of the challenge of militant Islam was internal as well as external, and that, given the relative ease of cross-border movement between EU states, 'internal' meant the European Union, rather than Britain alone (though Britain has tried to maintain its inviolable border). A terrorist operation in one country has often been supported by a logistics network in another. The French were among the first to realize this following a series of bombings by Algerian militants in Paris, Lyon and elsewhere in the mid-1990s. But they were initially unable to persuade other countries that those were anything more than a unique national problem produced by French support for the Algerian junta – referred to as *le pouvoir* or *les décideurs*. The contrasting British intelligence view was articulated by the 1997 report of the Parliamentary Intelligence and Security Committee:

> Elsewhere, there is increasing concern over Islamic terrorist threats. Whilst we may not have been so affected ourselves by these groups, some of them have used Britain as a base to raise funds and equipment and recruit new members. We have been significantly helped by many

other countries in countering Irish terrorism, and we have a clear duty to help them in return.[10]

In other words, militant Islam was essentially a liaison matter and not an urgent priority for British intelligence. It had not been elevated to what was then termed the First Order of Importance – now known as a Band One priority. (Britain's three operational intelligence agencies grade by importance the annual 'Requirements and Priorities' assigned by the Joint Intelligence Committee. Band One is the highest; Band Seven is intelligence of 'opportunity'.[11])

After 9/11, the Americans opted for a simple 'lock-down' solution – keep the bad guys out and solve a problem which was exclusively external. Initially, the EU and most of its member states adopted a similar approach. After M-11, the penny dropped; after 7/7, the pound coin dropped. Denis MacShane, formerly a junior Foreign Office minister, subsequently lamented that 'before 7/7, Whitehall was asleep.'[12] British intelligence themselves have since admitted that, as late as 2004, they were still expecting the primary threat to come from abroad. The investigations known as Operation Crevice, notably including a home-grown fertilizer bomb plot thwarted by MI5 and the police, was apparently 'the moment when the lights came on and you could see the state of the kitchen'.[13] By the end of 2006, MI6 was sufficiently awake to establish a 'specialist operational team' designed to 'illuminate … the interface between al-Qaeda and radicalized British Muslims, essentially to catch the connection between … the domestic aspect of the threat and the overseas aspect of the threat.'[14]

The external component, which we have tracked in the course of this book, is evident; the internal component is less so. The objectives of the 'home-grown' groups are vague, almost intangible. The prospect of a European polity based on Islamic sharia law is clearly fanciful, but there appears to be a developing conception – taken seriously in some quarters – that Islamic militants seek to 'turn already separate communities into 'no-go' areas where adherence [to Islam] ... has become a mark of acceptability'.[15]

These remarks, by the Anglican bishop Michael Nazir Ali, were echoed by the academic Anthony Glees of Brunel University, who observed that 'we have now got Islamic enclaves where a self-selecting apartheid system is emerging under the banner of 'celebrating diversity'.[16] And in the view of the BfV, the German security service, 'Islamist groups ... are endeavouring to create enclaves for their supporters in Germany so that they can lead their lives according to sharia law.'[17]

The creation of quasi-ghettos run on sharia principles might be considered a feasible objective. Europe's largest Muslim populations are in France (6 million), Germany (3 million) and Britain (2 million). There are also large Muslim communities in Italy, Spain, the Netherlands, Sweden and Austria. Like immigrant or immigrant-descended groups throughout history, they tend to be concentrated in relatively small districts, dictated by the demands of work and housing. These communities are drawn from all quarters of the globe and are anything but homogenous, either in themselves or between nations: Britain's largest Muslim communities emanate from the Asian subcontinent; France's from North Africa; Germany's from Turkey. The relative attraction of militant Islam in each area varies as much as the communities themselves, but, as the security and intelligence services eventually realized, social exclusion, marginalization and disaffection were equally significant factors in attracting recruits to violent jihad whilst the often closely-knit nature of the communities cemented its appeal.

Allied to ethnic, familial and geographical ties and the inherent importance of religion, the security services also saw the perceived injustices inflicted by the Christian world upon Islam as a powerful motivator. A vogue theory, especially among American sociologists, is the 'communal humiliation' model.[18] Suicide bombers, for example, seek to cause the occupying or dominant population the same level of fear and suffering as they have experienced themselves. Class and economic interests do not enter into the equation. The sufferings of Palestinians, Chechens and other Muslim populations, as well as the wars in Iraq and Afghanistan, have been constantly highlighted in media throughout the Islamic world. The civil war in Algeria and French support for *le pouvoir* provided a strong incentive to North African militants based in France.

A particular problem for the intelligence services was working out the structure of the Islamic militant movement. Left- and right-wing groups, active in the 1970s and 1980s, and nationalist groups such as the IRA and the still-active Corsicans and Basques, have tended to run well-defined, structured organizations. Mosques and the Internet were clearly the principal vehicles for propaganda and recruitment, but, lacking a formal system of membership, militant Islam was a far more amorphous and flexible entity than the terrorist groups to which Europe's security services had been accustomed. Its cross-border methodology was also a problem: again, rival national intelligence services were forced into collaboration. Researchers in the field have experienced the same problem. Perhaps the most apposite model is that of a franchise operation, under which aspirant jihadis approach the core al-Qaeda leadership through a network of 'fixers' and, if approved, are provided with such support as is deemed appropriate. This may account for the wide variety in the nature, quality and range of attack plans employed by Islamist militants. As the German BfV expresses it, 'al-Qaeda's role in this is to offer an ideal with which its members can identify and provide operational guidance.'[19]

To summarize, three major themes dominate the European response in the War on Terror: the nature of al-Qaeda and the jihadi movement; the conflict between national, bilateral and supranational operational approaches; and the differing perceptions of the jihadi threat as internal and/or external.

The European response: enter NATO,
the 'liaison game' and the bilateral conundrum

The first key development involving Europe after 9/11 was, in some ways, a surprising one. On 4 October 2001, the Americans called a meeting of the North Atlantic Council, the governing body of NATO. Here they invoked Article 5 of the 1949 North Atlantic Treaty, which decrees that 'an armed attack against one or more of them [i.e. members of NATO] ... shall be considered an attack against them all.'

Article 5 was originally conceived by NATO's Europeans as a guarantor that, should any of them come under attack by the Soviet Union, the Americans would be obliged to respond immediately. The last thing anyone expected – short of thermonuclear war – was a non-nuclear attack on the USA and that it would be the Europeans who had to respond. The 9/11 attack was construed as such an attack and, when Article 5 was invoked for the first time in NATO's history, the Europeans fell into line.[20] However, the degree to which they did so was a matter of interpretation and public relations, especially as much of the subsequent War on Terror was conducted covertly. Several European countries maintained a studied neutrality in public, pointing out that Article 5 did not place an automatic obligation on them to take part in military operations, while simultaneously providing copious clandestine support. The French and Germans, in particular, had to bite hard on their tongues in putting up with delinquent abuse from across the Atlantic ('cheese-eating surrender monkeys' etc.)[21] while their intelligence services tried to help fill some of the gaps arising from the Americans' chronic and well-documented lack of agents in the Middle East.

Enhanced intelligence cooperation was the most obvious of the eight measures agreed at the 4 October meeting. Others were drafted in deliberately vague or oblique terms: 'backfill selected

Allied assets ... required to directly support operations against terrorism'; 'provide ... assistance to Allied and other states which are or may be subject to increased terrorist threats as a result of their support for the campaign against terrorism'. Yet others presaged the extraordinary rendition programme, as well as invasion: 'provide blanket overflight clearances for the United States'; 'provide access to ports and airfields ... for operations against terrorism'.[22] For this, as Dick Marty demonstrates, was the real purpose behind the exploitation of Article 5. The USA did not particularly want or need NATO support for its military campaigns. Article 5 was the 'platform from which the United States obtained the essential permissions and protections it required to launch CIA covert action in the 'War on Terror'.[23]

Poland and Romania, both now members of the EU and of NATO, were the only European countries[24] prepared to house 'black sites' under agreements brokered with the CIA which guaranteed absolute discretion to the Americans and non-interference by the host government. However, in the wake of the 4 October 'eight measures' agreement, other European states were quite prepared to assist in whatever ways they could, subject to the vagaries of their own domestic politics. SISMI, the former Italian military intelligence service (see below), directly assisted the kidnapping from a Milan street of the Islamic cleric Hassan Mustafa Osama Nasr (known as Abu Omar).[25] The former SISMI chief, Nicolo Pollari, has since been sacked, along with divisional head Mancini, and indicted along with the two-dozen-strong CIA rendition team. Marty also identifies Germany and the former Yugoslav republic of Macedonia as complicit in the rendition programme, and points to 'concurring confirmations' that the British Indian Ocean territory of Diego Garcia[26] has been used to hold American captives (later confirmed: see Chapter 4 above). And all have supplied intelligence on request or under existing arrangements.

A subtle distinction here is that, while NATO provided a broad platform of agreement, the rendition programme relied on one-to-one contacts between the Americans and cooperating European states. As Dick Marty points out, 'it is important to emphasize that the key arrangements for CIA clandestine operations in Europe were secured on a *bilateral level* [emphasis in original]'.[27]

In the years following 9/11, most EU governments poured an ever-increasing amount of extra resources into their counter-terrorist police and intelligence apparatuses. Britain's MI5 received a budgetary increase of nearly 30 per cent between 2004/05 and 2005/06.[28] However, a different approach was needed as well. Given the ease of cross-border movement within the EU and the perceived threat from indigenous Muslim populations, European governments concluded that improvements to pan-European intelligence systems were required, especially intelligence liaison (where possible and appropriate) but also at the basic levels of data exchange and judicial procedures. A 2005 paper published by the Paris-based European Union Institute for Security Studies (EUISS), a think-tank that reflects official EU thinking, summarized the position: 'Developing international and cross-agency intelligence cooperation has become imperative in today's security environment.'[29] But the EU in particular was ill-equipped to cope, given that 'the [European] Union has only limited intelligence capabilities, in particular collection capabilities, and depends on the support of national agencies.'[30] Overall, the situation regarding intelligence liaison was probably best expressed by Michael Herman, formerly a senior British intelligence officer, as being 'a patchwork of bilateral and multilateral arrangements of all kinds and all degrees of intimacy'.[31]

The 'liaison game' is a critical aspect of the intelligence business. Sharing information with other intelligence services is commonplace among the larger agencies; for small and medium-sized intelligence services with limited resources – which applies to the bulk of European security and intelligence services – it is vital. Charles Grant, in a seminal paper for the Centre for European Reform, expands on this: 'There is a large amount of intelligence sharing among European governments. Some of this sharing is multilateral ... However, governments are generally reluctant to circulate the highest grade material ... They tend to be more willing to share sensitive material bilaterally.'[32]

Britain is in an invidious position here by virtue of its exceptionally close intelligence and foreign policy links with the USA. Nowhere is this more evident than in the relationship between the British signals intelligence agency, GCHQ, and its American counterpart, the National Security Agency (NSA). In many respects, GCHQ functions as a branch of a US multinational corporation.

Signals intelligence, or SIGINT, has two aspects. The first is Communications Intelligence, meaning intelligence acquired from monitoring domestic and foreign communications: the target may be an individual terrorist, a foreign government, a bank or a troublesome NGO. The second aspect is Communications Security: protecting one's own communications from the SIGINT activities of others (now also known as Information Assurance).

The particular importance of SIGINT in the War on Terror is that communications are central to the jihadis' operational and propaganda functions, especially given the diffuse nature of the network. Ex-MI5 director-general Stella Rimington put it at its simplest: 'These people do have to talk to each other and they have to communicate and that makes them vulnerable.'[33] In some estimates, 80 per cent of 'actionable' intelligence derives from SIGINT: monitoring phone calls and messages between suspect individuals and groups, website contents and other parts of the plethora of cyber-traffic. The War on Terror is fought as much in cyber-space as in the wider world.

The role of SIGINT and the wider exploitation of data exchange between governments are areas where the EU has the technical and economic resources to make an appreciable contribution to the War on Terror. While there is a reasonable amount of publicly available information about Europe's 'traditional' intelligence services, engaged in agent-running and close surveillance, the more abstract world of European SIGINT is little known. We look at this later in this chapter.

Given their technical expertise, SIGINT agencies have also acquired a central role in handling the Internet aspects of the War on Terror: first, by detecting hidden or disguised communications between activists, who can use a technique known as steganography (the use of hidden messages that are undetectable by anyone other than the sender and recipient); and second by monitoring access to websites carrying militant Islamist propaganda and material such as bomb-making instructions. According to the EU's former counterterrorism coordinator, Gijs de Vries, 'The Internet has been identified as a key vector for the spread of terrorist propaganda and recruitment. Germany has launched an initiative ("Check the Web") to tackle terrorist incitement.'[34]

The flip side of intelligence-gathering is propaganda, and the EU has now developed a Media Communication Strategy of its own. Approved by the EU's heads of government in July 2006, it seeks to undermine 'inaccurate depictions of EU policies and terrorist propaganda which distorts conflicts around the world as a supposed proof of a clash between the West and Islam', whilst asserting that 'improved communication should contribute to countering … radicalization and recruitment'.[35]

Later on that year, justice and home affairs commissioner Franco Frattini announced a plan to render the Internet a 'hostile environment for terrorists … I think it is very important to explore further possibilities of blocking websites that incite terrorist acts.'[36] A year on, in October 2007, Frattini was still doggedly pursuing his plan. The main problem, though, is that Frattini and his cohorts appear to have not the slightest idea how to go about taking down

Internet sites.[37] The most likely outcome, therefore, is that the EU will lay down a broad set of directives, probably in the form of a Framework Decision, and leave individual countries to work out how and what to do. In anticipation, several countries have already moved in this direction, establishing lists of 'forbidden' websites and looking to persuade Internet Service Providers (ISPs) to block access to them. (The term 'Framework Decision' appears several times in this chapter. This is a slightly different legislative procedure under which the EU lays down a broad set of principles – the 'framework' – and leaves it to individual states to tailor the detail according to their own domestic law and circumstances.)

The proliferation of national and EU-wide databases has evolved under a similar enveloping cloak of secrecy. These relatively new systems allow for the exchange of information which, although low-level in intelligence terms, often contains sensitive personal information such as identity and vehicle data, criminal records and immigration status, bank account and credit-card transactions, travel details, and communications data. Finally, the EU is also able to make an important contribution in the fast-developing field of Open Source Intelligence (OSINT), which attempts to refine the arts and skills of sifting through the enormous quantity of public information that has become easily available through the Internet. These issues, which have an important bearing both on the conduct of the War on Terror and on the future of civil rights in Europe, are also explored in this chapter.

The European Union and the G6

We have already seen how the CIA worked through bilateral intelligence links to establish their rendition architecture. Multi-national intelligence set-ups are rare and selective but have often functioned successfully when organized to deal with a particular topic or set of circumstances and constructed around a community of interest and a coherent and well-defined sense of purpose. During the Cold War this was straightforward. Subsequently, issues such as nuclear proliferation have served as a unifying force.[38] Since the 1970s, several 'clubs' have held regular get-togethers to exchange information and provide junkets for senior intelligence officials. Some of those held a counterterrorism brief, such as the TREVI group and the Club of Berne. Formed in 1971, the Club of Berne held rotating twice-yearly summits for the directors and senior officials of selected European intelligence services. TREVI, established five years later, was structured more formally with working groups, committees of senior officials, and ministerial meetings which met shortly before the six-monthly meetings of the EU heads of government. TREVI's functions gradually expanded to cover other areas of police and intelligence cooperation before being absorbed into EUROPOL (see below). Also worthy of mention are the Kilowatt Group, another creation of the 1970s which brought in the Israeli intelligence services and dealt specifically with Palestinian and Arab terrorism, and the little-known Megatonne group, apparently a French initiative set up in the mid-1990s to tackle Algerian radicals. (Kilowatt has since been disbanded, but doubtless continues under a different rubric.) A more recent arrival is the Egmont Group, which has a network of Financial Intelligence Units: originally set up to tackle money laundering, it has switched its focus to terrorist financing. Inside the EU, these groupings have been supplemented and to some extent superseded by the mixture of formal and informal intelligence and anti-terrorist entities which have sprouted since the 1990s.[39]

Effective supranational intelligence systems are built on strong bilateral links, and so the tone of liaison within the EU tends to be set by the matrix of bilateral relationships between individual services, especially those of the G6. This group – Britain, France, Germany, Italy, Poland and Spain – largely dictate the overall direction of the EU in all policy fields. Using their superior resources and diplomatic leverage, they have sufficient diplomatic and voting clout to push through most of their proposals and certainly to block those of which they disapprove. The G6 hold regular, informal, virtually secret meetings two or three times a year. The last meeting held in Britain, near Stratford-on-Avon in October 2006, was almost entirely devoted to terrorism, and this continues to be a major item on the G6 agenda.[40]

On the intelligence front, of the six, only Britain, France and Germany aspire to something approaching global coverage. Britain, of course, enjoys considerable advantages over its European counterparts through the UKUSA alliance, which allows access to material from American high-tech operations far beyond the scope and budget of the French and Germans. And while senior American, Australian and Canadian intelligence officers are a regular presence at meetings of the Joint Intelligence Committee, the appearance of a non-anglophone is extremely rare.[41] The French and Germans have compensated to some extent by forging their own bilateral arrangements. During the late 1990s, they reached an understanding about a territorial carve-up under which the Direction Générale de la Securité Extérieure (DGSE, French foreign intelligence service) would have precedence in Southern Europe and North Africa – France's *précarré* (backyard). Meanwhile the German foreign intelligence service, the Bundesnachrichtendienst (BND) would take the lead in Northern and Eastern Europe.[42] The agreement applied to agent-running and close surveillance operations, and is often honoured in the breach. The French have, for example, encroached on German 'territory' in the former Warsaw Pact, notably Hungary.[43] More seriously, the BND foreign intelligence service sought to take advantage of the situation in Algeria by supplying weapons and radio equipment to Algerian Islamists. According to the right-wing German politician Franz-Josef Strauss, the BND's objective was to break France's economic stranglehold on North Africa in the event of an Islamic government taking power in Algiers. The BND operation came to an end after furious objections from the French.[44]

More important than these squabbles, which are typical of intelligence service relationships, the two countries have worked together to develop their own joint and complementary SIGINT and space-based intelligence capabilities. (The latter form the core of the European Union Satellite Centre – see below). One important advantage that the French enjoy over the Germans is a network of overseas territories and ex-colonies, which provide 'suitable pieces of real estate'[45] for locating intelligence facilities. 'Shadow' earth stations, used for monitoring the downlinks of orbiting satellites, and radio monitoring facilities have been set up in French Guiana (at Kourou, home of the European Space Agency launch site and jointly operated with the Germans), Djibouti, Réunion, New Caledonia and, somewhat surprisingly, the former British fiefdom of the United Arab Emirates. These are supplemented by a variety of mobile platforms and the Helios satellites which conduct both visual and electronic surveillance. Responsibility for these is divided between the DGSE and the military.[46]

French domestic intelligence and surveillance was until recently handled by two bodies: the Direction de la Surveillance du Territoire (DST) national internal security service and the regionally organized Renseignements Généreaux (RG) political police. With counterterrorism dominating the agendas of both, the French found, as have the British, that the roles and functions of the two were increasingly 'indistinguishable ... You can't tell any more now who's the cop and who's the spook.'[47] A merger between the DST and RG had long been proposed but foundered on historic rivalries, turf squabbles and political conflicts. It was finally effected in September 2007 when, shortly after his electoral victory, new President Nicolas Sarkozy announced the formation of the Direction Centrale du Renseignement Intérieur (DCRI).[48]

The German intelligence system is similar to that of the French. Foreign SIGINT operations are divided between the military and the BND foreign intelligence service. Lacking a significant post-colonial legacy, the Germans have relied mainly on liaison agreements and technical prowess to establish a quasi-global SIGINT presence. On top of joint projects with the French, the UKUSA alliance and other European agencies (see below), the BND has agreements with countries as diverse as Taiwan, Turkey, Lebanon and Brazil, providing advanced technology and training in exchange for access to telecommunications traffic from those territories. Moreover, in 1985 the Chinese government allowed the Germans to set up a facility in the Pamir mountains near the Chinese–Afghan border, which allowed them to monitor radio traffic throughout the Middle East; in this case, the trade was for information on dissident Chinese exiles based in Germany.[49]

Much of the information on Chinese dissidents would have been produced by the Germany's BfV internal security and intelligence agency. Counterterrorism, on which it works closely with the BND, is a major part of the BfV's remit. However, there is a crucial difference between the French and German models. While the French state apparatus is highly centralized, Germany's federal structure gives substantial powers to the country's sixteen *Länder* (provinces), and to their independent security entities, the Landesbehörden für Verfassungsschutz (LfV). So, as well as fulfilling its national role, the BfV acts a clearing house and coordinating body for the regional LfVs. An advantage of this system in dealing with militant Islam is that it allows for a directed concentration of intelligence resources on those cities and regions with relatively large Muslim populations, notably Berlin, Duisberg, Frankfurt and Hamburg.[50] Britain's MI5 has recently opted for a similar approach by establishing regional offices which can be focused on the major Muslim population centres outside London in the West Midlands, Greater Manchester and Yorkshire.[51]

Though they do not seek to match the global ambitions of
Britain, France and Germany, the Spanish and Italians dispose of
considerable intelligence resources in specific regions. Both are
heavily involved across Northern Africa and the Middle East. One
of the most valuable assets of the principal Spanish intelligence
agency, the Centro Nacional de Inteligencia (known until 2002
as CESID), is the monitoring station at Conil de la Frontera,
30 kilometres south of Cadiz. This provides access to the traffic
carried on several main transoceanic sub-marine telecoms cables.
Still in operation today, the facility was originally set up and run
jointly with the Germans until 1992. The CNI also maintains a
satellite eavesdropping complex at Fresnedillas, outside Madrid.[52]

Geography alone gave the Italian intelligence services an important role during the Balkan wars of the 1990s. The Italian
military and foreign intelligence agency at the time, SISMI, ran
a major satellite monitoring station at Cerveteri, near Rome, and
other facilities at Lecce, at the major airbase at Aviano and on
Sicily.[53] In terms of human intelligence, the Italians have often
been effective in North Africa, the Horn of Africa and the Middle
East. Had the Americans heeded Italian warnings, they might have
avoided the worst consequences of their Somali imbroglio which
famously culminated in the 'Black Hawk Down' fiasco of October
1993.[54] Historically, the Italian services have been widely distrusted
at home through their close relationship with the CIA, their involvement in the 'strategy of tension'[55] and in the P2 scandal.[56] It
took several major incidents during the premiership of the pro-
American Silvio Berlusconi to bring about long overdue reform.
One was the kidnapping of Abu Omar, described above. A second
was a large-scale illegal mobile phone-tapping operation directed
against Berlusconi's political opponents.[57] A third was the Niger
yellowcake forgery.

This last Byzantine tale centres on a set of documents, passed to
the Italian weekly magazine *Panorama* in 2002 via SISMI, purport-

ing to illustrate Iraqi attempts to buy uranium oxide ore from the former French West African colony of Niger. The importance of these documents was that the 'Niger uranium' story became a centrepiece of American efforts to persuade a sceptical world that the Iraqis were still in clandestine pursuit of a nuclear programme. However, the documents were quickly shown to have been forgeries. There are several theories as to the purpose of this classic Information Operation but none is conclusive or definitive and much remains unclear.[58]

Yet more obscure was the killing in 2005 of a senior SISMI officer, Nicola Calipari. The Italians have a deserved reputation for adept hostage negotiation in the Middle East. Calipari, an experienced operational officer, had secured the release of the kidnapped Italian journalist Giuliana Sgrena, from an Iraqi militia. After she was freed from captivity, the car carrying Calipari and Sgrena to Baghdad International Airport unexpectedly came under American gunfire at a checkpoint inside the American-controlled 'Green Zone'. The circumstances are disputed but the incident caused serious ructions within the Italian intelligence community, parts of which were already deeply unhappy about Italian engagement in Iraq.[59]

The combined effect of these scandals was a long overdue reform and overhaul of the Italian intelligence services. Italy has now adopted the standard domestic–foreign division in the form of the Agenzia Informazioni e Sicurezza Interna (AISI) and the Agenzia Informazioni e Sicurezza Esterna (AISE). The Dipartimento delle Informazioni per la Sicurezza (DIS) covers SIGINT and information security. This triad are overseen and directed by the Comitato Interministeriale per la Sicurezza della Repubblica, chaired by the prime minister.[60]

The newest member of the G6 is Poland. Sandwiched between Germany and Russia, the Poles have need of good intelligence. The country also enjoys the unique position of being a former Soviet bloc state with a legitimate claim on a 'special relationship' with the USA. Warsaw's diplomatic support for the Americans has been 'constant and uncritical'[61] and, as noted earlier, Poland was one of only two EU states prepared to host CIA 'black sites'. The Poles had already earned their spurs in Washington during the 1990s in the Balkans and the Middle East. The post-Soviet era intelligence services are the Agencja Bezpieczenstwa Wewnetrznego (ABW, Internal Security Agency) and the Agencja Wywiadu (AW, the foreign intelligence service). If anything, these 'new model' intelligence outfits have been even more enthusiastic than their immediate predecessors in their support for the Americans and the War on Terror. In 2002, faced with reorganization, the chiefs of both agencies resigned on the grounds that this would 'limit Poland's ability to help Washington combat terrorism'.[62] However, the politicians, with no doubt a little gentle persuasion from Moscow, had clearly urged restraint. The Poles also have good historical relationships, forged during World War II, with the British and French. And it is to this pair that we now turn.

The *mésentente cordiale*

The bilateral relationship between the British and French intelligence communities lies at the heart of Europe's War on Terror. It is close but often fraught; one experienced observer described it as a *mésentente cordiale*.[63] History, psychology and political philosophy all play their part: the French retain their mild paranoia about the 'Anglosphere' while the British are perennially suspicious of French motives. However, the realities of the War on Terror – not least geography – demanded that they work together as closely as possible.

The two countries host two of the largest and most politically active Muslim communities in Europe, but their initial responses to the rise of Islamic militancy were very different. We have already seen how in the early stages the British attitude was desultory and dismissive; not so the French. As America reeled in the trauma and humiliation of 9/11, there was sadness, sympathy, but little surprise in Paris.

The French had been warning since the mid-1990s of the threat posed by militant Islam and advocates of jihad. This followed the killing of five French officials at the French embassy in Algiers in September 1994, a series of bomb attacks on trains in Paris and Lyon between 1995 and 1997, and the kidnapping and murder of seven French monks from a monastery in Algeria in 1997. These attacks were accredited to the Algerian Groupe Islamique Armé (GIA).

Particularly galling for the French was their belief that much of the planning and logistic support for the GIA's campaign in France was arranged by North African exiles in what French intelligence dubbed 'Londristan'.[64] France was concerned to alert the British to the perceived threat. The French further believed that despite the variegated nature of their Muslim communities, there was a rapid cross-fertilization and spread of militant ideas among people linked by a common faith, marginalization and alienation. French intelligence was therefore determined to try and persuade the British that they faced a genuine and serious home-grown Islamist threat. At the same time, the French badly wanted more information about the London support networks: not least because they were extremely worried about possible attacks in the period before the 1998 football World Cup, a tournament of enormous prestige, which was to be hosted by France.

In 1997, the London station of the DGSE French foreign intelligence service, based at its Knightsbridge embassy, began an operation against Islamic militants in Britain. It was run by the station head, who used the workname 'Jerome'. His principal agent was Reda Hassaine, an Algerian journalist and publisher, then in his mid-thirties, who had arrived in London in 1994. He was already working for Algerian intelligence – the price of securing exile from the Algerian cauldron for himself and his family – gathering low-level intelligence on Algerian militants in London. The Algerians passed him on to the DGSE. Lacking either a French or a British passport, the promise of a French passport was sufficient inducement for the continuation of his intelligence work.[65]

In dealing with Islamic militants, residency status is a regular pressure point used by intelligence services to assist recruitment of agents. (Even if the immediate recruitment target is secure, there may well be a close relative whose position is less so.) Both the French and the British exploited this in their dealings with Reda Hassaine and with numerous other potential and actual recruits.

The DGSE's main targets were, not surprisingly, the two best-known radical Islamic clerics in London, Abu Hamza and Abu Qatada. The pair were felt by the French to be key attractors for ex-Algerian and Afghani militants. (Abu Hamza was jailed in Britain 2006 for seven years for inciting murder and racial hatred. He is also wanted by the Americans. Home Secretary Jacqui Smith approved his extradition in February 2008.). Hassaine collected such information as he could, taking notes of speeches, identifying worshippers and, when the opportunity presented itself, copying or removing documents and other material from the mosques. He also set up a newspaper, financed by the French, promoting the views of Osama bin Laden. This was intended to tempt militants to make contact.

Hassaine was a small part of a much larger enterprise which in early 1998 saw half a dozen DGSE personnel cross the Channel to monitor both Abu Hamza and a Saudi national, Abu Walid, suspected of being a key GIA organizer. One of the group, Pierre Martinet, was a member of a reconnaissance unit from the DGSE's Service Action, the paramilitary unit that was to prepare the ground for, subject to orders from Paris, the assassination of suspected militants.

The team was divided into two units, each devoted to one of the main targets. Both were exposed within months of their arrival and returned to France. The World Cup then passed without major incident (France won). The DGSE station head, 'Jerome', closed the operation down shortly afterwards. Contact with Reda Hassaine, who now had been working for DGSE for about a year, was precipitately cut off in November 1998. The promised French passport never materialized.

Apparently upset by his betrayal, Hassaine went public and gave an account of his intelligence work to the London *Sunday Times*, which was published in October 2000. One crucial aspect was left out: that in May 1998 Hassaine had hedged his bets by contacting the Metropolitan Police Special Branch, who passed him on to MI5. The British were happy to take on the 'walk-in' and – with the promise of asylum – ran him as an agent from July 1998 until April 2000. By this point, he had come under suspicion in militant circles, which led to his being severely beaten up. This brought British interest in him to an end. Asylum was initially refused although Hassaine remained in Britain; after a nerve-racking delay he was eventually granted British citizenship in late January 2008.

Both of the DGSE's pre-World Cup operations in Britain cast light on Anglo-French intelligence relations. 'Jerome' regularly voiced his concerns to Reda Hassaine: "'Jerome" was always telling me that if the British found out what he was up to, he would be in trouble ... on the first ferry back to France.'[66]

Martinet claims to have operated without British knowledge until 'nosey parkers' reported him to the police, who wondered why he had spent two hours sitting in his car in the same place eating the same burger. However, he also states, somewhat obliquely, that 'We were not the only ones watching ... If we had been co-operating together we might have saved a lot of time.'[67] British intelligence were certainly interested in Abu Hamza by this time, but probably more concerned to find out what the French were doing. Hassaine's MI5 handler had told him that 'Abu Hamza was harmless and MI5 thought he was a clown.'[68]

This suggests that DGSE had largely failed in its objective of persuading the British to take their domestic threat seriously. After 9/11, the situation changed dramatically, as Britain was swept along in the American tsunami of counterterrorist activity. The DST, the French internal security service, which generally had good relations with MI6, rolled up the French support network behind would-be 'shoe bomber' Richard Reid.[69] Rivalry with the DGSE, however, continued unabated. As Martinet put it: 'the English can't stand us and we return the compliment.'[70]

Some mystery surrounds alleged warnings from the Renseignments Généraux, the French Special Branch, of an imminent al-Qaeda attack in London shortly before 7/7. The May 2006 parliamentary inquiry into the prior performance of British intelligence dismisses information from the Saudis, but makes no mention of the French.[71] British prime minister Gordon Brown and French president Nicolas Sarkozy subsequently announced in July 2007 the formation of a bilateral 'joint committee to exchange terrorism intelligence'.[72] Vive la *mésentente cordiale*.

EU decision-making

At this point, we must take a short but necessary detour to describe something of the EU's labyrinthine decision-making processes. This is complicated and a full account is beyond the scope of this book, but some essential points must be made. The starting point is the 1992 Maastricht Treaty which converted the European Community – essentially a glorified free-trade bloc – into the European Union, a fledgling political alliance with considerable economic resources at its disposal. Under Maastricht, the EU's realm was divided into three 'pillars'. These pillars still pertain today, although their position within the overall structure of the EU has been gradually modified and will change again if the member states accept the provisions of the 2007 Lisbon Treaty.

The first pillar is the Single European Market. The second pillar covers the EU's Common Foreign and Security Policy (CFSP). The third pillar deals with police and judicial cooperation, immigration and asylum and similar matters – collectively referred to as Justice and Home Affairs (JHA).

The principal decision-making entity in the EU is the Council of Ministers, usually referred to as 'the Council'. This is a flexible body whose membership depends upon the issue at hand. So, if the issue falls under the second pillar, the Council will bring together the foreign ministers of the twenty-seven member states to agree it. Under the third pillar, interior and/or justice ministers (for the UK, ministers from the Home Office and the Department of Justice) are involved. In total, there are nine different Councils covering the typical range of ministerial portfolios at national level – agriculture, industry, transport, and so on.

The Council also has a General Secretariat which effectively serves as its 'civil service'. The head of the Council's Secretariat, the general secretary, is an especially powerful position within the EU. This is because the same individual also acts as the so-called High Representative of the Common Foreign and Security Policy (the second pillar). The post is officially known as the High Representative/Secretary General, though for the sake of convenience it will be referred to here as the High Representative. Since October 1999, the post has been held by Javier Solana Madariaga, previously a member of the Spanish government of Felipe Gonzáles and then secretary general of NATO. Solana, a strong proponent of a distinctive EU foreign policy, has been a major driving force behind the development of an EU intelligence system. If the Lisbon Treaty is fully ratified, Solana will become the EU's 'foreign minister'.[73]

There is one other important factor. Decisions taken under the second and third pillars require the unanimous agreement of all EU governments. As the EU steadily grows, this will necessarily become harder to obtain. First pillar (single market) decisions are adopted under a procedure known as 'co-decision'. This requires both a simple majority in the European Parliament and a 'qualified majority' in the Council. The latter is a system of weighted voting where each country is allocated a number of votes according to their relative size: Germany, the largest EU country, has 29 votes in the Council; Malta, the smallest, has 3. The idea is to prevent a single veto from blocking a measure acceptable to the other 26 countries, while mitigating the smaller countries' fear of being constantly steamrollered by the gorillas on the block.

For first pillar decisions, the Parliament has equal powers to the Council – in principle. In practice, co-decision is blanketed in secrecy with decisions taken behind closed doors and often passed without debate. On occasion, the Parliament's decision is simply bypassed. Under the second and third pillars, decisions are taken at 'inter-governmental level' – although they must be approved *unanimously* – and the Parliament need only be 'consulted.' Again, its opinion is usually ignored. Since most counterterrorism measures fall under the second or third pillars, this means most measures are introduced in near-secrecy without debate or scrutiny. Some changes are due if the Lisbon Treaty is ratified: much of Justice and Home Affairs (the third pillar) will be transferred to the first pillar. However, it is far from clear that this will result in an increased role for either the European or national parliaments.

The EU intelligence system

Although they recognize the present system's flaws and limitations, the G6 are reasonably content with the EU's policy- and decision-making structures as regards counterterrorism and are in no mood for radical reform. The same cannot be said of the smaller and newer countries, which lack the resources, capability and experience to deal with a serious terrorist threat. It is they – especially Belgium and Austria – that have lobbied hardest for a fully fledged European intelligence service primarily devoted to counterterrorism.[74]

Inasmuch as an EU intelligence community exists, most analysts consider it to comprise four components.[75] Technologically, the most advanced of these is the satellite reconnaissance programme. The EU Satellite Centre, based at Torrejón de Ardoz, east of Madrid, does not own or operate any spacecraft; these remain firmly under the control of national governments. The Centre processes downlinks from a variety of national and joint satellite projects, including imaging using optical, radar and infrared frequencies and signals intelligence. It reports to the office of the High Representative, which is responsible for its tasking. Although it contributes little directly to counterterrorism, the Centre's product offers a useful means of targeting other resources more accurately.

Similar considerations apply to the second part of the nascent EU intelligence community: the Intelligence Division of the EU Military Staff, known as INTDIV. Much of the EU's tasking for the Satellite Centre originates here. The EU Military Staff provides specialist military advice to High Representative Solana, who is responsible for the EU's foreign and security policy, and coordinates EU military operations. These are not extensive but are growing in number and scope: defined as the 'Petersburg tasks', these include humanitarian and rescue operations, crisis management and peacekeeping. EU-sponsored military teams and formations have been a regular presence in the Balkans but are also active in Moldova, Ukraine, the Darfur region of Sudan, the Middle East and as far afield as the troubled Indonesian province of Aceh. The thirty-strong Intelligence Division is the largest single component of the Military Staff and draws on secondees from the military intelligence services of EU member states. It is currently headed by the Lithuanian brigadier-general Gintaras Bagdonas. Once again, the INTDIV is not an operational agency with its own collection capability: it draws on national military intelligence agencies to compile its reports.[76]

A similar consideration applies to the SITCEN (the EU loves its acronyms). This is the Joint Situation Centre, a political and diplomatic corollary to INTDIV. The Situation Centre compiles risk analyses and intelligence support for the EU's diplomatic missions, as well as specific reports on some two dozen geographical regions (e.g. the African Great Lakes). A small and secretive body which started work in early 2002, SITCEN is staffed by twenty-five analysts plus support staff, drawn from member states' national foreign intelligence services. High Representative Javier Solana confirmed that the EU's national foreign intelligence services, including Britain's MI6 and GCHQ, were working in tandem with SITCEN.[77]

SITCEN's original brief was confined to matters outside the EU, but in the flurry of activity following the M-11 Madrid train bombings Solana announced that strategic and policy aspects of counterterrorism had been added to SITCEN's brief, focusing on the ideology, organization, finance and likely targets of particular groups. These issues fall largely within the purview of domestic intelligence services rather than police, and Solana confirmed that MI5 and its European counterparts would join their sister foreign intelligence agencies in working with SITCEN.[78]

The deliberate blurring of the boundary between internal and external is characteristic of the smokescreen behind which much EU policy is conducted. The status of and tasking arrangements for SITCEN are similarly hazy. It has no statutory basis, no governing instrument and no formal rules governing its activities.

In practice, SITCEN supplies information to any EU or member-state body which has an apparently legitimate reason. The main 'customers' are the EU Counter-Terrorism Coordinator, the High Representative, the office of the EU Presidency, the Commission (the EU's 'civil service') and the Council of Ministers. SITCEN also regularly supplies material to member states with relatively little counterterrorist experience. This creates a problem for SITCEN inasmuch as all reports and products must be made available to all member states, irrespective of who originally asked for them. The result is that 'national intelligence services do not yet completely trust SITCEN's ability to handle classified documents ... [or] the newer EU member states who are able to access such information.'[79] Nevertheless, for newer member states, 'SITCEN products provide a wealth of information which would be costly and ... lengthy for their own intelligence and security services to collect.'[80] This goes at least some way to satisfying the concerns of smaller and newer EU nations.

SITCEN is the most likely basis for a future EU intelligence service. It already enjoys limited cooperation from national intelligence and security services and, subject to the ratification by member states of the 2007 Lisbon Treaty, it will also acquire an expanded reporting role briefing the Standing Committee on Internal Security (COSI). This will cover 'operational cooperation', taking it beyond its current function of a glorified information exchange. Moreover, 'internal security' is defined much more widely than counterterrorism, as it also includes public order, the activities of lobbying and protest groups, and, in a rather sinister phrase, people 'pursuing a common purpose'.[81]

SITCEN's only rival for pre-eminence in European counterterrorism is the fourth element of the EU intelligence quartet. This is EUROPOL, the European Police Office. Counterterrorism is part of a remit which covers most forms of organized crime, including trafficking in drugs and stolen vehicles, illegal immigration and people-trafficking, fraud and forgery, and the illicit trade in radioactive and nuclear materials. But it has also made significant inroads into 'internal security'. EUROPOL differs from the other three inasmuch as it is the only one that does not belong to the realm of the High Representative.

EUROPOL started out and still primarily functions as a clearing house for the exchange of information between EU police forces; it provides also technical expertise and advice. Created in 1992 and based in The Hague, EUROPOL is much larger than the other members of the quartet. Its personnel consist of a mainly locally recruited central staff, liaison officers and secondees from member states. EUROPOL works through a system of 'National Units' with a single point of contact in each country, typically a national police organization. (In Britain, this is now the Serious Organized Crime Agency.)

Significantly, EUROPOL has also developed a mechanism for operational cooperation between several national police forces engaged in complex multinational investigations: these are the Joint Investigation Teams which bring together EUROPOL and national police personnel, particularly to carry out so-called 'high impact operations' designed to bring down organized multinational criminal networks.

Yet again, EUROPOL's system of governance is typical of EU-style administration. It does at least have a governing instrument, the 1992 EUROPOL Convention, which came into force two years later and has since been ratified by all member states. Although set up around the same time as the Maastricht Treaty, it does not come under any of the pillars, and answers to the EU Council of Ministers in its Justice and Home Affairs version. The result of this regime is that EUROPOL is wholly unaccountable to the European and national parliaments, the Commission and the European Court of Justice. Many details of its establishment, finance and activities are secret. (In 2007 it had 580 staff and a budget of €67 million.[82])

EUROPOL's counterterrorism work is mainly geared to its policing aspects. Although the line between 'cops' and 'spooks' is becoming increasingly blurred, the EU's national intelligence services tend to be wary of EUROPOL and direct such demands as they have for information through the single point of contact. As Tony Bunyan of *Statewatch*, an astute observer of the European security scene, explained:

> It is quite obvious you are never going to get any real intelligence sharing by EUROPOL; that it was never, ever going to happen in a million years because the intelligence and security services will not share – apart from in specific cases – real information with police agencies because they do not trust them.[83]

The prospects for a future European intelligence agency can be summarized as follows. The EU Satellite Centre has its own specialized brief; INTDIV, the military component, is in its infancy. Given that national intelligence services have begun to work, albeit tentatively, with SITCEN, it is the more likely candidate to prevail than the larger and better-established EUROPOL. The attitude of the intelligence services has been well described as follows:

> They concur that European cooperation is important to ensure the security of European citizens, but are very hesitant to allow European interference in their mandate. Most importantly, they do not want to be forced to submit intelligence to a European agency. They see SITCEN and EUROPOL as a good platform, a useful forum to meet other intelligence officers and receive updates about ongoing European investigations.[84]

Again, issues of trust and the minutiae of the 'liaison game' prevail. Turf wars have also stunted the effectiveness of the post of EU Counter-Terrorism Coordinator (mentioned above), created as an urgent response to M-11. The Coordinator's role was and is a potentially valuable one in bringing together EU's disparate counterterrorist functions and going some way to tackling the national/pan-European schism. However, the Coordinator's mandate was ill-defined, and the justice and home affairs ministers resented the encroachment into their territory. The first holder of the post, Dutchman Gijs de Vries, departed in March 2007 after three years of frustration. The Coordinator's role was revamped following agreement by JHA ministers in September 2007 and a new incumbent installed in the form of Gilles de Kerchove d'Ousselghem, a Belgian academic and Euro-mandarin.[85] At the time of writing it is too early to say how effective this post will or can be.

There are several other EU entities that impact on counterterrorist policy, strategy and operations, mostly functioning under the roof of the EU Council in its third pillar JHA variant: the Police Chiefs' Task Force; the Strategic Committee on Immigration, Frontiers and Asylum; the European Border Agency; the Counter-Terrorism Group; the Internal Crisis Management working party; and the Article 36 Committee of senior interior ministry officials. None of these bodies has any formal legal basis or enabling instruments and their uncontrolled proliferation is typical of EU administrative structures. Gauging their power and influence, let alone keeping track of their activities, is all but impossible.[86]

Important as it is, the EU's counterterrorism effort is not simply confined to intelligence. National governments have found that the obscurantism of the EU's policy machinery provides an ideal vehicle for pushing through repressive laws with a minimum of scrutiny. Using a process which has come to be known as 'policy laundering', civil liberties and democratic accountability have been bypassed and stifled. As Gus Hosein of the campaign group Privacy International observes,

> Governments are increasingly pushing illiberal policies through international treaty organizations, then bringing them back home ...

> The UK has recently laundered communications surveillance policies through the EU and ID cards through the United Nations. The Government then returns home to parliament, holding up their hands saying 'we're obliged to act because of international obligations' and get what they want with little debate.[87]

The net result of these elaborate procedures is a serious democratic deficit. Worse, it also affords the opportunity for governments to engage in what has been neatly described as 'policy laundering'. Binding decisions taken at EU level become incumbent on member states, whose governments can then avoid deliberation by national parliaments by presenting these as faits accomplis. Another standard technique used by the British government is to release EU-authorized measures shortly before a Westminster parliamentary recess, preferably as a statutory instrument, although in this regard Britain behaves no differently to its fellow EU members.

Policy laundering and the proliferation of databases

Two striking but very different examples of policy laundering were the European Arrest Warrant and the introduction of measures to store communications data.

The European Arrest Warrant (EAW) is a fast-track pan-European extradition procedure which came into effect throughout the EU in mid-2005. The measure was rapidly agreed after 9/11 by the EU Council (Justice and Home Affairs version). European and national parliaments were bypassed; in Britain, a statutory instrument device was used to bring it into force.

The new system of European Arrest Warrants has removed many previous safeguards. Uneven standards of justice, different procedures and translation difficulties all work against the defendant. The double criminality rule – that the alleged offence must be a crime in both the countries concerned – is dispensed with for a large category of offences, including all those related to 'terrorism' but also 'computer-related crime' and 'facilitation of unauthorized entry and residence' (i.e. illegal immigration). Crucially, the previous right of appeal to political authority is removed: the decision to extradite is simply a matter for a judge to decide whether the warrant is properly completed and that the offence qualifies under the relevant criteria. It must be exercised within ninety days and the right of appeal is strictly circumscribed.[88]

A more involved instance of EU policy laundering took place in the spring of 2006, when the Council passed a framework decision on the retention of communications data.[89] Known in the SIGINT business as 'externals', communications data consists of all facets of a communication *except* the content: who is in contact with whom (irrespective of method), when, for how long, from where and to where, and which websites have been accessed. Much intelligence can be derived from the data without the laborious and expensive process of listening to phone calls and reading emails or faxes. All telephone companies and Internet Service Providers are now required to record and store the communications data of every phone call, fax and Internet session to, from, within and passing through the EU for a period of up to twelve months. This process evades many legal restrictions on the monitoring of conversations while providing a large amount of personal information.

In 2003, a simple contact with a commercial supplier of agricultural fertilizer (a standard component of certain types of improvised explosive) triggered an investigation into a possible bomb plot. At the other end of the scale, network analysis tools, assisted by specialized software, can be applied to raw communications data to allow intelligence and police agencies to work out links between individuals, network structures and hierarchies. According to Roger Gaspar, formerly deputy chief of Britain's National Criminal Intelligence Service (since absorbed into the Serious Organized Crime Agency), 'it is difficult to overstate the value of communications data ... [in] the intelligence officer's toolbox of techniques.'[90]

The creation of new systems storing vast quantities of personal information across the EU will demand either a network of inter-connected national databases or the creation of a custom-built centralized EU database. The likely result is a combination of both, depending on the nature and volume of the information and the degree of security demanded. There are no legal constraints: since the passage of the 2005 Prüm Treaty – another little-known but critical EU agreement – all EU members are entitled to access and search each others' databases without restriction.

In the case of communications data, the Euro-parliamentarian Alexander Nuno Alvaro has offered this perspective:

> The network of a large Internet provider would, even at today's traffic levels, accumulate a [traffic] data volume of 20–40,000 terabytes ... equivalent to ten stacks of files each reaching from the earth to the moon ... One search, using existing technology, would take 50 to 100 years.[91]

The EU has therefore placed the primary obligation for data storage upon the telecoms companies and Internet Service Providers, and required them to design suitable administrative systems to allow easy access for police and intelligence agencies.

By contrast, the position with European Arrest Warrants, which run into a few hundred at present, is less demanding in terms of data volume. However, a secure network is required to transmit the warrants from one jurisdiction to another, along with supporting documentation. For this purpose, the EU is able to call upon its principal pan-European policing and intelligence computer network: the Schengen Information System (SIS).[92]

The creation of the SIS was a key aspect of the 1985 Schengen Agreement – named after the Luxembourg town where it was signed – which allowed for the removal of frontier controls. This completed the set of 'four freedoms' envisaged by the founders of the EU. By the end of 1995, after a decade of intergovernmental wrangling and some modifications to the Agreement, all EU countries apart from Britain and Ireland, which had refused to divest their border controls, had signed up to Schengen. Two non-EU members, Norway and Iceland, also became parties.

In the next stage of evolution, the 1999 Amsterdam Treaty made the Schengen Agreement one of the thirty-one *acquis*, or basic conditions, which all countries must fulfil to qualify for EU membership.[93] All ten countries in the 2004 EU influx, plus Bulgaria and Romania three years later, were therefore obliged to sign up to Schengen: following several delays, it will now probably come into force in these countries in 2009.

In its original form, the Schengen System consisted of a central database, known as C-SIS and located in Strasbourg with a backup in Austria. Each Schengen country possesses an exact copy of the database, known as an N-SIS, which is updated from C-SIS every few minutes. In Britain this is held by the Serious Organized Crime Agency. Statistics about the SIS are difficult to acquire, 'poorly presented and insufficiently informative'[94] – in line with the pervasive secrecy which surrounds the system as a whole. At the beginning of 2007, it contained 17 million entries divided into various classes of 'alert' – wanted persons, firearms, forged banknotes, and lost or stolen vehicles and identity documents; 'wanted persons' are further broken down into people wanted for extradition, missing persons and potential witnesses, convicted felons and 'third-country' nationals (i.e. from outside the Schengen area) to be refused entry; this last category includes individuals whose exclusion 'may be based on a threat to public order or national security'. Of the total database, 895,000 entries concerned individuals; of these, 752,000 were people earmarked to be refused entry into Schengen.[95]

So SIS contains not only basic factual information about individuals, but also intelligence data based on alleged 'threats'.

Following the Prüm Treaty, this information can now be freely exchanged between any EU national police or intelligence services. Furthermore, the Schengen regime allows for more extensive searches of national databases under a procedure known as SIRENE (Supplementary Information Request at the National Entry). If, for example, an officer from a provincial English police force conducts a search on the Police National Computer for a person or item with a SIS entry, the search will be flagged at the Serious Organized Crime Agency, and the officer will be put in contact with the SIRENE UK Bureau. This is staffed by police officers and specialist lawyers who will inform the officer of what action to take, what information is available from the SIS and, if more information is available from other nationally held databases abroad, liaise with the relevant foreign agency.[96]

In its original form, the SIS started operations in 1995. By 2001, the EU was looking to overhaul and modernize the System. There were two ostensible reasons. The first was to take account of the large influx of new members; the second was to take advantage of new technologies to store fingerprint and other biometric data from iris scans, facial recognition and DNA coding. The 9/11 attack of 2001 merely gave an impetus to plans already in train. In addition, under its 'anti-terrorism roadmap', the EU proposed two new databases: a register of all 'third country' nationals resident in the EU and a database of 'potentially dangerous persons … notoriously known by the [EU's] police forces for having committed recognized acts of public order disturbance'.[97]

SIS II has experienced technical difficulties and will now probably start up in 2009. Despite an unsuccessful effort by the EU Commission to take control, the upgrade will, as before, retain the same structure as its precursor with a central database in France, a backup in Austria and national points of contact. Some €30 million will be needed to cover the costs of setting up and running SIS II up to 2012.[98]

In addition to SIS II, the EU is developing several other large databases geared to the interlinked issues of immigration, public order and terrorism. In 2004, the Council agreed to the establishment of the Visa Information System, which will operate on the same 'technical platform' as SIS II and hold extensive personal data on the 20 million visa applicants who have entered the EU. As originally designed, the Visa Information System was intended to store biometric information in the form of finger-prints and digitized facial images. These would be recorded in a chip attached to individual passports as well as being held on a central database. Due to come online by the end of 2008, the Visa Information System has also experienced technical problems and delays. Its ultimate format is currently uncertain.[99]

By contrast, another biometric database, the EURODAC finger-print system, is up and running. The 1990 Dublin Convention established common EU procedures for the handling of asylum-seekers and illegal immigrants: all must now provide fingerprints to be stored digitally on EURODAC. Laying claim to being the first Automatic Fingerprint Identification System in Europe, EURODAC processes over a quarter of a million requests a year. It is housed and run by the European Commission in Brussels and in 2006 enjoyed an annual budget allocation of €16.7 million.[100]

Throughout the research, development and implementation stages of these and other databases, the influence and demands of the Americans were never far from the minds of EU planners. Answering media enquiries during discussions on the type of data to be held on SIS II, a German government spokesman ob-served that 'it depends on the United States and on which features they require'.[101] In discussing EURODAC, the 'US side wished to explore the possibility of exchanging data with EURODAC, both for analysis and for searching for people'.[102] Apart from that, the demands of the USA provided another useful pretext for pushing through measures which might otherwise prove controversial in Europe – again, more policy laundering.

Nowhere was this more apparent than in the introduction of the Passenger Name Record (PNR) system. Under American pressure after 9/11, the EU set about creating a system for passing detailed information about all transatlantic airline travellers using European airlines to the US Customs Service (which is now part of the Department of Homeland Security).

On pain of a €6,000 fine per passenger, European airlines operating flights to, from and in transit through the USA were instructed to supply information in forty separate data fields about each passenger at least fifteen minutes before departure. As well as basic biographical data, the range of data covered contact phone numbers, email addresses, credit-card details, connecting flights in the USA, seating arrangements and meal preferences. This provisional arrangement came into force in March 2003 pending the establishment of a firm legal basis for it. However, given that issues of the transfer of personal data fell under the first pillar (single market), the PNR plan had to have the endorsement of the European Parliament (under the co-decision rule).[103] The Parliament's Article 29 Committee, which deals with data protection, produced several highly critical assessments of the arrangement. One of their main observations was that the United States government has no data protection legislation as such, and promises that its agencies would abide by EU standards of data protection were at least questionable and definitely unenforceable. Consequently, the European Parliament voted against the PNR plan, not once but three times.[104]

The final outcome was typical of the way the EU works. With a European election campaign under way in May 2004, the EU Council and the Commission simply ignored the otherwise pre-occupied Parliament and settled the PNR agreement with the Americans anyway.[105] Furious Euro-parliamentarians took the

Council and the Commission to the European Court of Justice.[106] As expected, American data-protection assurances proved worthless. In the summer of 2005, it transpired that the US Transportation Security Administration (again, part of the Department of Homeland Security and privy to US Customs PNR data) had been exchanging PNR material with private firms engaged in data-mining and brokerage.[107] In May 2006, the Court ruled in favour of the Parliament. The Council responded with a simple gambit. The original PNR plan had been arranged under the EU's first pillar, the single market, which covers transport. The Council now revised its original conclusion to the effect that, given that PNR was a matter of public security and criminal law, it should come under the third pillar, which avoids parliamentary scrutiny, although it does demand unanimity among EU member governments. Given heavy US pressure (to which the Czechs, for one, were subject) there were no dissenters and the PNR agreement came into force in its present form in June 2006. The data may be stored for up to fifteen years and made available to any American law enforcement or intelligence agency.[108]

The few watchers of the PNR process were slightly baffled by the EU's limp negotiating with the USA, before realizing that the EU Council and Commission had their own agenda. This was, yet again, a classic piece of policy laundering. Through a subtle change in the manner in which the PNR data was collected, the EU acquired the ability to establish its own PNR surveillance system through the back door. Initially, US Customs were to be granted direct access to individual airline databases and download such information as they wanted. Under the final arrangements, with the encouragement of the EU, a centralized database would be set up, to which all transatlantic operators would contribute after installing 'filters' to remove 'sensitive data'. US Customs could then extract what it wanted from this database. In sociology jargon, this change from a 'pull' to a 'push' architecture 'seems ... to the

Commission to offer advantages in terms of cost and efficiency'.[109] Privacy International, which published a forensic analysis of the PNR proposals in early 2004, delivered an uncompromising verdict on the Commission, which

> has engaged in the process of systematic deception and subterfuge … Not only has it allowed key privacy rights to be extinguished … but it has failed to disclose its own intention to establish a more extensive regime in the EU. The proposed EU surveillance system will be used not only for purposes of anti-terrorism, but also for immigration, law enforcement and customs.[110]

Sure enough, having skirted the obstacles erected by the European Parliament and the Article 29 Working Party, the Commission unveiled its own PNR plan in November 2007. Justice Commissioner Franco Frattini stated that the EU 'was at least as much of a target of a terrorist attack as the United States, and the use and analysis of passenger name records is an important *law enforcement* tool [emphasis added].[111]

Meanwhile, the British government was already engaged in its own pet scheme, Project Semaphore, set up in 2005 as part of Home Secretary David Blunkett's 'e-borders' initiative. The Home Office has claimed that this PNR data, which was passed to police, immigration and customs for analysis, resulted in 1,200 arrests in a single six-week period. Figures for the number of charges and convictions are unavailable.[112]

One little-noticed aspect of these PNR schemes is in creating 'traveller profiles'. The best known of these is the US Automated Targeting System, which uses the data acquired through PNR to calculate a 'score' that assesses the supposed likelihood of an individual's connection to terrorism. Britain's Project Semaphore has a similar sub-programme. Under the Frattini plan for the EU central PNR database, the information accumulated will be examined by 'analysis units' which will conduct a 'risk assessment' of each traveller. In the European case, the information will be kept for five years in an active form and a further eight on a 'dormant' database.[113]

Aside from the civil rights implications of establishing yet another mass surveillance tool, the value of 'terrorist profiling' is questionable. Edwin Bakker, a Dutch researcher at the Clingendael Institute in The Hague, has conducted a detailed study of 242 Islamist militants convicted or accused of involvement in terrorism in Europe. From his results, published in early 2007, Bakker concluded that no reliable profile existed: 'There is no standard jihadi terrorist in Europe ... For the secret services, it doesn't give them a clue.'[114]

The growth of this type of database is ominous. In an extraordinary exercise conducted in 2002, German authorities sought employee files from several thousand companies engaged in infrastructure industries, defence and scientific work. The aim was to check the workers against a standard terrorist profile to identify potential miscreants. However, memories of authoritarianism run deep in Germany and civil liberties are taken seriously. Only 5 per cent of the 4,000 companies and institutions approached complied with the police request.[115]

Another, American-led, initiative involves SWIFT, the Society for Worldwide Interbank Financial Telecommunication. Headquartered at La Hulpe in Belgium, this important financial consortium provides a secure message service between banks and financial institutions. SWIFT carries 12 million messages daily, moving around €5 trillion between more than 8,000 users, through its two major operations centres in Belgium and New York.[116] (It does not engage in or facilitate the actual transactions.) Within a month of 9/11, SWIFT in New York received a subpoena requiring it to submit all messages to the Terrorist Finance Tracking Program, a joint project between the US Treasury department and the CIA which attempts to identify terrorists' 'financial footprints'.[117] It complied without demur. SWIFT's managing board comprises representatives of ten of the world's leading central banks. A spokesman for the Bank of England, one of the ten, pronounced insouciantly: 'It was a matter of security and not of finance. It had nothing to do with us.'[118]

The SWIFT monitoring operation was a direct arrangement between the institution itself and the Americans. Even the EU Council and Commission were unaware of it until its public exposure in 2006. But the EU and SWIFT were equally culpable in their failure to contemplate the data-protection implications of their various actions in the wake of 9/11. As is often the case with governments, data protection is treated as an inconvenient administrative add-on to be dealt with when the main business has been concluded.

The EU does at least have some data-protection safeguards which do not exist in the USA, where the information – especially that acquired from foreign countries, including Europe – can be used for any administrative purpose the US government wishes. It can also be sold, without restriction, to commercial information brokers. This is one of the legacies of the War on Terror: the rapid unaccountable growth of vast databases of personal information, accessible to their subjects, if at all, only with difficulty and persistence – assuming the subjects are even aware of their existence. The other important consequence, for both society and the individual, is an increasingly pervasive culture of secrecy in which even basic information is denied to elected representatives on notional, spurious grounds, typically national security.

A House of Lords Select Committee inquiring into SIS II in 2006/07 was told that eighty UK 'authorities' had access to the system and that most were constabularies. The Committee was provided with the list but 'asked to treat it as confidential'.[119] As for entering data into the system, the Committee found 'a wide divergence in differing national approaches to listing a person on the current SIS'.[120] It also encountered constant difficulty while trying to find out about the progress of the SIS II project, and noted that 'the lack of transparency in [EU] Council proceedings and in co-decision negotiations between the Council and the European parliament [i.e. under the first pillar] is an issue relevant to all areas of EU policy-making, and has been particularly notice-able in the negotiations on the SIS II legislation.'[121]

The last word on this should perhaps go to Statewatch, which has done most to illuminate the murky precincts of EU decision-making: 'there is no formal requirement to publish an agenda or minutes, there is no system of access to documents, there is no process of public consultation or impact assessment', while, overall, the system is 'utterly lacking in the rudiments of accountability as understood at EU or national level'.[122] In years to come, this will be seen as a suitable epitaph for the European contribution to the War on Terror.

Illiberal democracy
and 'manufactured risk'

The war isn't going as advertised. (Congressman Jack Murtha, November 2005)

Some six years after George W. Bush and Tony Blair declared 'global war on terror', word went out that the term was to be quietly dropped from public discourse. Not un-coincidentally, this happened with the departure of Donald Rumsfeld, Paul Wolfowitz and the most vocal warriors from the US stage – and the reluctant exit of Tony Blair himself. Although, as we have seen, Blair was to remain adamant to the last, there were two outstanding factors in play: the ill-fortune of actual wars in Iraq and Afghanistan and the eager uptake of the concept by radical Islamists themselves, whose fractious cause had found apparent vindication. But to unpack the unfortunate and overworked metaphor, it would perhaps be more accurate to characterize three wars hosted under the same banner: (i) a conventional theatre conflict in the Middle East, concerning US hegemony and, yes, 'the oil, stupid';[1] (ii) a parallel 'war' on civil liberties in the West, driven by power-seeking government agencies and headline-chasing politics; and (iii) the acute, but circumscribed, intelligence struggle in the day-to-day field of counterterror. In this essay, we have attempted a modest disentanglement of these trends. But we have also sought to factor in the feedback – and, indeed, blowback – of consequential unity.

It has become commonplace in contemporary historical writing to hold that contending powers in the world system have tended towards similarity.[2] In a striking fashion, it can be argued that something very close to this process was at work in the commencement of the Global War on Terror – with the emergence of an avowedly faith-based global movement matched by the (hopefully, brief) ascendancy of 'faith-based decision-making' from their declared opponents in London and Washington. What is also striking, however, is the way 'an enemy of tiny proportions and relatively meagre resources' was able to seize upon and mould these diffuse currents towards its desired outcome. Indeed, as one experienced Arab commentator points out, 'In many ways, al-Qaeda has effected more change in Western societies than *vice versa*.'[3]

This should not, though, have come as any surprise. The technology of spin, or 'strategic communications', is as widely understood globally as the physical technology of distribution. Unlike Saddam's absent WMD, this is not rocket science. Islamist radicals have their own well-developed media operations. Al-Qaeda themselves have an in-house production team – 'al-Sahab' (the clouds) – that puts out commentary, jihadi videos and 'instant rebuttal' of whatever White House line happens to be the message of the day. At a more street level, there is an extensive promotional literature, under such headings as the 'Great Jihad Encyclopaedia', devoted precisely to misleading interrogators and steering embedded bias.[4] As we have seen, this was an approach that was also highly successful in corralling Western politicians and opinion-formers 'on message'. With awareness of any possible ironies almost wilfully absent, George Bush's 'bring 'em on' throwaway at the start of the Iraq insurgency was fielding only a particularly egregious example.

If Bush's stump presentation drew all too closely from the jihadis themselves, the overall US/allied policy dynamic was not exclusive to the two-term White House incumbent and his neocon outriders with their own preset agenda. There was also a deeper resonance. For decades, as al-Qaeda and the Islamist coalition well knew, the notion of US primacy in the world was considered something of a settled axiom for the policy community across the West. Where differences were in view, they concerned the nuances of stewardship. After the shock of 9/11, these were shelved – at least in the moment – in favour of an uncompromising exercise of force. Unfortunately for those uneasily signing up to the 'Coalition of the Willing' in the Bush administration's military ventures, al-Qaeda itself views its conflict with the USA as a conventional struggle for world hegemony, albeit one conducted in asymmetric terms. The tactics, though, are textbook 'realism'. As seasoned Middle East journalist and analyst Abdel Bari Atwan explains, al-Qaeda senior strategist Ayman al-Zawahiri puts great store by Yale historian Paul Kennedy's 1987 classic *The Rise and Fall of the Great Powers.*[5] Kennedy's thesis, widely circulated at the time, holds that empires fall for three main reasons: open-ended internal security costs; an ever-expanding military budget and international presence; the rise of rival powers in trade and commercial competition.

Given the evident presence of these factors, it is arguably the case that the flat rejection of a more selective, long-term approach by Bush and Blair has given radical Islamist terrorism all it was aiming for. Henry Kissinger's contention that US policy after 9/11 needed a response 'essentially more than proportionate' – and one necessary 'in order to make the point' – captures all too well the combination of perceived military omnipotence and untroubled confidence in outcomes of the immediate post-9/11 era. It is also worth recalling that Kissinger's 'madman theory' – the conscious cultivation of irrationalism as a tool in politico-military threat-bargaining – has seen a somewhat ill-starred rerun in the 'shock and awe' tactics that opened the Iraq War. Although those such as Richard Perle, Michael Ledeen and the ascendant neoconservative caucus of the early Bush administration were fierce opponents of Nixon-era policies towards the Soviets, this was one aspect of the Kissinger legacy they embraced. But a fatal weakness here was the sheer disconnect between expressing 'will', belief and, indeed, utter ruthlessness in demonstrative military form and the stage-presence this can bestow – empowering, in direct proportion, for those in the target cross-hairs and their standing before the wider target audience.

As the Pentagon and its global allies rushed to promote strategic communication and I/OPS to a 'core military competency', the pace was clearly being dictated elsewhere. It was the instant uptake of the terrorists' own terms of reference that 'they hate us for our freedoms' and 'our way of life' – true, but essentially irrelevant – that was, in every instance, fresh grist to an ill-understood mill. As pointed out by the UK Defence Academy, 'you cannot make war on an idea'.[6] But as the War on Terror itself became a brand identity, it was the prospect of reflected military kudos and media grandstanding that had proved irresistible.

The scramble by politicians, on both sides of the Atlantic, to make tabloid capital out of the atmosphere of crisis saw an immediate expression in the push for ever more curbs on civil liberties. As elsewhere in the War on Terror bandwagon, a multitude of lobby interests and daily demands of expediency were clearly at issue here. But there is also an underlying structural dimension. The Gordon Brown government's pressure for 42-day detention and yet wider police and security service powers – the *fifth* terrorism bill from 2000 to date from New Labour – has been justified by not any admitted present need, but on the grounds that such measures might be needed in so-far-unspecified future scenarios.[7] With threats of climate change, resource wars and uncontrolled mass migration on the agenda, it can be reasonably assumed that these proposals have been in ministerial in-trays for some time.

Indeed, as far back as the 1970s, governments and private think-tanks have been focusing on population flow, resource depletion and – certainly not least – peak oil. If the uptake of these concerns has moved emphatically mainstream, so have arguments for a new authoritarianism and scrapping the 'rules of the game'. We have had a glimpse of what this entails. In the USA, the Pentagon grab for decisive authority at policy and departmental levels was matched by a determined drive to enhance domestic presence. With the newly affirmed (if not uncontested) doctrine of presidential prerogative providing legal sanction, the framework was in place for parallel systems of law enforcement, surveillance and – in embryo – internment without trial on a mass scale. The groundwork and technical feasibility for schemes such as the locally based, anonymous 'threat reporting' network by the Counter Intelligence Field Activity and rejigged Cold War ENDGAME provisions have had thorough market testing at Guantánamo Bay and the worldwide network of black sites and covert transportation.

As we have shown in this book, the War on Terror grew out of the failures and failings of intelligence and has in turn profoundly shaped and redefined the meaning of intelligence. Today, intelligence is more than ever a coin with two sides: a tool for gaining knowledge and a tool for the exercise of government power. Government now comes into areas of our lives once thought private: who we talk to, what we think, where we meet. Calls are monitored, travel is circumscribed, and torture is once again becoming routinized. All this is done in the name of security in the War on Terror. Perhaps more ominously, where the evidence that such tactics produce isn't available, but is deemed necessary to achieve greater political ends in the War on Terror, it is assembled from hearsay, speculation and selective presentation. Governments accrue power to themselves by doing this, demanding that societies put faith in them in the face of risks too great to be discussed or even imagined. Yet, at the same time, the inevitable doubt and mistrust this creates serves to undermine government power. The new reliance on intelligence in the face of this, and the resultant casualties of free speech and thought, are far greater and may have more lasting and damaging implications. Our spies and their lies may in the end completely undermine the kind of freedom that the War on Terror ostensibly seeks to defend and expand.

Throughout, the advent of a 'Global War on Terror' of seemingly unlimited duration has, like wars past, been a gift for arms manufacturers, mercenary contractors, demagogy and authoritarians of every stripe. A comprehensive audit on the Global War on Terror bottom line has yet to be established, although George W. Bush's $515 billion defence budget of February 2008 surely gives a sense of the sums involved. A ballpark figure for the likely span of conflict runs into decades – about the same figure offered, as we have seen, by the US Defense Science Policy Board for America's image and standing in the world to even approximately recover. This has profound implications for us all. The term 'manufactured risk' was coined by Tony Blair's Third Way guru Anthony Giddens to characterize liberal capitalism and modernity. Latterly, it has become perhaps unintentionally telling.

Notes

Introduction

1. Talk of 'World War Four' was widely current among US neoconservatives in the build-up to war in Iraq. For a telling analysis of these trends, see Robert Dreyfuss, *Devil's Game: How the United States Helped Unleash Fundamentalist Islam* (New York: Metropolitan Books, 2005), pp. 304–12.
2. Vice President Richard Cheney interviewed on 'Meet the Press', NBC News, 16 September 2001; see 'The Dark Side' interviews, *Frontline*, 20 June 2006; see also Oliver Burkeman, 'Rumsfeld's Progress', *Guardian*, 10 November 2006.
3. The term has gained currency through its use by such administration critics as former UN weapons inspector Scott Ritter. See, for example, 'Target Iran: White House Plans for Regime Change', interview with Seymour Hersh and Scott Ritter, *Democracy Now*, 28 December 2006.
4. See Ron Suskind, 'Without a Doubt', *New York Times* magazine, 17 October 2004.

Chapter 1

1. See Steven Strasser (ed.), *The 9/11 Investigations: Staff Reports of the 9/11 Commission* (New York: Public Affairs, 2004), pp. 132–51 *passim*.
2. McCormick Tribune Foundation, 'Understanding the Privatisation of National Security', Conference Proceedings, 11–12 May 2006, p. 3, at www.abanet.org/natsecurity/understanding_privatization_2006.pdf.
3. See Michael Scheuer, *Imperial Hubris* (Dulles, VA: Brassey's, 2004); see

in particular, Abdel Bari Atwan, *The Secret History of Al Qa'ida* (London: Abacus, 2007), pp. 115–45.

4. See Robert Dreyfuss, *Devil's Game: How the United States Helped Unleash Fundamentalist Islam* (New York: Metropolitan Books, 2005).

5. See Amir Tahiri, *Holy Terror* (London: Sphere, 1987), pp. 159–63.

6. See Fred Halliday, *Threat from the East? Soviet Policy from Afghanistan and Iran to the Horn of Africa* (London: Penguin, 1982).

7. See Zbigniew Brzezinski, interviewed in *Le Nouvel Observateur*, 15–21 January 1998.

8. David Holden and Richard Johns *The House of Saud* (New York: Holt, Rinehard & Wilson, 1982), p. 271.

9. See UN General Assembly, GA Resolution ES-6/2, 9 January 1980.

10. See Charles Kupchan, *The Persian Gulf and the West* (London: Allen & Unwin, 1987), pp. 68–99.

11. *Department of State Bulletin*, vol. 80 (March 1980), p. 65.

12. Brzezinski, *Le Nouvel Observateur*.

13. See 'New Evidence on the War in Afghanistan', *Cold War International History Bulletin* 14/15 (Winter 2003–Spring 2004), pp. 139–232.

14. See Stephen Dorril, *MI6* (London: Fourth Estate, 2000), pp. 751–2.

15. See Robert Gates, *Out of the Shadows* (New York: Simon & Schuster, 1996), pp. 319–21.

16. George Crile, *My Enemy's Enemy* (New York: Grove Atlantic, 2003), p. 348.

17. Ibid., p. 20.

18. Ibid., pp. 517–19.

19. See 'US Declassifies Report on Yugoslavia's Break-up', *Associated Press*, 22 December 2006.

20. See J.M. Berger, 'Bush Nominee Turned Blind Eye as Arms Flowed to al-Qaeda in 1994', Intelwire.com, 12 May 2006.

21. See David Buckley, 'Scratching the Surface', *The American Monitor*, 16 November 2006; see also David Pallister and Jamie Wilson, 'Muslim Relief Groups Caught in Crossfire', *Guardian*, 26 September 2001.

22. See US Congress, Senate, *The BCCI Affair, Report to the Committee on Foreign Relations*, Senator John Kerry and Senator Hank Brown, 2d Congress, 2nd Session, December 1992, Senate Print, 102–40.

23. See *The 9/11 Commission Report –Authorized Edition* (New York: Norton, 2004), pp. 58–9.

24. Alex de Waal (ed.), *Islamism and Its Enemies in the Horn of Africa* (Bloomington, IA: Indiana University Press, 2004), p. 68.

25. Ibid., pp. 68–9.

26. See Berger, 'Bush Nominee'; Radu Tudor, 'Izetbegovic Backed Terrorists', *Jurnalul*, 9 April 2006.

27. See Patrick Thorne, 'The Rise of the Islamic Lenin', *Casablanca*, London, Autumn 1994.

28. See Ali Farassati, 'Iran and al-Qaeda', *Terrorism Monitor*, vol. 1, no. 1, 11 September 2003.

29. See Stephen L. Burg and Paul S. Shoup, *The War in Bosnia-Herzegovina* (New York: M.E. Sharpe, 1999), pp. 307–16.

30. See *New York Times*, August, 12 1994, A3; *Washington Post*, 12 August 1994, A33.

31. See Burg and Shoup, *The War in Bosnia-Herzegovina*, p. 307; Berger, 'Bush Nominee'.

32. Burg and Shoup, *The War in Bosnia-Herzegovina*, p. 308.

33. See Cies Weibes, *Srebrenica – A Safe Area?*, report published on behalf of the Dutch government, 10 April 2002, Appendix II and ch. 4.

34. Ibid.

35. Al Fadhl was then a central figure in al-Qaeda's financial operation in the Sudan and visited Croatia in autumn 1992. He defected to the USA in spring 1996 after being pursued for embezzling al-Qaeda funds. See Berger, 'Bush Nominee'; Richard Clarke, *Against All Enemies: Inside America's War on Terror* (London: Simon & Schuster, 2004), pp. 148–9.

36. See Tudor, 'Izetbegovic Backed Terrorists'.

37. These were Khalid Almidhar and Nawaf Alhamzi, who had notoriously been allowed into the USA, despite being on the State Department watch list. See James Bamford, *Pretext for War* (New York: Doubleday, 2004), pp. 221–31.

38. This apparently had been issued by a CIA undercover official. Rahman was a leading recruiter for the Afghan Mujahideen. See Peter Bergen, *Holy War Inc.* (New York: Free Press, 2001), p. 67.

39. Tony Blair, speech to the Economic Club of Chicago, 22 April 1999.

40. See, for example, Sofia Damm, 'The Limits of Violent Intervention', in Michael Waller, Kyril Drezov and Bulent Gokay (eds), *Kosovo: The Politics of Delusion* (London: Frank Cass, 2001), pp. 130–37.

41. See Alan Little, 'Moral Combat', BBC2 television, 12 March 2000.

42. See 'The Kosovo Liberation Army: Does Clinton Policy Support Group with Terror, Drug Ties', US Senate Republican Policy Committee, 31 March 1999, www.senate.gov/~rpc/releases/1999/fr033199.htm.

43. See 'More Assets on Hold in Anti-Terror Efforts; 39 Parties Added to List of Al-Qaeda Supporters', *Washington Post*, 13 October 2001.

44. See Jean-Charles Brisard and Guillaume Dasquie, *Forbidden Truth: US–Taliban Secret Oil Diplomacy and the Failed Search for Bin Laden* (New York: Nation Books, 2002), pp. 128–9.

45. James Dettmer, 'Al-Qaeda's Links in the Balkans; Macedonian Officials Contend the Bush Administration Largely Is Ignoring Intelligence

Information that Has Connected al-Qaeda Elements to Albanian Separatists – World: War on Terror', *Insight on the News*, 22 July 2002.

46. See Jerry Guidera and Glenn Simpson, 'US Probes Terror Ties to Boston Software Firm', *Wall Street Journal*, 6 December 2002. Of further concern to US investigators, Ptech had apparently conducted a major risk-assessment survey for the Federal Aviation Authority (FAA) prior to 9/11. It will be recalled that a series of air defence exercises and emergency simulations were in progress at the time of the hijackings themselves. See, for example, Daniel Hopsicker, 'FBI Shut Down Investigation into Saudi Terror Cell in Boston', Mad Cow Morning News, 5 February 2003, www.madcowprod.com/mc5422004.html.

47. See Thanasis Cambanis and Ross Kerber, 'Ptech CEO Says Probe Put Firm on Ropes', *Boston Globe*, 13 September 2002.

48. See US Library of Congress, Federal Research Division, 'A Global Overview of Narcotics-funded Terrorist and Other Extremist Groups', report prepared in agreement with the DoD, May 2002, p. 90.

49. See 'Albania Seizes Assets of Alleged Bin Laden Associate', AP, 22 December 2006.

50. See '*Terrorism Weekly* claims Wartime Bosnian President Linked to al-Qaeda', Vpr/Aki, 8 September 2006.

51. See Alban Barra, 'Albania: Officials Crack Down on Terror Suspects', Radio Free Europe/Radio Liberty, 22 January 2002.

52. A 2005–06 investigation by the counterterrorism unit in the New York Police Department found that Bakri's Al Muhajiroun had formed eighty-one front groups and support networks in six countries, most of them based in London. See Nafeez Mosaddeq Ahmed, 'Inside the Crevice', *Institute for Policy Research and Development*, June 2006.

53. See Stephen Ulf, 'Londonistan', *Terrorism Monitor*, vol. 2, no. 4, February 2004.

54. See 'The Links of Terror Suspect to MI6', interview with former FBI investigator John Loftus, Fox News, 1 August 2005; at www.globalresearch.ca/index.phpcontext=viewArticle&code =20050801&articleId=783.

55. See B. Rahman, 'Daniel Pearl and the London Blasts', South Asia Analysis Group, Paper no. 1458, 15 July 2005. HUA were a faction of Jamait e-Ulema, junior partners in the Bhutto government. See also Ahmad Rashid, *Taliban* (London: I.B. Tauris, 2001), pp. 90–91.

56. Whether Omar Sheikh was himself recruited by MI6 and became a double agent is considered in Michael Meacher, 'Britain Now Faces Its Own Blowback', *Guardian*, 10 September 2005.

57. Mahan Abedin, 'Al Muhajiroun in the UK: An Interview with Sheikh Omar Bakri Mohammed', *Terrorism Monitor*, vol. 2, no. 5 (March 2004).

58. This provision had been overturned by the House of Lords in December 2004. See Andrew Blick and Stuart Weir, *The Rules of the Game: The*

Government's Counter Terrorism Laws and Strategy, Joseph Rowntree Trust, November 2005.

59. See Sean O'Neil and Yakov Lippin, 'Britain's Online Imam Declares War as He Calls Young to Jihad', *The Times,* 17 January 2005.

60. See 'The Links of Terror Suspect to MI6'.

61. This charge was finally brought on Awsat's 2005 deportation.

62. 'The Links of Terror Suspect to MI6'.

63. See Ahmed, 'Inside the Crevice'.

64. See Zahid Hussein, David McGrory and Sean O'Neill, 'Top al-Qaeda Briton Called Tube Bombers before Attack', *The Times,* 24 July 2005; Michael Isikoof and Mark Hosenball, 'Worldwide Conspiracy', *Newsweek,* 21 July 2005.

65. See Richard Woods, David Leppard and Mick Smith, 'Tangled Web that Still Leaves Worrying Loose Ends', *The Times,* 30 July 2005.

66. See Jessica Ashooh and Mark Burgess, 'In the Spotlight: Jaish-e-Mohammed', *Center for Defense Information* (Washington DC), 28 August 2006.

67. See *Pitsburgh Tribune-Review,* 3 March 2002.

68. 'Who Really Killed Danny Pearl?', Salon.com, 22 October 2003.

69. See 'UPI Exclusive: Pearl Tracked al-Qaida', *UPI,* 30 September 2002.

70. See Zubair Ahmed, 'Face to Face with Sheikh Omar', BBC News South Asia, 7 February 2002, news.bbc.co.uk/hi/English/world/south_asia/newsid_1806000/1806001.stm.

71. See Zahid Hussein and Daniel McGrory, 'London Schoolboy Who Graduated to Terrorism', *The Times,* 16 July 2002.

72. BBC News, 'Militant Free to Return to UK', 3 January 2000, news.bbc.co.uk/1/hi/uk/588915.stm.

73. See James Taranto, 'Our Friends, the Pakistanis', *Wall Street Journal,* 10 October 2001; *Press Trust of India,* 8 October 2001; Agence France-Presse, 10 October 2001.

74. See Press Trust of India, 13 March 2002.

75. See Jim Hoagland, 'Pakistan: Pretence of an Ally', *Washington Post,* 28 March 2002.

76. See http://news.bbc.co.uk/go/pr/fr/-/1/hi/programmes/newsnight/5388426.stm; Jenny Booth, 'Angry Musharraf to Raise ISI Collusion Claims with Blair', *Times Online,* 28 September 2006.

77. BBC News 24, 'Bomb Suspect Halts Evidence', 18 September 2006.

78. Booth, 'Angry Musharraf to Raise ISI Collusion Claims with Blair'.

79. Pervez Musharraf, *In the Line of Fire* (New York: Simon & Schuster, 2006); see also 'How We Found Pearl in Pieces', *The Times,* 26 September 2006.

80. See *Dawn* (Karachi), 3 March 2002.

81. Musharraf, *In the Line of Fire.*

82. See Ahmed, 'Inside the Crevice'.
83. See Julian Borger, 'Britain Lacks Counterterrorism Policy, Says Musharraf', *Guardian*, 29 January 2008.
84. See Jamie Doward and Mark Townsend, 'US Pushed MI5 into Airport Terror Swoop', *Observer*, 1 October 2007.
85. See Ian Cobain, 'The Mysterious Disappearance of an Alleged Terrorist Mastermind', *Guardian*, 28 January 2008.
86. See Meacher, 'Blowback'.
87. See *The 9/11 Commission Report: Authorized Edition* (New York: Norton, 2004).
88. Musharraf, *In the Line of Fire*, ch. 6 n64; 'Interview with Sandy Berger', p. 503.
89. 'Without Precedent', Lee H. Hamilton interviewed by Evan Saloman, CBC, 21 August 2006.
90. For a wide-ranging account of the rise of Islamic banking, see Dreyfuss, *Devil's Game*, pp. 168–90.
91. See Rashid, *Taliban*, pp. 158–82.
92. Graham Fuller, *The Future of Political Islam* (New York: Palgrave, 2003), p. 141.
93. Richard Perle and David Frum, *An End to Evil: How to Win the War on Terror* (New York: Random House, 2003), pp. 140–41.
94. Arthur Bright, 'Study Calls Iran "Main Beneficiary" of War on Terror', *Counter Terrorism Monitor*, 26 August 2006.
95. See M.K. Bhadrakumar, 'Foreign Devils in the Iranian Mountains', *Asia Times*, 23 February 2007.
96. Brian Ross and Richard Esposito, 'Bush Authorises New Covert Action Against Iran', ABC News, 23 May 2007.
97. See James Bamford, 'Iran – The Next War', *Rolling Stone*, 24 July 2006.
98. See Ali Akbar Dareini, 'Explosion Kills Eleven Members of Iran's Elite Revolutionary Guard', AP, 14 February 2007.
99. See James Brandon, 'PJAK Claims Fresh Attacks in Iran', *Global Terrorism Analysis*, 6 March 2007.
100. See Guy Dinmore, 'US Marines Probe Tensions among Iran's Minorities', *Financial Times*, 23 February 2006.
101. See William Lowther and Colin Freeman, 'US Funds Terror Groups to Sow Chaos in Iran', *Sunday Telegraph*, 25 February 2007.
102. See Seymour Hersh, 'The Redirection', *New Yorker*, 25 February 2007.
103. See Anatol Kaletski, 'An Unholy Alliance Threatening Catastrophe', *The Times*, 4 January 2007.
104. See Con Coughlin and Tony Harnden, 'CIA Gets the Go-ahead to Take On Hizbollah', *Sunday Telegraph*, 10 January 2007.
105. Hersh, 'The Redirection'.

106. See Lisa Myers and Robert Windrem, 'CIA Warned of Middle East War', NBC News, 25 May 2007.
107. Michael Ledeen, *The War against the Terror Masters* (New York: St Martin's Press, 2002), pp. 212–13.

Chapter 2

1. See Paul Rogers, 'It's the Oil, Stupid', *Open Democracy*, October 2005.
2. Henry Kissinger in conversation with Bush speechwriter Mike Gerson, cited in Bob Woodward, *State of Denial* (New York: Simon & Schuster, 2006), pp. 204–5.
3. Ibid.
4. See, for example, Roger Morris, *Uncertain Greatness: Henry Kissinger and American Foreign Policy* (New York: Harper & Row, 1977).
5. See Joseph S. Nye, *Bound to Lead: The Changing Nature of American Power* (New York: Basic Books, 1990).
6. See Fred Landis, 'CIA Media Operations in Chile, Jamaica and Nicaragua', *Covert Action* 16 (March 1982).
7. Ibid.
8. Ibid.
9. The term 'full spectrum dominance' was first widely used in the Clinton administration. See Secretary Les Aspin, *Report on the Bottom-up Review*, US Department of Defense, Washington DC, 1993.
10. As an independent executive branch agency, USIA was at least formally equivalent in advisory terms with the CIA and Joint Chiefs and entitled to representation on the National Security Council. See *Report of the Defense Science Board Task Force on Strategic Communication* (Washington DC: DoD, September 2004), pp. 60–63.
11. Ibid., p. 70.
12. Ibid., p. 71.
13. Secretary of State Colin Powell, *Statement before the House Budget Committee*, 7 March 2002; see *Report of the Defense Science Board Task Force*, p. 21.
14. See 'Impressions of America 2004: How Arabs View America, How Arabs Learn About America', six-nation survey conducted by Zogby International.
15. See US Department of State, Office of Research, April 29, 2004; *Views from the Muslim World: Opposition to US Foreign Policy Contrasts with Admiration for American Innovation and Education*, DoS, 31 March 2003.
16. See *Report of the Defense Science Board Task Force*, p. 41.
17. Ibid., p. 50.
18. Ibid., p. 14.
19. Ibid., p. 30.
20. Ibid., p. 40.

21. Ibid.
22. Ibid., p. 36.
23. Ibid., p. 51.
24. Ibid., p. 2.
25. Ibid., p. 39.
26. Ibid., p. 50.
27. See *Managed Information Dissemination*, Report of a Defense Science Policy Board Task Force sponsored by DoS/DoD, September, 2001, at www.acq.osd.mil/dsb/.
28. See *Report of the Defense Science Board Task Force*, p. 25.
29. Ibid., p. 24.
30. See Jeff Gerth, 'Military's Information War is Vast and Often Secretive', *New York Times*, 11 December 2005.
31. Ibid.
32. See James Bamford, 'The Man Who Sold the War', *Rolling Stone*, 17 November 2005.
33. See Paul Todd and Jonathan Bloch, *Global Intelligence: The World's Secret Services Today* (London: Zed Books, 2003), pp. 81–6.
34. See Veronica Loeb, 'US Revives Old Dream of Saddam Overthrow', *Washington Post*, 21 October 1998.
35. See Bamford, 'The Man Who Sold the War'.
36. See John Prados, *Hoodwinked: the Documents that Reveal how Bush Sold Us a War* (New York: New Press, 2004), pp. 13–15.
37. See Elizabeth Bumiller, 'Traces of Terror: The Strategy', *New York Times*, 7 September 2002.
38. According to chief US weapons inspector David Kay, the precision tooling was employed simply to make more money for the Iraqi middlemen getting a cut from the deal. See Woodward, *State of Denial*, pp. 278–9.
39. See Bumiller, 'Traces of Terror'.
40. See, for example, David Morey and Scott Miller, *The Underdog Advantage: Using the Power of Insurgent Strategy to Put Your Business on Top* (New York: McGraw-Hill, 2004), pp. 35–50
41. See *Report of the Defense Science Board Task Force*, p. 20.
42. US Central Intelligence Agency, *Iraq's Weapons of Mass Destruction Programs* (Washington: GPO, October 2002), hereafter CIA White Paper.
43. See *Iraq WMD – the Assessment of the British Government* (London: HMSO, 2002), at www.fco.gov.uk/resources/en/pdf/pdf3/fco_iraqdossier.
44. UK Cabinet Office, Iraq Options Paper, 8 March 2002, at http://downing streetmemo.com/docs/iraqoptions.pdf.
45. See Michael Smith, 'Blair Planned Iraq War from Start', *Sunday Times*, 1 May 2005.
46. See Barton Gellman and Walter Pincus, 'Depiction of Threat Outgrew Supporting Evidence', *Washington Post*, 10 August 2003.

47. See memorandum from Peter Ricketts, Political Director FCO to Jack Straw, Foreign Secretary, 22 March 2002, at downingstreetmemo.com/docs/rickets.pdf.

48. Bumiller, 'Traces of Terror'.

49. See Sam Tannenhaus, 'Bush's Brains Trust', *Vanity Fair*, July 2003.

50. See James Bamford, *Pretext for War* (New York: Doubleday, 2004) pp. 333–4.

51. *The Commission on the Intelligence Capabilities of the United States Regarding Weapons of Mass Destruction*, Report to the President of the United States, Co-chairmen Charles S. Robb and Laurence H. Silberman (Washington DC: GPO, 31 March 2005), p. 6, www.whitehouse.gov/wmd/.

52. See Jonathan S. Landay, 'CIA Leak Illustrates Selective Use of Intelligence on Iraq', Knight-Ridder Newspapers, 26 October 2005.

53. As James Bamford observes, the CIA had admitted to having only three Iraqi sources 'who often contradicted each other', none of whom was actually in Iraq at the time. See Bamford, *Pretext for War*, pp. 340–42.

54. See Douglas McCollum, 'The List: How Chalabi Played the Press', *Columbia Journalism Review*, July/August 2004.

55. See Jim Dwyer, 'The Reach of War: The Weapons; Defector Reports Were Embellished, Exile Asserts', *New York Times*, 9 July 2004, A1.

56. See Minority Report of H.Com. on Gov't Reform, 108th Cong., *Report on Iraq on the Record* (Comm. Print, 2004), p. 10.

57. See Laura Miller, John Stauber and Sheila Rampton, 'War is Sell', *PR Watch*, Winter 2002/Spring 2003.

58. See President George W. Bush, 'Iraq: Denial and Deception', speech to Veterans of Foreign Wars, Cincinnati OH, 7 October 2002.

59. Jim Lobe, 'The Men Who Stole the Show', *Foreign Policy in Focus*, October 2002.

60. See Study Group on a New Israeli Strategy towards 2000, *A Clean Break: A New Strategy for Securing the Realm* (Jerusalem: IASPS, 1996), at www.israeleconomy.org/strat1.htm.

61. See *Rebuilding America's Defenses*, at www.newamericancentury.org; Robert Kagan and William Crystal (eds), *Present Dangers: Crisis and Opportunity in American Foreign and Defence Policy* (San Francisco: Encounter Books, 2000).

62. See DSBTF, *Managed Information Dissemination*, October 2001, viewed at www.acq.osd.mil/dsb/; emphasis in the original.

63. See Bill Berkowitz, WorkingForChange.com, 14 October 2002.

64. See www.whitehouse.gov/ogc/index.html.

65. See Judith Miller, 'Iraqi Defector Tells of At Least 20 Hidden Weapons Sites', *New York Times*, 20 December 2001.

66. See US Senate: *Report of the Select Committee on Intelligence on Postwar Findings about Iraq's WMD Programs and links to International Terrorism and how*

they compare to Prewar Assessments, 109th Cong. 2d sess., 8 September 2006. Al-Haideri was returned to Iraq in early 2004 with the Iraq Survey Group and failed to identify any claimed CBW facilities. The Senate Intelligence Report observes his 'prolific' reporting as 'not due to his wealth of knowledge, but ... to a conscious effort to produce as many reports as possible' (p. 55).

67. See Bryan Burrough, Evgenia Peretz and David Rose, 'The Path to War', *Vanity Fair,* May 2004.

68. Secretary of State Colin Powell, remarks to the UN Security Council, 5 February 2003, at www.whitehouse.gov/news/releases/2003/02/20030205-1.html.

69. Remarks of President George W. Bush, Elizabeth NJ, 16 June 2003, at www.whitehouse.gov/news/releases/2003/06/20030616-html.

70. Ibid.

71. See US Senate, *Report of the Select Committeee on Intelligence,* p. 67.

72. Al-Zarqawi led an independent jihad network, affiliated to al-Qaeda, and was responsible for the killing of USAID official Lawrence Foley in Amman on 28 October 2002. He became prominent as leader of 'al-Qaeda in Iraq', playing an active role in the insurgency.

73. See Roland Flamini, 'German Spy Scandal Heats Up', *UPI/World Peace Herald,* 4 February 2006.

74. See US Senate, *Report of the Select Committeee on Intelligence,* p. 90. There were apparently five named individuals on the IIS list, one of whom, Abu Yassim Sayyem, was indeed arrested but released on the eve of invasion, according to debriefed Iraqi officials, to 'participate in striking US forces when they entered Iraq' (p. 93).

75. See US Department of Defense, *Information Operations Roadmap,* Washington DC, 30 October 2003.

76. This was of a total $385 million. See ibid., p. 1.

77. Ibid.

78. Ibid., p. 65. Thousands of 'iPod-like devices' – blue for women, silver for men – were scattered in Iraq and Afghanistan in the run-up to elections. See also Jeff Gerth, 'US on the Attack in the Information War', *International Herald Tribune,* 12 December 2006.

79. See *Information Operations Roadmap,* p. 59.

80. Ibid., p. 13.

81. Ibid., p. 26.

82. See Morey and Miller, *The Underdog Advantage,* pp. 2–8, cited in *Report of the Defense Science Board Task Force,* p. 49.

83. Ibid., p. 52.

84. See *Hedge World Daily News,* 15 November 2002; *Alternative Investment Newsletter,* 1 March 2003. See also Andrew Buncombe, 'So, Just Who Is Christian Bailey?' *Independent,* 3 March 2006.

85. See Jeff Gerth, 'US on the Attack'.

86. See Mark Mazzetti and Borzou Daragahi, 'Troops Write Articles Presented as News Reports', *LA Times*, 30 November 2005.

87. See 'More Money Goes to Iraq's Development' (unsigned), *Add'ustor* (Baghdad), 2 August 2005.

88. Abdul Zahara Zaki, managing editor, *Al Mada*, cited in ibid.

89. See UK House of Commons, Foreign Affairs Select Committee, ninth report, *The Decision to Go to War in Iraq*, HC 813–1, 7 July 2003.

90. See Douglas Quenqua, 'White House Prepares to Feed 24-hour News Cycle', *PR Week*, 24 March 2003.

91. See John Williams, 'Dodgy Judgements', *Guardian*, 18 February 2008. Williams was press secretary at the Foreign Office from 2000 to 2006 and wrote the first draft of the dossier *Iraq's Weapons of Mass Destruction*.

92. See *Iraq's Weapons of Mass Destruction: The Assessment of the British Government*, 24 September 2002. See also Richard Norton-Taylor, 'Iraq Weapons Dossier Draft Reveals Role of Spin Doctor', *Guardian*, 19 February 2008.

93. See *Iraq's Infrastructure of Concealment, Deception and Intimidation* (HMSO, February 2003), www.number-10.gov.uk/output/page1470.asp.

94. See Glen Rangwala and Dan Plesch, *A Case to Answer: A First Report on the Potential Impeachment of the Prime Minister for High Crimes and Misdemeanours in Relation to the Invasion of Iraq* (Nottingham: Spokesman Books, 2004).

95. See memorandum from David Manning to PM, 14 March 2002, at downingstreetmemo.com/docs/manning.pdf.

96. Ibid.

97. See memorandum from Christopher Meyer to David Manning, 18 March, 2002, at afterdowningstreet.org/?q=node/837.

98. See Memorandum from Cabinet Office, 21 July 2002, at timesonline. co.uk/article/0,,2089–1648758_1,00.html.

99. See Alastair Campbell, evidence to HCFA, 23 June 2003.

100. See Senate Select Committee on Intelligence (S.Rep 308–101), Report on SSCI Activities in the 109th Congress (2005–06), 7 July 2004, at www. fas.org/irp/congress/2007_rpt/srpt110-57.html.

101. See John J. Mearsheimer and Stephen Walt, *The Israel Lobby and US Politics* (New York: Farrar, Strauss, 2005), p. 40.

102. See Samuel G. Freedman, 'Don't Blame Jews for this War', *USA Today*, 2 April 2003; Ori Nir, 'Poll Finds Jewish Political Gap', *Forward*, 4 February 2005.

103. See, for example, Richard Clarke, *Against All Enemies: Inside America's War on Terror* (London: Simon & Schuster, 2004). Clarke records Paul Wolfowitz pressing for an Iraq invasion at the administration's first NSC meeting (p. 232).

104. See, for example, Benjamin Netanyahu, 'The Case for Toppling

Saddam', *Wall Street Journal*, 20 September 2002; Ehud Barak, 'Taking Apart Iraq's Nuclear Threat', *New York Times*, 4 September 2002; 'Next Stop Baghdad', *Jerusalem Post*, 15 November 2001. See also virtually every column by Charles Krauthammer, Irving Kristol, Robert Kagan et al. during this period.

105. See 'Israel Knew Iraq Had No WMD, Says MP', *Guardian*, 4 February 2004

106. See Karen Kwiatkowski, 'Open Door Policy', *American Conservative*, 19 January 2004.

107. See Julian Borger, 'The Spies that Pushed for War', *Guardian*, 17 July 2003.

108. See *Jane's Foreign Report*, 19 September 2004.

109. See Ephraim Halevy, 'On September 11, World War 3 Started', transcript in *Yediot Aharanot*, 28 June 2002.

110. See Gen (retd) Schlomo Brom, 'An Intelligence Failure', *Strategic Assessment*, vol. 6, no. 3 (November 2003), Jaffee Institute for Strategic Studies, University of Tel Aviv.

111. A February 2003 poll records some 77.5 per cent of Israelis in favour. See Ephraim Yaar and Tamar Hermann, 'Peace Index: Most Israelis Support Attack on Iraq', *Ha'aretz*, 6 March 2003.

112. Philip Zelikow, speech at the University of Virginia, 10 September 2002. See 'Emad Mekay, Iraq Was Invaded "To Protect Israel" – US Official', *Asia Times Online*, 23 March 2004. Zelikow was a member of the President's Foreign Intelligence Advisory Board (PFIAB) and co-author of the 2002 National Security Strategy of the United States.

113. See Parliament of the Commonwealth of Australia, Joint Committee on ASIO, ASIS and DSD, *Intelligence on Iraq's Weapons of Mass Destruction* (Canberra, December 2003), p. 97.

114. Ibid., p. 46.

115. The Office of National Assessments had successfully resisted including Tony Blair's '45 minute' claim. Ibid., p. 94.

116. John Howard, address to the House of Representatives, 4 February 2003.

117. *Managed Information Dissemination.*

118. Bamford, 'The Man Who Sold the War'.

119. See *Report of the Defense Science Board Task Force*, p. 57.

Chapter 3

1. See Michael Ledeen, *The War on the Terror Masters* (New York: St Martin's Press, 2002), p. 172.

2. For an elaboration of these themes and comparison with the Bush admin-

istration, see *US Foreign Policy for the 1970s: Building for Peace*, A Report to the Congress by Richard M. Nixon (Washington DC: GPO, 1971).

3. See George W. Bush, *The National Security Strategy of the United States* (Washington: GPO, September 2002), p. 19.

4. Ibid. The document observes: 'The United States has long maintained the option of preemptive actions to counter a sufficient threat to our national security.'

5. See (Field Marshall) Michael Carver, *Tightrope Walking: British Defence Policy since 1945* (London: Hutchinson, 1992), pp. 36–40.

6. See Peter Hounam, *Operation Cyanide* (London: Vision, 2003), pp. 120–23, 270; see also Paul Todd, 'Robert Kennedy and the Middle East Connection', *Lobster* 51 (Summer 2006), pp. 31–4.

7. James Mann, *The Rise of the Vulcans: The History of Bush's War Cabinet* (London: Penguin, 2004), pp. 32–4.

8. Henry Kissinger, *The Years of Upheaval* (London: Weidenfeld, 1982), p. 983.

9. See Paul H. Nitze, 'Deterring Our Deterrent', *Foreign Policy* 25 (Winter 1976–77), p. 208. Nitze was a leading member of Team B.

10. See Murray Marder, op-ed, *Washington Post*, 2 January 1977.

11. See Secretary Harold Brown, *Defense Department Final Report for FY 1982* (Washington: GPO, 1981).

12. See Harold Brown, *Remarks to the Council on Foreign Relations* (New York, 6 March 1980).

13. See Paul Wolfowitz and Geofrey Kemp, *Capabilities for Limited Contingencies in the Persian Gulf*, 15 June 1979; declassified 23 April 2003.

14. See Colin S. Gray, 'A Case for a Theory of Victory', *International Security*, vol. 4, no. 1 (Summer 1979), pp. 54–87.

15. See Defense Secretary Richard Cheney, *Defense Strategy for the 1990s: The Regional Defense Strategy* (Washington: GPO, January 1993), p. 3.

16. See Michael Putzel, 'Battle Joined on Peace Dividend', *Boston Globe*, 12 January 1992.

17. See Charles Krauthammer, 'The Unipolar Moment', *Foreign Affairs*, vol. 70, no. 1 (1990–91).

18. See Patrick E. Tyler, 'US Strategy Plan Calls for Insuring No Rivals Develop', *New York Times*, 8 March 1992.

19. See Charles Krauthammer, 'What's Wrong with the Pentagon Paper?', *Washington Post*, 13 March 1992.

20. See Barton Gellman, 'Keeping the US First: Pentagon Would Preclude a Rival Superpower', *Washington Post*, 11 March 1992.

21. Cheney, *Defense Strategy for the 1990s*, p. 9.

22. See Paul Wolfowitz, 'Remembering the Future', *The National Interest* 59 (Spring 2000).

23. See Michael E. O'Hanlon, 'Limiting the Growth of the US Defense

Budget', Brookings Institution, *Policy Brief 95* (March 2002).

24. Michael Killan, 'Panel Disputes CIA Assessment; Fears Attacks by Rogue States', *Chicago Tribune*, 16 July 1998.

25. See David Sanger and Elizabeth Busmiller, 'US to Pull Out of ABM Treaty, Clearing Path for Anti-missile Tests', *New York Times*, 12 December 2001.

26. See Steve Boggin, 'Space – The Final Frontier in a New and Terrifying Arms Race', *Independent*, 8 August 2001.

27. See Loring Wirble, 'NRO, Space Command, NASA Tout Common Language of "Space Supremacy" at Conference', *Global Network against Weapons and Nuclear Power in Space*, 11 April 2002. Peter Teets was head of the National Reconnaissance Office (NRO).

28. See Julian Borger, 'US Plan for New Nuclear Arsenal', *Guardian*, 19 February 2003, Michael R. Gordon, 'US Nuclear Plan Seeks New Targets and New Weapons', *New York Times*, 10 March 2002.

29. See T.A. Mehuron, 'The Defense Budget at a Glance', *Air Force Magazine*, April 2005; O'Hanlon, 'Limiting the Growth'.

30. See 'Remarks by the President at 2002 Graduation Exercise of the United States Military Academy', 1 June 2002, at www.whitehouse. gov./news/releases/2002/06/20020601-3.html.

31. See Presentation by American Petroleum Institute President and CEO Red Cavaney held at the USAF/API Awards Banquet, Arlington VA, 15 July 2004; E.C. Aldbridge and D.M. Etter testimony before the US Senate Armed Services Committee on 5 June 2001; see the Hon. E.C. Aldridge, 'Mastering the Ultimate High Ground', at www.rand.org/ pubs/monograph_reports/MR1649/MR1649.sup.pdf. For Congress testimony, see www.afspc.af.mil/shared/media/document/AFD-061128-043.pdf. See also G.J. Gilmore, 'DoD Has Enough Petroleum', American Forces Information Service News Article.

32. See Office of the Deputy Undersecretary of Defence, *Base Structure Report* (A Summary of DoD's Real Property Inventory) (Washington: DoD, 2002); US Department of Defense, *Worldwide Manpower Distribution by Geographical Area* (Washington: DoD, 30 September 2001).

33. See Office of the Deputy Undersecretary of Defence, *Base Structure Report*; US Department of Defense, *Worldwide Manpower Distribution by Geographical Area*.

34. See US Department of Defense, *Quadrennial Defense Review* (Washington: DoD, January 2006), Sec.1 p. vi.

35. Ibid., p. 38.

36. Ibid., p. 27.

37. Ibid., p. 84.

38. See Eric Schmitt, 'General Backs More Policing Power for Military', *San Diego Union Tribune*, 21 July 2002.

39. See Jeffrey St Clair, 'Rumsfeld's Enforcer: The Secret World of Stephen Cambone', at counterpunch.org/stclair02072006.html.

40. See Robert Dreyfuss, 'The Pentagon Muzzles the CIA', *American Prospect*, 16 December 2002.

41. See Walter Pincus, 'Pentagon Intelligence Authority Grows', *Washington Post*, 19 December 2002.

42. See St Clair, 'Rumsfeld's Enforcer'.

43. 'DOD kills TALON database', Network World, 22 August 2007, networkworld.com/community/node/18609.

44. Walter Pincus, 'CIFA: Unverified Reports of Terror Threats Linger', *Washington Post*, 31 January 2006.

45. Charlie Savage, 'Spy Net May Pull In All US Calls Overseas', *Boston Globe*, 23 December 2005.

46. Interview with former Senate Intelligence Committee chair Bob Graham. See Barton Gellman and Dafna Linzer, 'Pushing the Limit of Wartime Powers', *Washington Post*, 18 December 2005.

47. See press briefing by Attorney General Alberto Gonzales and General Michael V. Hayden, Principal Deputy Director of National Intelligence, White House, James S. Brady Briefing Room, 19 December 2005.

48. See Gelman and Linzer, 'Pushing the Limit'.

49. See William Norman Grigg, 'Suspending Habeas Corpus', *New American*, 15 July 2002; John C. Boniface, 'War Powers: The White House Continues to Defy the Constitution', tompaine.com, 4 February 2003.

50. See interview with former US Navy general counsel Alberto Mora, in Jane Mayer, 'The Memo', *New Yorker*, 27 February 2006.

51. See Jane Mayer, 'The Experiment', *New Yorker*, 11 July 2005.

52. Ibid.

53. See Richard Norton-Taylor, 'Al-Qaeda Planted Information to Encourage US Invasion', *Guardian*, 17 November 2006; 'Torture: The Dirty Business', *Dispatches*, Channel 4 television, 1 March 2005.

54. See James Risen, 'Bush Secretly Lifted Some Limits on Spying in US', *New York Times*, 15 December 2006.

55. For detail on the Geneva Conventions and their status in US law, see Jennifer K. Elisa and Julie Kim, 'Undisclosed US Detention Sites Overseas: Background and Legal Issues', *Congressional Research Service*, RL33643, 12 September 2006.

56. See Jennifer K. Elisa, 'Hamdan v. Rumsfeld: Military Commissions and the 'Global War on Terror', *Congressional Research Service*, RS22466.

57. See *US Army Field Manual* FM 3–24 (Department of the Army, 15 September 2006), at www.fas.org/irp/doddir/army/fm3–24.pdf, App. D, pp. 204–6. The text notes that 'the term 'cruel, inhuman, or degrading treatment or punishment' means the cruel, unusual, and inhumane treatment or punishment prohibited by the fifth, eighth, and fourteenth

amendments to the Constitution of the United States, as defined in the U.S. reservations, declarations, and understandings to the United Nations Convention Against Torture and Other Forms of Cruel, Inhuman, or Degrading Treatment or Punishment established in New York, NY, December 10, 1984.'

58. Wells Dixon of the Center for Constitutional Rights, interviewed by Julian Borger. See 'US Lawyers Challenge Clampdown on Immigrant Rights', *Guardian*, 15 November 2006.

59. Gonzales and Hayden press briefing.

60. President George W. Bush, remarks of 17 December 2005, in Gelman and Linzer, 'Pushing the Limit'.

61. Peter Dale Scott, '10 Year US Strategic Plan for Detention Camps Revives Proposals from Oliver North', Pacific News Service, 22 February 2006.

62. Richard Halloran, 'Pentagon Draws Up Strategy for Fighting a Long Nuclear War', *New York Times*, 30 May 1982.

63. James Mann, *The Rise of the Vulcans*, pp. 138–44.

64. Shane Harris, 'Rolling Back Pentagon Spies', *National Journal*, 9 March 2007.

65. Eric Lichtblau and Mark Mazzetti, 'Military Expands Intelligence Role in US', *New York Times*, 14 July 2007.

66. Eric Schmitt, 'Clash Foreseen between CIA and Pentagon', *New York Times*, 10 May 2006.

67. Dan Eggan, 'Lawsuits May Illuminate Methods of Spy Program', *Washington Post*, 14 August 2007.

68. J. Nicholas Hoover, 'Can Data-mining Catch Terrorists?' *Information Week*, 22 May 2006.

69. Ibid.

70. Paul Todd and Jonathan Bloch, *Global Intelligence: The World's Secret Services Today* (London: Zed Books, 2003), pp. 212–13.

71. Tim Shorrock, 'America under Surveillance', Salon.com, 10 August 2007.

72. Scott Shane and David Johnson, 'Mining of Data Prompted Fight over Spying', *International Herald Tribune*, 28 July 2007.

73. Alberto Gonzales, letter to the Senate Judiciary Committee, 1 August 2007, cited in Robert Parry, 'Bush's Secret Spying on Americans', *Middle East Online*, www.middle-east-online.com/english/?id=21652.

74. Shorrock, 'America under Surveillance'.

75. Hoover, 'Can Data-mining Catch Terrorists?'

76. Ryan Singel, 'DHS Data Mining Program Suspended', *Wired*, 20 August 2007.

77. 'NSA to Spy on 38 per cent of World Telecom Traffic', *Computer Weekly*, 9 August 2007.

78. Walter Pincus, '325,000 Names on Terrorism List', *Washington Post*, 15 February 2006.
79. Ibid.
80. Singel, 'DHS Data Mining Program Suspended'.
81. 'DOD Kills TALON Database'.
82. See Jeff Stein, 'Spying without Warrants: What's the Rush?' *GQ Home Security*, 16 December 2006.
83. See Richard Clarke, *Against All Enemies: Inside America's War on Terror* (London: Simon & Schuster 2004).
84. See Rumsfeld, *Quadrennial Review*, Sec. 1 (vi).
85. See Philip Zelikow, 'Legal Policy for a Twilight War', Annual Lecture, *Houston Journal of International Law*, 26 April 2007.

Chapter 4

1. Christopher Meyer, *DC Confidential* (London, Weidenfeld & Nicolson, 2005), pp. 171–82.
2. For a comprehensive survey, see Andrew Blick and Stuart Weir, *The Rules of the Game: The Government's Counterterrorism Laws and Strategy* (York: Joseph Rowntree Reform Trust, November 2005).
3. Shadow home secretary Oliver Letwin, interviewed in *Guardian*, 10 December 2001.
4. Section 1 of the Terrorism Act 2000.
5. Amnesty International, *United Kingdom Human Rights: A Broken Promise*, 23 February 2006.
6. These were Article 5(1) of ECHR and Article 9 of the International Covenant on Civil and Political Rights. See The Human Rights Act, 1998 (Designated Derogation) Order 2001, No 3644 (13 November 2001).
7. Bill Hayes, 'There is No "Balance" Between Security and Civil Liberties – Just Less of Both', *European Civil Liberties Network (ECLN) Essays* 12 (2005).
8. Amnesty International, *United Kingdom Human Rights*, p. 10.
9. Parliamentary Intelligence and Security Committee (UK), *The Handling of Detainees by UK Intelligence Personnel in Afghanistan, Guantánamo Bay and Iraq*, Cm 6469, March 2005.
10. Ibid., pp. 57–60.
11. See David Rose, 'I Helped MI5', *Observer*, 29 July 2007.
12. See Parliamentary Intelligence and Security Committee (UK), *Rendition*, Cm 7171, July 2007, pp. 36–46.
13. Ibid.
14. See *Hansard*, v. 431, col. 1512, 9 March 2005.
15. Peter Hain, *BBC Breakfast*, BBC 1, 24 November 2004.

16. Prime Minister's Press Conference, 5 August 2005, www.number-10.gov.uk/output/Page8041.asp.

17. See *Notes on the Judgement of the Special Immigration Appeals Commission in the Case of 2 Libyan Nationals Facing Deportation*, at peaceandprogress.prg (SJC/21/05/2007).

18. *First Report of the Independent Reviewer Pursuant to Section 14(3) of the Prevention of Terrorism Act 2005*, 2 February 2006, 42–43 (p. 13)

19. Jack Straw, 11 November 2004, in Amnesty International, *United Kingdom Human Rights*, p. 18.

20. *Report of the Special Rapporteur on the Question of Torture to the 62nd Session of UN Commission on Human Rights*, E/CN.4/2006/6, p. 10.

21. *A and Others (Appellants) (FC) v. the Secretary of State for the Home Department (Respondent) (Conjoined Appeals)*, UKHL 71, 8 December 2005.

22. Peter Oborn, *The Use and Abuse of Terror* (London: Centre for Policy Studies, February 2006).

23. See *Sun*, 3 August and 6 August 2005, *passim*.

24. Amnesty International, *Deportations to Algeria at All Costs*, 26 February 2007.

25. *Guardian*, 8 April 2005.

26. Habib Souadia, *Dirty War: The Testimony of a Former Officer of the Special Forces of the Algerian Army* (Paris: La Découverte, 2001).

27. Amnesty International, *Algerians: Failed by Their Government and the International Community*, New York, 18 November 1997.

28. For a detailed analysis, see Richard Norton-Taylor, 'Terrorist Case Collapses after Three Years', *Guardian*, 21 March 2000.

29. Metropolitan Police, joint press statement from MPS Assistant Commisssioner David Veness and the Deputy Chief Medical Officer Dr Pat Toop with notes to editors, 6 January 2003.

30. Tony Blair speech, 7 January 2003, at www.news.bbc.co.uk/1/hi/uk_politics/2635807.stm.

31. Secretary Colin Powell, 'Remarks to the UN Security Council', 5 February 2003.

32. See interview with General Richard Myers, 'Late Edition with Wolf Blitzner', CNN, March, 30 2003, at www.edition.cnn.com/TRANSCRIPTS/0303/30/le.00.html.

33. Amnesty International, *Deportations to Algeria at All Costs*.

34. Ibid., p. 4.

35. *A and Others v. the Secretary of State for the Home Department*, exhibit EM 1 'Statement of Eliza Manningham-Buller', p. 6.

36. Amnesty International, *Deportations to Algeria at All Costs*, p. 7.

37. See Metropolitan Police Anti-Terrorism Branch (SO 13), 'Three Month Pre-Charge Detention', public correspondence to Home Secretary, 5 October 2005.

38. Interview with lawyer Gill Crossley, representing one of the suspects, in Oborn, *The Use and Abuse of Terror*, p. 26.
39. *Daily Mail* and *The Times*, 3 June 2006.
40. *Sunday Telegraph*, 11 June 2006.
41. Scrutiny by the Metropolitan Police Authority of Communications and Media at the Metropolitan Police Service, with particular reference to the handling of media and communications during the Forest Gate incident of June, 2006; Submission of Newham Monitoring Project, *Aftermath of the Anti-Terrorism Police Raids in Forest Gate on June, 2006* (27 September 2006).
42. Ibid., Executive Summary, pp. 3–4.
43. Tony Blair speaking on *Woman's Hour*, BBC Radio 4, February 2005.
44. David Morrison, 'What Became of Blair's Several Hundred Terrorists?', *Labour and Trade Union Review*, May 2005.
45. *Joint Committee on Human Rights – Eighteenth Report*, Session 2003–04, July 2004, para. 46.
46. In these provisions, Greater London is deemed a 'Designated Area', sanctioned by rolling 28-day authorizations. See Blick and Weir, *The Rules of the Game*, p. 18.
47. Privy Counsellor Review Committee, *The Anti-Terrorism, Crime and Security Act 2001 Review* ('the Newton Report'), HC 100, December 2003.
48. Ibid., para. 2076.
49. Ian Thomson, 'UK issued 439,000 Spying Orders Last Year', *VNU Net*, 22 February 2007.
50. See Tony Blair press conference, 11 October 2005, in Blick and Weir, *The Rules of the Game*.
51. Amnesty International, *United Kingdom Human Rights*.
52. Intelligence and Security Committee, *Rendition*, p. 57. The ISC was unable to obtain precise figures.
53. EU Parliamentary Assembly, Committee on Legal Affairs and Human Rights, *Report on the Alleged Use of European Countries by the CIA for the Transportation and Illegal Detention of Prisoners*, 26 January 2007, pp. 13–14. See also *Secret Detentions and Illegal Transfers of Detainees involving Council of Europe Member States*, second report, 7 June 2007.
54. Intelligence and Security Committee, *Rendition*, p. 10.
55. Remarks by the US Secretary of State, Condoleezza Rice, on her departure for Europe, 5 December 2005, at www.state.gov/secretary/rm/2005/57602.htm.
56. *A (FC) and Others* v. *the Secretary of State for the Home Department*.
57. Intelligence and Security Committee, *Rendition*, p. 13
58. SIS/MI5 oral evidence, cited in ibid., p. 11
59. SIS oral evidence, cited in ibid., p. 25.
60. FCO oral evidence, cited in ibid., p. 47.

61. SIS, ibid., p. 24.

62. Ian Cobain, 'Air Firm Accused of Rendition Flights Role', *Guardian*, 27 November 2007.

63. See EU Parliamentary Assembly, *Secret Detentions*, pp. 37–42.

64. See Larisa Alexandrovna aand David Dastych, 'US, Britain Asked Poland to Join Clandestine Program', *Raw Story*, 8 March 2007.

65. See Jane Mayer, 'Outsourcing: The CIA's Travel Agent', *New Yorker*, 30 October 2006.

66. EU Parliamentary Assembly, *Secret Detentions*, p. 13.

67. Duncan Campbell and Richard Norton-Taylor, 'Fresh Questions on Torture Flight Spark Demands for Inquiry', *Guardian*, 10 March 2008.

68. Intelligence and Security Committee, *Rendition*, p. 49.

69. Ibid., p. 54.

70. www.labour.org.uk/leadership/tony_blair_resigns.

71. www.cabinetoffice.gov.uk/publications/reports/isc/iwmdia.pdf (paras 123–7).

72. www.labour.org.uk/leadership/tony_blair_resigns.

73. Joint Intelligence Committee, 'International Terrorism: Impact of Iraq' (April 2005), *Sunday Times*, 2 April 2006, www.timesonline.co.uk/article/0,,2087-2114502,00html; see also www.intelligence.gov.uk/central_intelligence_machinery/joint_intelligence_committee.aspx.

74. Ben Leapman, 'Muslims Are Not Doing Enough to Help This Country Fight Terror, Says Met Chief', *Sunday Telegraph*, 12 November 2006.

75. For details, see http://news.bbc.co.uk/1/hi/england/southern_counties/5310522.stm. See also Tim Pendry, 'Plots, Smoke and Mirrors – Managing Our Muslim Brothers', *Lobster* 52 (Winter 2006/7).

76. Chatham House, *Riding Pillion for Tackling Terrorism is a High-risk Policy*, 18 July 2005.

77. Letters page, *Guardian*, 27 April 2004.

78. Jack Straw MP, BBC News 24, 18 July 2005.

79. Peter Mandelson, BBC 1, *Question Time*, BBC 2, 10 May 2007.

Chapter 5

1. Unidentified EU Commission official, October 1998, quoted by Kenneth Cukier, 'Frenchelon', paper given at Computer, Privacy and Freedom conference, Washington DC, April 1999.

2. The other major European institution is the Council of Europe. This 47-nation body is based on common acceptance of the basic precepts of liberal democracy and human rights. It has nothing whatever to do with the EU or NATO.

3. M-11, like '9/11' and '7/7', is the customary term used in Spain to denote the train bomb attacks of 11 March 2004.

4. Michael Herman, *Intelligence Power in Peace and War* (Cambridge: Cambridge University Press, 1996), p. 203.

5. Bundesamt für Verfassungsschutz (BfV, German security service), *Annual Report 2005* (Berlin: Federal Ministry of the Interior, 2006), p. 194.

6. Press Association, 15 May 2006.

7. Michael Chertoff, US Secretary for Homeland Security, interview with BBC, 15 January 2008.

8. Council of Europe Parliamentary Assembly, Committee of Legal Affairs and Human Rights, *Secret Detentions and Illegal Transfers of Detainees Involving Council of Europe Member States: Second Report*, 7 June 2007; Rapporteur Dick Marty (henceforth Marty Report), para. 16.

9. Eliza Manningham-Buller, director general of Security Service (MI5), 2002–07, speech to Algemene Inlichtingen-en-Veiligheidsdienst (AIVD, Dutch intelligence service), Ridderzaal, Binnenhof, The Hague, 1 September 2005.

10. UK Parliamentary Intelligence and Security Committee, *Annual Report 1997/98*, Cm 4073 (London: Stationery Office, October 1998), p. 2.

11. See Parliamentary Intelligence and Security Committee, *Report into the London Terrorist Attacks on 7 July 2005*, Cm 4073 (London: Stationery Office, May 2006), paras 15, 118.

12. Foreign Office minister Denis MacShane, interview with Channel 4 News, 9 January 2008.

13. Unidentified British intelligence official, interview with Gordon Corera, BBC 4, *The Real Spooks*, 4 December 2007.

14. Secret Intelligence Service (MI6) evidence, in Parliamentary Intelligence and Security Committee (ISC), *Annual Report 2006–07* (London: Stationery Office, January 2008), para. 34.

15. *Sunday Telegraph*, 6 January 2008.

16. *Sunday Telegraph*, 13 January 2008.

17. BfV, *Annual Report 2005*, p. 189.

18. See, for example, Robert Pape, *Dying to Win: The Strategic Logic of Terrorism* (New York: Random House, 2005); *Christian Science Monitor*, 12 March 2007.

19. BfV, *Annual Report 2005*, p. 194.

20. Marty Report, paras 84–87.

21. *Guardian*, 11 February 2003.

22. Marty Report, para. 91.

23. See statement by George Robertson, NATO secretary general, 4 October 2001, cited in Marty Report, para. 90.

24. See Marty Report, para. 117.

25. Ibid., para 316ff.

26. Ibid., para 70.

27. Ibid., para 112.

28. See Parliamentary Intelligence and Security Committee, *Annual Report 2006/07*, para. 16.
29. See Björn Müller-Wille, 'For Our Eyes Only: Shaping an Intelligence Community Within the EU', European Union Institute for Security Studies Occasional Papers no. 5 (Paris: EUISS, January 2004), p. 30.
30. Ibid.
31. Michael Herman, *Intelligence Power*, p. 203.
32. Charles Grant, *Intimate Relations*, working paper (London: Centre for European Reform, April 2000), p. 4.
33. Stella Rimington, director general of Security Service (MI5), 1992–96, speech to RSA Europe conference, Vienna, 17 October 2005.
34. Memorandum, EU Counter-Terrorism Co-ordinator to COREPER/ European Council, *Implementation of the Strategy and Action Plan to Combat Terrorism*, 24 November 2006, para. 11.
35. Ibid., para. 16.
36. See *The Times*, 15 October 2006.
37. See correspondence between Commissioner Frattini and spyblog.org. uk, reported in *The Register*, 16 October 2007.
38. See Stephen Dorril, *MI6: Fifty Years of Special Operations* (London: Fourth Estate, 2000), p. 765.
39. See Shlomo Spiro, *The Communication of Mutual Security: Frameworks for European–Mediterranean Intelligence Sharing* (Israel: Bar-Ilan University, 2001), paras 16–22; Club de Madrid, 'Confronting Terrorism', paper to International Summit on Democracy, Terrorism and Security, Madrid, 8–11 March 2005, p. 30.
40. *Guardian*, 25 October 2006.
41. See Mark Urban, *UK Eyes Alpha* (London: Faber & Faber, 1996), p. 237; Grant, *Intimate Relations*, p. 4.
42. See Paul Todd and Jonathan Bloch, *Global Intelligence* (London: Zed Books, 2003), p. 126; *Intelligence* 40 (Paris, 24 June 1996), p. 1.
43. *Intelligence* 68 (Paris, 6 October 1997), p. 31 .
44. See Matthew Aid and Cees Wiebes, *Secrets of Signals Intelligence During the Cold War and Beyond* (London: Frank Cass, 2001), p. 155.
45. Des Ball, *A Suitable Piece of Real Estate* (Sydney: Hale & Iremonger, 1980).
46. See Aid and Wiebes, *Secrets of Signals Intelligence*, pp. 202–4; *Le Nouvel Observateur*, 4 May 2001; *Independent*, 9 July 2000.
47. Mike Todd, Chief Constable, Greater Manchester Police; interview with Gordon Corera, BBC Radio 4, *The Real Spooks*, 11 December 2007.
48. *Intelligence* 505 (Paris, 8 October 2007), p. 1.
49. Aid and Wiebes, *Secrets of Signals Intelligence*, pp. 154–62; *Independent*, 9 July 2000.
50. See, for example, Open Society Institute, *Muslims in the European Union*

    – *Cities Report (Germany)*, EU Monitoring and Advocacy Programme, 2007.

51. ISC *Annual Report 2006/07*, para. 28.

52. See Nacho Garcia Mostazo, *Libertad Vigilada: El Espionaje de las Comunicaciones* (Madrid: Ediciones B, 2002).

53. See Cees Wiebes, *Intelligence and the War in Bosnia 1992–1995* (Münster: Lit Verlag, 2003), p. 239.

54. Ibid., p. 50.

55. The 'strategia della tensione' refers to the state exploitation of terrorism to control and manipulate public opinion. See for example Philip Willan, *The Puppetmasters: The Political Use of Terrorism in Italy* (London: Constable, 1991).

56. 'Propaganda Due' (P2) was a pseudo-masonic lodge composed of leading politicians, business executives, media figures and government officials which comprised an Italian 'state within a state'. See Tobias Jones, *The Dark Heart of Italy* (New York: North Point Press, 2003).

57. Associated Press, 26 October 2006; *Guardian*, 13 December 2006; *The Register*, 25 January 2007.

58. See George W. Bush, State of the Union Address, 28 January 2003; see also *Sunday Times*, 1 August 2004; *Guardian*, 4 January 2005; *La Repubblica*, 24 October 2005. The Niger yellowcake affair also led to a major political storm in the USA. Joseph Wilson, a veteran ex-US ambassador with African experience, was despatched to investigate the veracity of the reports of Iraqi purchases. Wilson concluded that they were false. Infuriated by his report, disgruntled elements within the administration took revenge by 'outing' Wilson's wife, Valerie Plame, as a covert CIA operative. In the investigation that followed, a senior administration official, Lewis 'Scooter' Libby, was convicted of perjury.

59. *Washington Post*, 24 February 2005; *La Repubblica*, 10, 22 March 2005; *Le Figaro*, 2 May 2005.

60. *Observer*, 13 December 2006; *Intelligence 503* (Paris, 3 September 2007), p. 1.

61. See Marcia Zabarowski and David H. Dunn, *Poland: A New Power in Transatlantic Security* (London: Routledge, 2003), p. 66.

62. Ibid., p. 69.

63. *Intelligence 85* (Paris, 21 September 1998), p. 18.

64. See, for example, *Guardian*, 12 July 2005; *Sunday Times*, 8 October 2000.

65. *Sunday Times*, 8 October 2000; *Observer*, 18 February 2001.

66. *Sunday Times*, 8 October 2000.

67. Ibid.

68. *Sunday Times*, 12 February 2006.

69. *Intelligence 413* (Paris, 16 December 2002), p. 22.

70. Philippe Lobjois and Pierre Martinet, *DGSE Service Action: Un Agent sort de l'ombre* (Paris: Broché, 2005).

71. See *Guardian*, 9 August 2005; Parliamentary Intelligence and Security Committee, *Report into the London Terrorist Attacks on 7 July 2005* (May 2006), paras 44–45.

72. *Daily Telegraph*, 21 July 2007.

73. See Javier Solana, Higher Representative for the Common Foreign and Security Policy, *Remarks on Terrorism and Intelligence Co-operation*, press conference, meeting of the EU JHA Council, Brussels, 8 June 2004, document SO159/04.

74. See John Nomikos, 'The European Union's Proposed Intelligence Service', *Power and Interest News Report*, 17 June 2005.

75. See Müller-Wille, 'For Our Eyes Only', p. 3; Eveline Hertzberger, *Counter-Terrorism Intelligence Co-operation in the European Union*, United Nations Inter-regional Crime and Justice Research Institute (UNICRI), July 2007, pp. iii, 51.

76. See Treaty on the European Union, article 17(2); Müller-Wille, 'For Our Eyes Only', p. 23; Hertzberger, *Counter-Terrorism Intelligence Co-operation*, pp. 84–5; Lithuanian government press release, 11 April 2007.

77. Hertzberger, *Counter-Terrorism Intelligence Co-operation*, pp. 66–73; William Shapcott, director, European Union Joint Situation Centre (SITCEN), evidence to House of Lords European Union Select Committee, 5th Report, Session 2004–05, 3 November 2004, published as *After Madrid: The European Union Response to Terrorism* (London: Stationary Office, March 2005); *Statewatch*, vol. 14 no. 5 (August 2004).

78. *Statewatch*, vol. 14, no. 5 (August 2004).

79. Hertzberger, *Counter-Terrorism Intelligence Co-operation*, p. 72.

80. Ibid., p. 73.

81. *Statewatch*, vol. 17, no. 3–4 (October 2007); *Statewatch*, vol. 15, no. 3–4, May 2005.

82. See Draft Budget 2007 for Europol, The Hague, 31 March 2006, file no. 2210–200r4, Limité.

83. Tony Bunyan, evidence to House of Lords Select Committee on the European Union, 5th Report, Session 2004–05, 17 November 2004, qu. 320, p. 112.

84. Hertzberger, *Counter-Terrorism Intelligence Co-operation*, pp. 76–7.

85. Reuters, 19 September 2007; John Nomikos, *Power and Interest News Report*, 5 October 2007.

86. *Statewatch*, vol. 14, no. 5 (August 2004).

87. See Privacy International, *Background on Policy Laundering*, 8 April 2005; quoted in Gus Hosein, *Privacy International*, 20 April 2005.

88. Steve Peers, 'Proposed Framework Decisions on European Arrest Warrants', *Statewatch*, no. 3 (16 October 2001); Statewatch.org/news/2004/jan/01/euro-arrest-warrant.htm.

89. See European Directive 2006/24/EC, 15 March 2006.

90. See Roger Gaspar, deputy director general, National Criminal Intelligence Service, 'Looking to the Future: Clarity on Communications Data Retention Law', submission to Home Office, 21 August 2000, para 2.1.6.

91. See Alexander Nuno Alvaro, Rapporteur of the European Parliament's Civil Liberties, Justice and Home Affairs Committee, Explanatory Statement to Plenary Session of European Parliament, 7 June 2005.

92. SIS is also the acronym for Britain's Secret Intelligence Service, colloquially known as MI6. There is no direct connection between the two. Here, SIS denotes Schengen Information System.

93. See Article 2.15, Amsterdam Treaty 1999.

94. House of Lords Select Committee, Ninth Report, *Schengen Information System II*, 20 February 2007, para. 63, Tables 1 and 2.

95. See Tony Bunyan (ed.), *Statewatching the New Europe* (London: Statewatch, 1993), Appendix 5, p. 193; Council of Europe Parliamentary Assembly, Political Affairs Committee, *Democratic Oversight of the Security Sector in Member States*, 2 June 2005, Rapporteur Lluis Maria de Puig, para 83; Schengen Agreement 1985, Articles 95–99.

96. See Ben Hayes, 'From the Schengen Information to SIS II and the Visa Information System (VIS)', *Statewatch*, February 2004.

97. Council of the European Union, Anti-Terrorism Roadmap, version of 15 November 2001, item 45; quoted in *Statewatch*, vol. 11, no. 6 (November 2001).

98. House of Lords Select Committee, Ninth Report, *Schengen Information System II*, 20 February 2007, para. 28–31.

99. Council of the European Union, Decision 2004/512/EC, 8 June 2004.

100. EU Commission, *Third Annual Report to the Council and Parliament on the Workings of the EURODAC Central Unit*, SEC(2006)1170, Brussels, 15 June 2006.

101. See *Frankfurter Allgemeine Zeitung*, 27 June 2003; *European Digital Rights* newsletter, vol. 1, no. 12 (2 July 2003).

102. *Statewatch*, vol. 17, no. 1 (January 2007).

103. *Wired News*, 31 March 2004.

104. *European Digital Rights* newsletter, vol. 2, no. 9 (5 May 2004).

105. *European Digital Rights* newsletter, vol. 2, no. 10 (19 May 2004); vol. 2 no. 11 (2 June 2004).

106. *European Digital Rights* newsletter, vol. 2, no. 12 (16 June 2004).

107. *European Digital Rights* newsletter, vol. 3, no. 14 (14 July 2005).

108. *European Digital Rights* newsletter, vol. 1, no. 12 (2 July 2003); vol. 4, no. 11 (7 June 2006); Silicon.com, 30 May 2006.

109. Frits Bolkestein, EU Commissioner for the Internal Market, address to European Parliament Committee on Citizens' Freedoms and Rights, Justice and Home Affairs, 1 December 2003, out-law.com, 23 August 2006.

110. Privacy International, press release, London, 1 February 2004.

111. *European Digital Rights* newsletter, vol. 5, no. 21 (7 November 2007).

112. See Home Office press release, 28 September 2004; *The Register*, 29 September 2004.

113. *European Digital Rights* newsletter, vol. 1, no. 12; vol. 5, no. 21 (7 November 2007); *Guardian*, 2 December 2006.

114. Quoted in *Washington Post*, 12 March 2007.

115. See *Wall Street Journal*, 9 August 2002.

116. See *The Register*, 17 October 2006.

117. *New York Times*, 22 June 2006.

118. *Guardian*, 21 August 2006.

119. See House of Lords Select Committee, Ninth Report, *Schengen Information System II*, 20 February 2007, para. 96.

120. Ibid., para. 70.

121. Ibid., para. 49.

122. Statewatch evidence to House of Lords Select Committee, Ninth Report, *Schengen Information System II*, quoted in *Statewatch*, vol. 16, no. 3/4 (May 2006), p. 1.

Conclusion

1. See Paul Rogers, 'It's the Oil, Stupid', *Open Democracy*, October 2005.

2. See, for example, Kenneth Waltz, *Theory of International Politics* (Reading, MA: Addison-Wesley, 1979); Robert Gilpin, *War and Change in World Politics* (Princeton, NJ: Princeton University Press, 1981).

3. Abdel Bari Atwan, *The Secret History of Al Qa'ida* (London: Abacus, 2007), p. 2.

4. See Abdul Hameed Bakier, 'Jihadis Adapt to Counter-terror Measures and Create New Intelligence Manuals', *Jamestown Terrorism Monitor*, 14 July 2006, www.jamestown.org/terrorism/news/article.php?articleid=2370062.

5. Bari Atwan, *The Secret History of Al Qa'ida*, p. 258.

6. See http://news.bbc.co.uk/go/pr/fr/-/1/hi/programmes/newsnight/5388426.stm.

7. See Vikram Dodd and Nicholas Watt, 'Terror Remands Over 28 Days Will Be Rare, Minister Tells Rebel MPs', *Guardian*, 27 February 2008. The Bill passed its first Commons reading (315–3056) on 11 June 2008. See 'Brown Buys Time with Deals on Terror Vote', *The Times*, 12 June 2008.

Select bibliography

Books

Aid, Matthew, and Cees Wiebes, *Secrets of Signals Intelligence during the Cold War and Beyond*, London: Frank Cass, 2001.

Atwan, Abdel Bari, *The Secret History of Al Qa'ida*, London: Abacus, 2007.

Bamford, James, *Pretext for War*, New York: Doubleday, 2004.

Blick, Andrew, and Stuart Weir, *The Rules of the Game: The Government's Counter Terrorism Laws and Strategy*, Joseph Rowntree Reform Trust, York, November 2005.

Brisard, Jean-Charles, and Guillaume Dasquié, *Forbidden Truth: US–Taliban Secret Oil Diplomacy and the Failed Hunt for Bin Laden*, New York: Nation Books, 2002.

Bunyan, Tony (ed.), *Statewatching the New Europe*, London: Statewatch, 1993.

Burg, Stephen L., and Paul S. Shoup, *The War in Bosnia-Herzegovina*, New York: M.E. Sharpe, 1999.

Carver, Michael, *Tightrope Walking: British Defence Policy Since 1945*, London: Hutchinson, 1992.

Cheney, Richard, *Defense Strategy for the 1990s: The Regional Defense Strategy*, Washington DC: GPO, January 1993.

Clarke, Richard, *Against All Enemies: Inside America's War on Terror*, London: Simon & Schuster, 2004.

Crile, George, *My Enemy's Enemy*, New York: Grove Atlantic, 2003.

de Waal, Alex (ed.), *Islamism and Its Enemies in the Horn of Africa*, Bloomington, IA: Indiana University Press, 2004.

Dorril, Stephen, *MI6: Fifty Years of Special Operations*, London: Fourth Estate, 2000.

Dreyfuss, Robert, *Devil's Game: How the United States Helped Unleash Fundamentalist Islam*, New York: Metropolitan Books, 2005.

Fuller, Graham, *The Future of Political Islam*, New York: Palgrave, 2003.

Gates, Robert, *Out of the Shadows*, New York: Simon & Schuster, 1996.

Halliday, Fred, *Threat from the East? Soviet Policy from Afghanistan and Iran to the Horn of Africa*, London: Penguin, 1982.

Herman, Michael, *Intelligence Power in Peace and War*, Cambridge: Cambridge University Press, 1996.

Holden, David, and Richard Johns, *The House of Saud*, New York: Holt, Rinehard & Wilson, 1982.

Hounam, Peter, *Operation Cyanide*, London: Vision, 2003.

Kagan, Robert, and William Crystal (eds), *Present Dangers: Crisis and Opportunity in American Foreign and Defence Policy*, San Francisco: Encounter Books, 2000.

Kissinger, Henry, *The Years of Upheaval*, London: Weidenfeld & Nicolson, 1982.

Ledeen, Michael, *The War against the Terror Masters*, New York: St Martin's Press, 2002.

Lobjois, Philippe, and Pierre Martinet, *DGSE Service Action: Un Agent sort de l'ombre*, Paris: Broché, 2005.

Mann, James, *The Rise of the Vulcans: The History of Bush's War Cabinet*, London: Penguin, 2004.

Marks, John, and Victor Marchetti, *The Search for the Manchurian Candidate: The CIA and Mind Control*, London: Allen Lane, 1979.

Mearsheimer, John J., and Stephen Walt, *The Israel Lobby and U.S. Foreign Policy*, New York: Farrar, Straus, & Giroux, 2005.

Meyer, Christopher, *DC Confidential*, London: Weidenfeld & Nicolson, 2005.

Morris, Roger, *Uncertain Greatness: Henry Kissinger and American Foreign Policy*, New York: Harper & Row, 1977.

Musharraf, Pervez, *In the Line of Fire*, New York: Simon & Schuster, 2006.

Nye, Joseph S., *Bound to Lead: The Changing Nature of American Power*, New York: Basic Books, 1990.

Oborn, Peter, *The Use and Abuse of Terror*, London: Centre for Policy Studies, 2006.

Pape, Robert, *Dying To Win: The Strategic Logic of Terrorism*, New York: Random House, 2005.

Perle, Richard, and David Frum, *An End to Evil: How to Win the War on Terror*, New York: Random House, 2003.

Phillips, Melanie, *Londonistan*, London: Gibson Square, 2006.

Prados, John, *Hoodwinked: The Documents that Reveal How Bush Sold Us a War*, New York: New Press, 2004.

Rangwala, Glen, and Dan Plesch, *A Case to Answer: A First Report on the Potential Impeachment of the Prime Minister for High Crimes and Misdemeanours in Relation to the Invasion of Iraq*, Nottingham: Spokesman Books, 2004.

Rashid, Ahmad, *Taliban*, London: I.B. Tauris, 2001.

Scheuer, Michael, *Imperial Hubris*, Dulles: Brassey's, 2004.

Souadia, Habib, *Dirty War: The Testimony of a Former Officer of the Special Forces of the Algerian Army*, Paris: La Découverte, 2001.

Strasser, Steven (ed.), *The 9/11 Investigations: Staff Reports of the 9/11 Commission*, New York: Public Affairs, 2004.

Tahiri, Amir, *Holy Terror*, London: Sphere, 1987.

Todd, Paul, and Jonathan Bloch, *Global Intelligence: The World's Secret Services Today*, London: Zed Books, 2003.

Urban, Mark, *UK Eyes Alpha*, London: Faber & Faber, 1996.

Wiebes, Cees, *Intelligence and the War in Bosnia 1992–1995*, Münster: Lit Verlag, 2003.

Woodward, Bob, *State of Denial*, New York: Simon & Schuster, 2006.

Zabarowski, Marcia, and David H. Dunn, *Poland: A New Power in Transatlantic Security*, London: Routledge, 2003.

Official reports and papers

Bundesamt für Verfassungsschutz (Germany), Annual Reports.

Bush, George W., *The National Security Strategy of the United States*, Washington DC: GPO, September 2002.

Council of Europe Parliamentary Assembly, Committee of Legal Affairs and Human Rights, *Secret Detentions and Illegal Transfers of Detainees Involving Council of Europe Member States: Second Report*, 7 June 2007, Rapporteur Dick Marty (Marty Report).

Council of Europe Parliamentary Assembly, Political Affairs Committee, *Democratic Oversight of the Security Sector in Member States*, 2 June 2005, Rapporteur Lluis Maria de Puig.

House of Commons (UK), Foreign Affairs Select Committee, Ninth Report, *The Decision to go to War in Iraq*, HC 813–1, 7 July 2003.

House of Lords Select Committee on the European Union (UK), *After Madrid: The EU's Response to Terrorism*, November 2004.

House of Lords Select Committee (UK), Ninth Report, *Schengen Information System II*, 20 February 2007.

Iraq's Weapons of Mass-Destruction: The Assessment of the British Government, London: Stationery Office, 24 September 2002.

Metropolitan Police Anti-Terrorism Branch (SO 13), *Three Month Pre-Charge Detention*, 5 October 2005.

Parliamentary Intelligence and Security Committee (UK), Annual Reports 1997/9, 2006/07.

Parliamentary Intelligence and Security Committee (UK), *Rendition*, Cm 7171, July 2007.

Parliament of the Commonwealth of Australia, Joint Committee on ASIO, ASIS and DSD, *Intelligence on Iraq's Weapons of Mass Destruction*, Canberra, December 2003.

Privy Council Review Committee, *The Anti-Terrorism, Crime and Security Act 2001 Review* (Newton Report), HC 100, December 2003.

UN Commission on Human Rights, 62nd session, *Report of the Special Rapporteur on the question of torture*, E/CN.4/2006/6.

US 108th Congress, Minority Report of House Committee on Government Reform, *Report on Iraq on the Record*, 2004.

US Department of Defense, *Report of the Defense Science Board Task Force on Strategic Communication*, Washington DC, September 2004 (DSB 2004).

US Department of Defense, *Defense Science Policy Board Task Force: Managed Information Dissemination*, Washington DC, September 2001, at www.acq.osd.mil/dsb.

US Department of Defense, *Information Operations Roadmap*, Washington DC, 30 October 2003.

US Department of State, *Views from the Muslim World: Opposition to US Foreign Policy contrasts with admiration for American innovation and Education,* Office of Research, 29 April 2004.

US Senate, *Report of the Select Committee on Intelligence on Post-War Findings about Iraq's WMD Programs and links to International Terrorism and how they compare to Pre-War Assessments*, September 2006.

US Senate, *The BCCI Affair, Report to the Committee on Foreign Relations*, Senator John Kerry and Senator Hank Brown, December 1992.

Other reports and papers

Ahmed, Nafeez Mosaddeq, 'Inside the Crevice', *Institute for Policy Research and Development*, June 2006.

Amnesty International, *Algerians: Failed by Their Government and the International Community*, 18 November 1997.

Amnesty International, *United Kingdom Human Rights: A Broken Promise*, 23 February 2006.

Club de Madrid, *Confronting Terrorism: The International Summit on Democracy. Terrorism and Security*, Madrid, 8–11 March 2005.

Grant, Charles, *Intimate Relations*, Centre for European Reform, April 2000.

Hertzberger, Eveline, *Counter-Terrorism Intelligence Co-operation in the European*

Union, United Nations Inter-regional Crime and Justice Research Institute (UNICRI), July 2007.

Müller-Wille, Björn, *For Our Eyes Only: Shaping an Intelligence Community within the EU*, Occasional Papers no. 50, European Union Institute for Security Studies, January 2004.

Newham Monitoring Project, *Aftermath of the Anti-Terrorism Police Raids in Forest Gate*, September 2006.

Open Society Institute, *Muslims in the European Union – Cities Report (Germany)*, EU Monitoring & Advocacy Programme, 2007.

Privacy International, *Background on Policy Laundering*, London, 8 April 2005.

Rahman, B., 'Daniel Pearl and the London Blasts', South Asia Analysis Group, Paper no. 1458, 15 July 2005.

Spiro, Shlomo, *The Communication of Mutual Security: Frameworks for European–Mediterranean Intelligence Sharing*, Bar-Ilan University, Ramat Gan, Israel, 2001.

Index